Abdominal Wall Surgery

Dalila Patrizia Greco • Elio Borgonovi
Editors

Abdominal Wall Surgery

How Reimbursement Systems Can Change Surgical Evolution

Springer

Editors
Dalila Patrizia Greco
Day&Week Surgery Unit
Ospedale Niguarda Ca' Granda
Milano
Italy

Elio Borgonovi
Department of Social and Political Sciences
Bocconi University
Milano
Italy

ISBN 978-3-030-02425-3 ISBN 978-3-030-02426-0 (eBook)
https://doi.org/10.1007/978-3-030-02426-0

Library of Congress Control Number: 2019933199

This Springer imprint is published by the registered company Springer Nature Switzerland AG
The registered company address is: Gewerbestrasse 11, 6330 Cham, Switzerland

Foreword

Over 100 years ago, Edoardo Bassini, a great pride of Italian surgery, asked whether it was still necessary to argue about hernia surgery. Actually, since Hippocrates until now, doctors have argued and debated about this topic and certainly will do so in the next decades.

In the last 30 years, during the progression of my personal academic, scientific and professional activities, I have had the honour and responsibility of the leadership of the European Hernia Society, a great society involving world-renowned key opinion leaders in hernia surgery that accounts for the largest part of the surgery carried out all over the world.

Hand in hand with this scientific expansion, technological and material evolution has been such as to merge the interest of patients, companies, media and especially surgeons. And of course, all this represented a real challenge for the health organizations in terms of cost/benefit ratio.

The fundamental objective in the surgery of the abdominal wall is the "restitutio ad integrum", that is to say a reconstruction as natural as possible, achieving at the same time a perfect repair in the different districts, and a relapse rate as low as possible, trying of course to control the expenses.

But today, there is something new: the concept of "Quality of life" (QOL) has become more and more important and appears in the most serious series as an essential item, whose measurement is requested to the individual patient after surgery; essentially, post-operative comfort for the recovery of normal life and work habits, in some cases the improvement of sports performances, and finally the natural cosmetic appearance are no more considered as collateral objectives but rather as essential ones.

For this reason, the concept of tailor-made surgery has been gradually developed, and, together with the acquisition of our international guidelines, it must permeate the training and the daily activity of surgeons who want to dedicate their professional life to this exciting journey.

This book has been realized thanks to the collaboration between surgeons and economists: Prof. Elio Borgonovi is a world-renowned expert in health administration and management and president of CERGAS, Bocconi University, Milan. Dr. Dalila Patrizia Greco is a surgeon who, as many other colleagues, has been challenged for years with the objective—as the same time difficult and beautiful—of obtaining the maximum satisfaction for her patients. She is also a great expert in management and administration, this following the virtuous path of super-specialization: the book I have the honour of presenting is the "summa" of their professional dedication.

I wish them and their collaborators the best of success with this book that has to be recommended for all individuals interested in abdominal wall surgery.

Madrid, Spain

Giampiero Campanelli
Past President of European Hernia Society

Preface

One of the main critical issues concerning health protection in modern systems is the development of parallel worlds unable to speak and understand each other: medical doctors, healthcare professionals, managers and policy-makers.

Doctors are focused on the development of scientific knowledge, clinical procedures and techniques and on the relationship with patients. Managers are focused on the functioning of hospitals and other structures delivering healthcare services and on their organization and financial balance. Policy-makers are focused on the identification of general rules concerning professionals and structures and on resource allocation.

The purpose of this book is to contribute to overcoming these crucial issues; it stems from the fruitful collaboration of the Editors, who come, respectively, from the world of abdominal wall surgery and from the world of management and health policies protection systems. This preface is written adopting the "narrative approach", which is gradually growing in different research fields.

The cultural exchange started about 30 years ago when Elio Borgonovi launched a master in economy and management (Ippocrate) addressed to medical doctors and healthcare administrative professionals at SDA Bocconi (School of Management). Health managers were the main audience, since clinicians' activity was not yet affected by the lack of resources, a problem that they have been facing in the last decades. At that time, Dalila Patrizia Greco, young surgeon, was already interested in abdominal wall surgery and in new models of care, such as Day Surgery, which was considered a way to contain spending, at the same time increasing the quality of service. She was convinced that in order to introduce a change, it was necessary to prove its benefits. The performance schemes adopted at that time were simple and simplicistic. Efficiency was emphasized independently from the clinical outcomes and from the perceived quality from the patient's point of view.

In a way, it was considered that new methods were automatically granting better solutions to patients' need, and hospital managers were focused on the comparison between direct costs of inpatient versus outpatient surgery.

The young surgeon was convinced of the need to overcome this gap. She considered Ippocrate programme as the best place to start a dialogue not only among researchers and teachers but also among people with heterogeneous professional experiences. She believed that everyone could bring a different perspective in the analysis of the reality.

On the other hand, for an academic interested in economy and management, the discussion with someone facing the requirements of the new medicine was both challenging and useful. CERGAS and SDA were in fact adopting a bottom-up approach (beginning from a problem to define actions and rules finalized to solve it) that required a debate with front-line professionals to propose realistic and feasible changes.

It was a fruitful meeting, which allowed them to exchange views on health system and helped them to deal with the difficulties involved in the healthcare system change. Several meetings, congresses and exchanges followed, enriching them and helping surgeons to learn those management skills which were, at that point, imperative.

The career development of the surgeon took her on the European Hernia Society quality board, whose aim is to investigate the topics of a better surgical performance and the possibility of developing tools to implement it. Different conditions are essential to improve quality: surgeon's skills, a well-organized system that allows to build multidisciplinary teams and the availability of resources to acquire good and appropriate technology.

The board has always claimed that abdominal wall surgery is penalized by inadequate reimbursement systems worldwide, above all by systems that require the so-called "silos" financing (reimbursement of the single procedure/performance). To be effective, abdominal wall surgery must produce advantages in terms of functional recovery, in particular, reducing risk factors for recurrence and complications, but these aspects are not considered by the "silos" reimbursement systems.

The board decided to study the consequences of the economy of the abdominal wall surgery evolution. A phone call and a series of meetings between the surgeon and the economist led to plan a conference where the surgeons had the task of explaining in simple terms what abdominal wall surgery is (in the collective imagination, it generally means only inguinal hernia), while the economists had the task of explaining to surgeons the functioning of complex organizations and how costs are determined.

The conference was held under the auspices of the EHS quality board and of the group of Italian surgeons who practise wall surgery and are affiliated with EHS (ISHAWS), and it took place in the prestigious headquarters of SDA Bocconi in January 2017.

During the conference, the delegates proposed to continue the discussion between surgeons and economists, and they thought to realize this through a book that would strengthen the communication channels between the two worlds.

It is difficult, if not impossible, for economists and management scholars to understand the differences between the various methods and surgical techniques and for surgeons to understand sophisticated aspects of economic analysis.

However, it was considered possible to identify a common ground that, avoiding the most technical aspects of both fields, allowed to communicate and think together about the improvement of this area of surgery.

In some cases, we found it interesting to exchange roles, planning contributions in which surgeons talk about organizational aspects, criteria and requirements of high specialization reference centres, while economists and management scholars deal with the correlation between costs and benefits of medical research, clinical evidence and health outcomes. This dialogue has later become a three-way discussion, since it was considered useful, or even necessary, to involve users and patients' associations, to represent the essential voice of people to whom the services are addressed.

Many different readers could be enriched from reading this book: surgeons can benefit from the knowledge of management principles, gaining incentives to find suitable solutions to overcome the restrictions, thus considering management as an opportunity, and not as an obstacle to their professional development and the adoption of advanced technologies. Economists and management scholars can be helped to better understand the complexity of abdominal wall surgery that, like other areas of health protection, has its distinctive features, different from other services. Users and patients' associations may receive a help to raise awareness about the cost impact of increasingly effective interventions.

To maintain a health system based on the principles of universality, solidarity and impartiality, patients must realize that any right involving an economic interest, such as health protection, can be concretely met also through their responsibility in the prevention and the adoption of behaviours leading to a fast recovery after surgery.

It was certainly a great effort to coordinate many people with different skills, but our hope is to have opened a new way, to have proposed a model for collaboration valid also for other areas of health protection. We thank everyone for accepting this challenge and for their collaboration.

Milan, Italy

Dalila Patrizia Greco
Elio Borgonovi

Contents

The Evolution of Surgery

1

Elio Borgonovi and Dalila Patrizia Greco

The term *surgery* derives from the Greek words χέρι (hand) and ἔργον (work). However, it is likely that surgical techniques first appeared before other medical practices. Indeed, there are archeological findings dating back to the Paleolithic which suggest that some sort of surgical activity was already being carried out, such as trepanning. Furthermore, there is evidence that the Egyptians were capable of performing highly specialized surgical techniques, with doctors benefiting from the anatomical knowledge of embalmers. The first regulation of the medical profession dates back to the Old Kingdom, whereas the world's oldest depiction of a surgical procedure—a circumcision—can be found at the entrance to the temple in Memphis. The first example of regulating the practice of physicians and surgeons can be attributed to some of the laws found in the Code of Hammurabi (1792–1759 BC), which provided for both monetary sanctions and corporal punishment in the event of medical errors.

In Europe, the "Hippocratic oath" was credited with bringing the medical practice out of the realm of magic and religion. The text attributed to Hippocrates (who lived in Greece around 450 BC) represents the first code of conduct for the medical profession, as well as the first time a distinction was made between physicians and surgeons. Indeed, the latter were held in lower regard than the former, but they were the only ones who could physically operate on patients.

After the barbarian invasions, medicine regressed during the Middle Ages. At that point, the practice was largely based on Greek and Roman texts that had escaped

E. Borgonovi (✉)
Department of Social and Political Sciences, Bocconi University, Milano, Italy
e-mail: elio.borgonovi@unibocconi.it

D. P. Greco
Day&Week Surgery Unit, Ospedale Niguarda Ca' Granda, Milano, Italy
e-mail: dalilapatriziagreco@gmail.com

D. P. Greco, E. Borgonovi (eds.), *Abdominal Wall Surgery*,
https://doi.org/10.1007/978-3-030-02426-0_1

destruction and which were now conserved in monasteries, making it the prerogative of monks, who also provided healthcare and took in patients. The Hippocratic distinction between physicians and surgeons still existed, with the former treating what were considered to be internal problems and the latter operating on external manifestations of disease. Surgeons mostly performed manual work, and indeed they were often described as *practici*, but they were not necessarily poorly educated people. Those with less training were the so-called barber-surgeons, who generally performed bloodletting, treated wounds or carried out simple operations. The famed medical school in Salerno (*Schola Medica Salernitana*) enjoyed its first period of splendor against this backdrop, towards the end of the eleventh century. Lastly, there were the so-called charlatans, commoners who lacked any formal training and who would provide mostly ineffective remedies at a lower price than licensed physicians.

As the study of human anatomy progressed, so too did surgery. Indeed, autopsies carried out during the Middle Ages began to explore anatomy in addition to discovering the cause of death. In any case, only with the revival of classical and humanist studies in the Renaissance would the study of the human body come to be recognized as an essential aid to surgery. In the sixteenth century, surgery was elevated to a higher social and scientific status, achieving the same recognition reserved for medicine. This was mainly thanks to the efforts of two major historical figures: Paracelsus and Ambroise Paré. The latter was a member of the barber-surgeon guild, but at the same time he worked at the Hôtel-Dieu in Paris, which was the area's main hospital. Paré started working as a surgeon in the French army, specializing in gunshot wounds. During the Damvillers campaign of 1552, he would perform the first ligation of arteries during a leg amputation. The introduction of firearms would have a significant impact on military surgery, leading to the development of revolutionary techniques and new ways of treating the wounded.

That same period was also witness to an important evolution in the regulation and supervision of the profession. Indeed, in 1540, two English guilds which up to that point had been separate—the barbers and the surgeons—were united to form a single Corporation (though each would retain its own coat of arms). The new charter not only addressed the quality and duration of training, but also established that surgeons could not perform the tasks of barbers, and that barbers would limit their practice to pulling teeth (the Corporation would be dissolved in 1745, leading to the formation of the independent Corporation of Surgeons; that body would then become the Royal College of Surgeons in 1843, which still exists today). A new decree in 1629 prohibited anyone from practicing medical professions unless they had been specifically licensed to do so following an examination conducted by four examiners, two of whom were to be master barber-surgeons.

As the Enlightenment unfolded and new ideas blossomed in all fields of human knowledge, surgery too came to be recognized as an independent medical discipline. Specialized texts written by renowned surgeons began to circulate, and the first scientific societies dedicated specifically to surgery were established, such as the Académie de Chirurgie in Paris (1731) and the Royal College of Surgeons in London (1800). Over the course of these centuries, surgeons, barber-surgeons, and military surgeons would achieve different degrees of social status, with some recognized as learned surgeons and others as untrained practitioners who learned on the job. In any case, the three categories would unite towards the end of the eighteenth century in most areas, and indeed French surgery was transformed from a craft guild to a liberal guild in 1750.

These developments would eventually reach North America as well, albeit a bit later on. While initially there were not so many physicians and professional surgeons in America, the great medical schools of the future would soon be founded at America's oldest universities, such as the University of Pennsylvania School of Medicine in 1765 and Harvard Medical School. In his *Discourse upon the Institution of Medical School in America* of 1765, John Morgan, the co-founder of the University of Pennsylvania School of Medicine, made a conceptual distinction between the practice of physic, surgery, and pharmacy.

Surgery was radically transformed towards the middle of the nineteenth century with the introduction of anesthesia (Humphry Davy 1830, Horace Wells 1844, Friedrich Trendelenburg with tracheal intubation 1881) and antisepsis (Holmes 1855, Semmelweis 1847, Lister 1865). These two practices led to an exponential increase in the kinds of operations that could be carried out. Other innovations followed, such as the introduction of surgical instruments to perform specific functions (Kocher, Pean) as well as the first use of surgical gloves (Halstead 1890). At the same time, there was a great change in the way patients were cared for, with women playing an increasingly important role. This culminated with the Crimean War and the nursing revolution led by Florence Nightingale. The technological innovation began with the introduction of anesthesia, the first electrocautery device, respirators and X-rays. At the beginning of the twenty-first century innovation in surgery was accelerated thanks to hemorrhagic management by mono and bipolar electrosurgery, lasers, radiofrequency or surgical innovations as ablation, laparoscopy, robotics, or innovative clinical management as preclinical assessment or ERAS. All of this has helped dispel the myth that surgery depends solely on the ability of the surgeon.

Just like medicine, as twentieth century surgery evolved, it came to encompass various specializations (from general surgery to specialist surgery) as well as the use of increasingly sophisticated, precise instruments and the presence of experts such as surgeons, anesthesiologists, surgical technologists, nurses, and other operating room technicians. What's more, the duties of each professional must be coordinated. In that regard, even the way a surgical team is coordinated has evolved, as the more complex surgery has become, the more a positive outcome has come to depend on the ability to work together and in harmony with the other professionals involved (the concept of teamwork).

Moreover, the complexity of surgery increases even further when one considers the hospitals and facilities in which it takes place. Indeed, the effectiveness of surgical procedures does not only depend on the knowledge, abilities, and actions of the individual team members or on the technology at their disposal, but also on how well the hospital is organized. This includes factors such as how the patient is prepared for surgery, or whether the hospital has an area for postoperative care or enough beds to accommodate the patient. There is more and more talk today about the importance of surgical blocks and patient logistics, as well as of the instruments and materials required for surgery. There is also another factor that has emerged, especially in the early twenty-first century: namely, the difference between "that which scientific knowledge and technology makes possible in theory" and "that which can realistically be done." On the one hand, this difference is attributable to the varying degrees of organizational efficiency or inefficiency of a given hospital; on the other hand, it depends on cost control and restrictions on financial resources.

Thus, it can be said that the surgeon–patient relationship has evolved. As long as the instruments were simple and rudimentary in nature, a successful surgical procedure mostly depended on the surgeon's skill. Later on, the surgeon's—and indeed the entire surgical team's—ability to use technology came to influence the effectiveness of surgery. The increasingly rapid evolution of technology has introduced new dynamics to the practice of surgery, as well as the need for every single surgical team to dialogue with other teams in order to share technology and keep pace with innovation. And the complex nature of new technology means that the concept of "team" must now include "team*work,*" meaning a group of professionals with individual skills who work together to ensure success in surgery. In other words, while a team is a group of experts who each have specific duties, teamwork is a group of people who, despite having specific duties, learn to work as an interdependent unit driven by a common goal: to resolve the patient's problem in the best way possible. In team-working non-technical skills (organization, leadership, etc.) are as important as technical ones (surgical, anesthesiological, etc.).

In addition to these technological factors, another element has subsequently come to influence the impact of a surgeon's (and surgical team's) skill on patient outcomes: hospital efficiency. Indeed, several organizational factors contribute to the creation of favorable conditions for a surgical team to meet patients' needs appropriately and effectively, including: good scheduling, satisfactory patient logistics and materials management, suitable rooms, systems capable of supplying the best materials in a timely fashion, and the availability of information.

Finally, the last link in the chain is the quality of policies, such as healthcare funding levels, hospital reimbursement criteria for services rendered, and the prioritization of different groups of patients. Surgery today takes place within a "long chain" that requires interdisciplinary knowledge. With changes in technology, organizational models, and healthcare settings (for example, intensive care units, subintensive care, etc.), as well as changes in funding methods and in the rules set forth in health policies, available healthcare processes have become more complex. For this reason, recovery outcomes have now come to be influenced by the sequence outlined below:

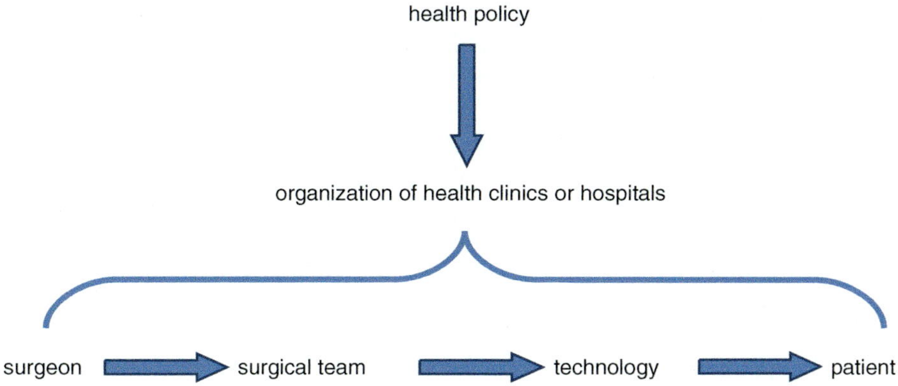

The increased complexity described in the flowchart above helps explain the reason behind publishing this book. Indeed, this publication represents the convergence of two fields of knowledge, skills and experiences, namely that of abdominal wall surgeons and that of experts in economics, management, economic evaluations, and health policy. There are a number of reasons why such a convergence is so necessary and useful. First of all, there is a need to establish a "virtuous alliance" in order to better deal with the restrictions that arise when healthcare demands and the opportunities provided by scientific progress come up against limited resources. After all, while knowledge is evolving at an exponential rate, economic growth rates have been limited when compared to the past. Just look at China and the emerging nations, which record an annual gross domestic product growth rate of 6–7%, while the USA and Europe—even after the recovery period following the recession of 2007–2008—record a 2–3% annual growth rate.

Secondly, an alliance between the two cultures will foster synergy and thus prevent vicious circles from arising when the two worlds are not able to dialogue with each other. If abdominal surgeons, like all other healthcare professionals, continue to support the principle of "providing everybody with the best"—which is understandable from a theoretical point of view—while managers and experts in economic evaluations focus their attention on restrictions and on the "impossibility of providing everybody with the best," then it is a waste of time and energy that would be better spent on the patient. However, if the two sides can understand each other and work together, it will be possible to find solutions that "provide more (quantity and quality to meet healthcare needs) with less (resources)." Such an alliance will lead to a better understanding of why health clinics and hospitals conduct themselves the way they do, as well as the reasoning behind health policy (on a regional and national level, and in terms of public finance). Indeed, all of these factors influence the healthcare context in a way that cannot be ignored.

Thirdly, it must be emphasized that the possibility of achieving more with less depends on the efforts of the two protagonists involved. The surgeon (and the healthcare professional in general) is focused on doing right by the individual—an approach that is best expressed as the "pursuit of the optimal solution for each patient." The expert in economic evaluations, the business manager, the health policy-maker, is focused on doing right by the population, or at least guaranteeing equity among social groups or groups of patients that have different healthcare needs. The surgeon/doctor/healthcare professional is in direct contact with the patient: when their approach prevails, they come up with optimal solutions for each phase of the patient's care, but only for those patients who have access to such services. Meanwhile, those who have no such access due to long waiting lists or lack of funding do not receive effective care. If the economic evaluations expert/business manager/health policy-maker's approach prevails, then that leads to solutions which on a theoretical level might indeed aim to guarantee a general level of equity, but in practice often turn into restrictions and inflexible rules that prevent patients from receiving appropriate, effective care. The two sides must be able to dialogue and establish a common ground for discussion: only then will it be possible to achieve better optimal solutions for individual patients and general equity (or at least, less inequality) for the population.

Fourthly, a lack of mutual understanding drives a wedge between "wanting to" and actually "being able to," because while scientific knowledge and available technology might make a certain solution theoretically possible, too often it cannot be done due to an inability to overcome the restrictions that stand in the way. To bridge this gap between "wanting to" and "being able to," both sides need to further develop their "knowledge" (i.e., the surgeon must better understand issues concerning economic evaluation and healthcare organization, management, and policy, while experts in these fields must better understand the issues facing those who have daily contact with patients) and their "know-how" (i.e., both sides need to work together to find realistic, concrete, applicable solutions).

Part I

Abdominal Wall

Anatomy of the Abdominal Wall

2

Cesare Stabilini and Ezio Gianetta

2.1 General Appearance

2.1.1 Superficial Layers

The superficial layers of the anterolateral abdominal wall include the skin, the subcutaneous tissue divided by Camper's and Scarpa's fascia. It contains lymphatic vessels and arteriovenous structures.

2.1.2 Myoaponeurotic Structures

The muscular components of the abdomen are represented by the two rectal muscles in central positions and a layer of three large lateral muscles namely external oblique, internal oblique, and transversus abdominis. This muscular complex is contained in a system of interconnected dense connective fibers which create the aponeurotical layers of the abdominal wall.

The rectus abdominis muscle (RA) has a proximal insertion in the V–VI–VII costal cartilage and xyphoid process, distally the muscle reaches the pubic crest. The RA has three transversal tendinous inscriptions which adhere firmly to the anterior rectus sheath as a result of the embryonal development. Anteriorly and caudally to the rectus muscle, inside of its sheath, the pyramidalis muscle exerts a tensive effect on the RA with its insertions on the pubic crest and linea alba.

The external oblique (EO) muscle takes its origin from the last eight ribs intermingling with latissimus dorsi and serratus anterior. The muscle has both a muscular and an aponeurotic part, the transition line is vertical downward medially to the emiclavear line, and below the anterosuperior iliac spine (ASIS) the muscle is

C. Stabilini (✉) · E. Gianetta
Department of Surgery, University of Genoa School of Medicine, Genoa, Italy
e-mail: gainetta@unige.it

D. P. Greco, E. Borgonovi (eds.), *Abdominal Wall Surgery*,
https://doi.org/10.1007/978-3-030-02426-0_2

totally aponeurotic. The direction of the fibers is oblique downward and internally, the distal part of the muscle is interlaced with fibers coming from the counterlateral internal oblique (IO) muscle and transversus abdominis (TA). Inferiorly, it contributes to the inguinal and lacunar ligaments and the pillars of the external oblique orifice (Colles ligament).

The internal oblique takes its origin from the thoracolumbar fascia, from the iliac crest and ASIS. The fibers are muscular in their origin and become tendinous creating a large aponeurotical structure which participates to the constitution of the aponeurosis of rectus abdominis muscle and linea alba. The more distal fibers of IO and TA merge to create the conjoined tendon, an inconstant structure of the inguinal canal.

The transversus abdominis muscle is fleshy in its middle part and tendinous at extremities, and its fibers depart from the inner surface of the last six ribs, thoracolumbar fascia, iliac crest, and from psoas fascia. From this region, the fibers run medially becoming aponeurotic along the semilunar line of Spigel. They run from the IX rib to the pubic tubercle, describing an arch with its convex part toward the midline. The Spigel fascia is the aponeurotical part between the semilunar line and the lateral aspect of the rectus muscle. The TA aponeurosis contributes to the constitution of the rectus abdominis aponeurosis, linea alba, and the transverse arch (conjoined area) of the inguinal region.

The three large muscles and their aponeuroses are separated by loose connective fibers, the outermost being called Gallaudet fascia which contributes to the external inguinal orifice, the innermost being the transversalis fascia originating from the endopelvic fascia.

Traditionally, the aponeuroses of each of the three lateral muscles are described as single laminar structures contributing on each side to the creation of anterior and posterior rectus sheaths. In reality, below the umbilicus halfway from the pubis, the deep aponeurotic layer is lacking, all the aponeuroses pass in front of the RA, and the posterior sheath of the muscle is represented only by the transversalis fascia with contribution from some fibers from the TA. The line of interruption has the shape of an arch and is called Arcuate Line of Douglas. The origin of this interruption could be caused by the presence of the urinary bladder in the retrorectus position at the embryonal stage, thus probably preventing development of the posterior sheath at this level.

Currently, this description is outdated, in particular after the studies of Askar and Rizk who modified the traditional theories on the rectus sheath and linea alba formation. They showed the two laminar components of each aponeurosis coming from the lateral muscles and their decussation at the midline. As a result, the RA is encased in a robust connective structure formed by the bilaminar aponeuroses of the three large muscles. These pass three anteriorly and three posteriorly, respectively, above the line of Douglas. Below this line, the anterior rectus sheath is formed by all six layers.

Thanks to this structure, the lateral muscle and RA abdominis are synergically connected and can exert their complementary function. An interruption of the tendinous midline center (such as after a laparotomy) carries as a consequence the functional loss of the RA.

2.1.3 Vascular Supply

The anterolateral abdominal wall is vascularized by two different systems, a deep and a superficial ones, connected by several perforator branches. The deep system is maintained mainly by the epigastric vessels: the deep superior epigastric artery (DSEA) originating from the internal thoracic artery as a terminal branch and the deep inferior epigastric artery (DIEA) coming from the external iliac vessels. These vessels create an anastomotic network connected to intercostal, subcostal, and lumbar arteries and to the ascending branch of the deep circumflex iliac artery. The main anastomotic connection between the DSEA and DIEA is at the level of the umbilical line, where the vessels bifurcate and trifurcate to join each other and give rise to inconstant umbilical branches.

The superficial system is similar and spreads longitudinally with a network created by superficial inferior and superior epigastric vessels, the type of interconnections being slightly different from that of the deep system. The superficial inferior epigastric artery, originating from the common femoral artery, vascularizes the anterolateral abdominal wall and joins the superior superficial epigastric artery in the subcutaneous tissue while communicating with the deep system via branches from its inferior surface and laterally with intercostal vessels and superficial circumflex iliac artery.

A particular attention is necessary on the subject of perforators. These vessels, originating from the anterior branches of the DSEA and DIEA, pierce the myoaponeurotic layers and reach the subcutaneous tissue. There is, according to several studies, clearly a significant periumbilical distribution of perforators, highlighting that the periumbilical skin has an effective circulation. All periumbilical and infraumbilical perforators are derived solely from the DIEA thus explaining the reliability of myoaponeurotic flaps derived from the infraumbilical region.

Tips The knowledge of this vascular supply is two-fold paramount in abdominal wall surgery. The first reason is related to the approach to complex defects and wide subcutaneous dissections typical of anterior component separations, where the interruption of perforating vessels is responsible for high rates of surgical site infections. The introduction of endoscopic approaches and open perforator sparing technique has reduced related morbidity. The second reason is explained by the increasing use of the abdominal wall in reconstructive surgery in which the areas with best vascularization (angiosomes) and the appropriate technique of harvesting must be owned by the operating surgeon for successful results.

2.1.4 Innervation

The major nervous structures of the abdominal wall are located in a neurovascular plane traditionally known as the Transversus Abdominis Plane. The intercostal, subcostal, and lumbar nerves run along with their vascular counterpart in the space between the internal oblique and transversus abdominis covered by a thin fascial layer. The segmental nerves of T6 to T12 enter the abdomen starting from the costal margin and then at increasingly lateral sites on the mid axillary line. They have extensive communication and interexchange of nervous fibers. This type of nervous architecture develops in a true plexus at level of the ascending branch of the deep circumflex iliac artery on each side. Muscular afferents arise from this structure directly providing innervation to the overlying oblique muscles and lateral aspect of rectus muscles. Nerves reappear after the plexus and encroach upon the rectus sheath from its lateral aspect, and they pierce the lateral margin of the linea semilunaris and enter the rectus sheath. The resulting truncal nerves are variable in number and, because of the communications noted previously, corresponded to multiple segmental origins.

Tips The knowledge of the innervation of the anterior abdominal wall has become increasingly important with the development of new surgical and anesthesiologic techniques which rely on the precise location of these structures to avoid direct irreversible damage or induce transient analgesic and relaxing effects.

Typical sequela of nerve section during lumbotomy for kidney surgery is atrophy of the lateral muscles due to denervation. Usually, practitioners misinterpret this condition with the presence of an incisional hernia, and the attempted repair of the affection is characterized by bad functional results. Similarly, denervation should be also taken in consideration whenever associated to a true incisional hernia since the bulging of the atrophied muscle could mimic an early recurrence.

The TAP block technique is an emerging and promising technique for the analgesia and anesthesia of the abdominal wall musculature. It is based on local anesthetic injection, under the US guidance, in the plane between transversus abdominis and oblique muscles paralyzing the aforementioned nervous structures.

2.2 Weak Areas of the Anterior and Posterior Abdominal Wall

While an incisional hernia can arise on the site of a previous surgical incision which can be placed everywhere in the abdominal surface, primary abdominal wall hernias take their origin in definite anatomical areas which, for several, reasons have reduced resistance to intra-abdominal pressure.

These so-called weakness areas are located mainly in anterolateral wall and less represented in the posterior part, that are:

- Linea alba
- Umbilical area
- Inguinofemoral region (or Fruchaud area or myopectineal orifice)
- Semilunar line of Spigel

Posteriorly, we can define a lumbar region, limited cranially by the 12th rib, caudally by the iliac crest, and its lateral margin is an imaginary vertical line from the extremity of the 12th rib to the iliac crest, medially by the latissimus dorsi. It is constituted by two weak areas:

- Triangle of Petit
- Triangle of Grynfeltt

2.2.1 Linea Alba

The linea alba is the central tendon of the anterior abdominal wall, it spans from the xiphoid process and reaches the pubic tubercle where it becomes wider including the pyramidal muscle.

Recent studies with electron microscopy examination of the linea alba contradict the description of the linea alba as a line of decussation of fibers (six aponeurotic layers, all oblique and crossing the midline). Instead, three layers have been identified:

1. The lamina fibrae obliquae consisting of intermingling oblique fibers (*on average, four to six layers of fibers*).
2. The lamina fibrae transversae containing mainly transverse fibril bundles (*on average, four to six layers of fibers*).
3. An inconstant, small lamina fibrae irregularium composed of one to two layers of oblique fibers.

Tips The traditional use of median laparotomy and incision of the linea alba affects the integrity and stability of the entire abdominal wall. The use of off-midline laparotomy to gain access to the peritoneal cavity is encouraged after the observation that it generates less incisional hernias and is endorsed by the current guidelines.

2.2.2 Umbilical Region

The umbilical region is a natural door to the abdominal cavity, surgeons use it as an entry point for laparoscopic port placement and more recently for single site surgery, it is a well-known weak point of the linea alba where hernias can be found at advanced age, in around 90% of patients.

Traditionally, the umbilical region is an anatomical structure of the linea alba surrounded by fibrous tissue belonging to rectus muscles aponeurosis and attached to the umbilical cord, created after the final rotation and internalization of the midgut into the abdominal cavity.

The distal two thirds of the ring are occupied by a bulk of fibrous tissue originated by fusion of urachus, umbilical artery, and skin after birth, and the superior third of the umbilicus is the true weak area reinforced by a fibrous lamina called fascia umbilicalis of Richet.

In more recent studies, it has been shown that different postnatal modifications in the development of the abdominal wall and liver can determine up to five different types of umbilical ring: in the most frequent of them (60% of cases), the urachus crosses the ring and protects from the development of an umbilical defect.

2.2.3 Inguinofemoral Region

2.2.3.1 General Description

Fruchaud's myopectineal orifice (MPO) is one of the anatomical regions with the highest number of eponyms used to describe each single structure of which it is composed. This observation reflects the overwhelming number of authors who tried to understand the anatomo-clinical correlations between the osteomuscular structures of this region and their role in the genesis of groin hernia. Most of the knowledge of this anatomical area comes from extensive studies performed by surgeons over the past 200 years describing their personal techniques of hernia repair.

The myopectineal orifice has a rhomboid appearance, the limits of this structure are:

1. Medial: rectus muscle and its insertion tendon, the condensed part of its anterior sheath, the pubic tubercle, and lacunar ligament
2. Lateral: iliopsoas muscle covered by fascia iliaca, the adjoining pelvic brim (part of iliac bone), genitofemoral nerve, and lateral cutaneous nerve of thigh
3. Superior: the arch formed by transversus abdominis muscle, internal oblique muscle, and fascia transversalis
4. Inferior: superior ramus of pubis with its pectineal ridge, Cooper's ligament, and pectineus muscle

The inguinal ligament divides this area in two compartments where we can identify an upper inguinal region and a lower femoral and muscular region. The knowledge of the MPO is crucial since various types of hernia arise in this region and the covering of the whole MPO with prosthetic material represents the real cure for these defects.

2.2.3.2 The Anterior View

During the embryonal development of the abdominal wall, which takes place between the 6th and 7th week of gestation, the testicle descent outside the abdominal wall in the scrotum creates the inguinal canal. In the early phase, the parietal peritoneum precedes the testicle creating a diverticular extrusion called the peritoneo-vaginal duct. This conduct obliterates after the testicle reaches its natural location; the failure of this process is the prerequisite for congenital inguinal hernias. In the female patient, the same duct is called Nuck's canal and it allows passage to the round ligament of the uterus.

The area inferior to the inguinal ligament and the femoral canal develops after the development of large muscles of the abdominal wall and the transversalis fascia.

The inguinal area from the ventral to dorsal has the following planes:

- Skin and subcutaneous tissue with Camper and Scarpa's fascia
- Innominate fascia of Gallaudet, investing the external oblique muscle and giving origin to intercrural fibers of the external inguinal ring and external spermatic fascias.
- External oblique aponeurosis, its inferolateral fibers forming the inguinal ligament, and those medial forming the lateral, medial, and posterior pillars of the external inguinal orifice.
- The spermatic cord
- Internal oblique muscle and transversus abdominis with their aponeuroses. The existence of a true conjoined tendon formed by the aponeuroses of IO and TA as classically described is questionable, being evident in only 3% of cases, most of cases the fibers of IO and TA form a conjoined arch which is the upper boundary of Fruchaud's orifice.
- Transversalis fascia with an anterior and posterior lamina delimiting the vascular space containing epigastric vessels.

In the inguino-abdominal part of MPO, the inguinal canal and spermatic cord (round ligament in the female) are the most important structures. The inguinal canal is a cylindrical opening of the abdominal wall oblique inferiorly and medially. The boundaries of inguinal canal are represented anteriorly by the aponeurosis of the EO muscle; superiorly by the transverse inguinal arch (fibers of TA and IO muscles), inferiorly by the inguinal ligament of Poupart and ileopubic tract, posteriorly by the transversalis fascia.

The inguinal ligament is the condensed reflection of the EO aponeurosis running from the anterior–superior iliac spine (ASIS) and the pubic tubercle. The ilio-pubic tract of Thomson corresponds to the inferior margin of the TF and inserts laterally on the pectineal arch and iliopsoas fascia, medially on the pectineal ligament.

The inguinal canal has two orifices, the internal and external inguinal rings. The external inguinal ring is near to the pubic tubercle and is created by the fibers of the external oblique aponeurosis which give rise to its medial and lateral pillars. The internal orifice is on the peritoneal aspect of the inguinal region, halfway between ASIS and pubic tubercle, and it is an opening in the transversalis fascia delimited from the aponeurotic fibers of the transversus abdominis, the inferior limit being the ilio-pubic tract. The transversalis fascia in the medial aspect of the ring forms a sort of sling (transversalis fascial sling) open laterally and cranially which acts with a shutter mechanism under contraction of the TA. This mechanism closes the inguinal ring during the abdominal contraction avoiding herniation of the peritoneal content in the inguinal canal.

The spermatic cord runs through the inguinal canal and is formed by the deferential artery, the internal spermatic artery (from the aorta), the external spermatic artery (from the inferior epigastric artery), by the venous anterior and posterior plexuses, and by lymphatics and spermatic nervous plexuses. Three fascias cover the spermatic cord: the external fascia from the external oblique muscle, the cremasteric fascia from the internal oblique fascia, and the internal spermatic fascia from the transversalis fascia.

The inferior part of myopectineal orifice is delimited superiorly by the inguinal ligament and divided perpendicularly by the ilio-pectineal arch. This latter is a thickening of the iliac fascia running from the inferior margin of the femoral arch and the ilio-pectineal eminence. Medially to the ilio-pectineal arch (lacuna vasorum) run the femoral vessels and the femoral ring, and laterally we have the ileopsoas muscle and the femoral nerve. The femoral ring is delimited by the inguinal ligament superiorly, laterally from the femoral vein, medially from the lacunar ligament of Gimbernat and terminal part of the ileopubic tract, and inferiorly by the ligament of Cooper. The pectineal ligament of Cooper is a rigid structure created by the thickening of the periostal tissue. The space between the femoral vein and the ligament of Gimbernat is posteriorly closed by the femoral sheet coming from the transversalis fascia; the weakening of this fascia is the cause of femoral hernia. The so-called femoral canal is a fibrous structure within Scarpa's triangle which goes from the femoral ring downward to the point of entry of the internal saphenous vein in the femoral vein.

2.2.3.3 The Posterior View

The current common knowledge of posterior inguinal region is linked to the great interest among surgical community elicited by minimally invasive approaches to inguino-femoral hernia repair, but it should be outlined that the majority of the anatomical descriptions comes from the early and mid-years of the nineteenth century from the study of Bogros and Retzius. Unaware of the theories of each other, Bogros and Retzius described two anatomical spaces that are complementary in the definition of the preperitoneal area.

From the inner aspect of the abdominal wall, three anatomical depressions called fossae (median, medial, and lateral) are delimited by three peritoneal folds created by chordal structures and covered by parietal serosa.

The three folds are the median umbilical fold, created by the urachus, the medial umbilical fold, represented by the obliterated umbilical arteries, and the lateral umbilical fold, represented by the inferior epigastric vessels.

The layers of the posterior view from the most inner are represented by the peritoneum. In front of it, there is, mainly in the midline, a preperitoneal fatty layer; a preperitoneal transparent membrane originating from the posterior rectus sheath at the arcuate line and leading to the bladder is considered as the dorsal component of the preperitoneal fascia complex. This membrane contains fat and is adherent to the peritoneum laterally. A white fascia supporting the inferior epigastric vessels is in front of this layer. This fascia also originates from the posterior rectus fascia at the arcuate line and leads to the pubic bone. Laterally, it fuses with the aforementioned.

The next layer is regarded as the ventral component of the preperitoneal fascia complex, and it is also generally known as the posterior layer of the transversalis fascia. The inferior epigastric vessels with surrounding fat lie in between of this layer and the anterior layer of the transversalis fascia. The rectus muscle is the limit with the anterior abdominal wall.

Bogros in 1823, in his dissertation of thesis on a new surgical approach to aneurysms of the epigastric artery, described a triangular space surrounding the iliac vessels. The space is limited laterally by the iliac fascia, anteriorly by the transversalis fascia, and posteriorly by the parietal peritoneum. A traditional description of the transversalis fascia as composed of a single layer that represents the anterior boundary of the Bogros space has been replaced more recently. According to the newer concept of a bilaminar FT, the Bogros space lies between the posterior lamina of the TF and the peritoneum.

The second space of the preperitoneal region was described in 1858 by Anders Adolph Retzius unaware of Bogros theories.

Triangle of pain: limited by the ileopubic tract superiorly and laterally, medially, and inferiorly by the gonadal vessels, the presence of several nervous structure suggests against direct fixation of the mesh in this area for the inherent risk of entrapment and cause of a severe postoperative pain syndrome.

Triangle of doom: It is laterally delimited by the gonadal vessels and medially by the vas deferens, inside this area run the external iliac vessels and the genital branch of the genitofemoral nerve. The electric dissection in this area must be done very cautiously for the actual risk of major vascular lesions.

Tips The traditional description of a dangerous zone for dissection during laparoscopic procedures emphasizes the risk of monopolar injury laterally to the vas deferens. In our opinion, an underestimated risk zone is represented by a somewhat ovalar region medial to the vas deferens and the medial aspect of the epigastric vessel delimited inferiorly by the obturator nerve. This part of the preperitoneal space contains the distal portion of the iliac vein, the corona mortis, and several little veins and anastomosis between the epigastric and obturator vessels that represent the real danger to the surgeon during dissection.

2.2.3.4 Innervation

The knowledge of nerve course in the inguinal region is important both in open and endoscopic technique to avoid direct injury to the nerves responsible for painful sequelae to the patients and, mainly for the open approach, to achieve effective nerve block during local anesthesia.

Nerves originating from the lumbar plexus in the anterior approach are characterized by several variations in position, course, and composition. The following structures are located in this area:

- Ilioinguinal nerve crosses the inguinal canal along its longitudinal axis anteriorly to the spermatic cord, and it can be joined by an inguinal branch of the iliohypogastric nerve;

- Genitofemoral nerve splits into a femoral and a genital branch, the latter entering the inguinal canal at the level of the deep inguinal ring. It runs the inguinal canal in close contact to the cremasteric vessels;
- Ilio-hypogastric originates from the lumbar plexus and pierces through the transversus abdominis near the iliac crest. It gives rise to branches for the internal oblique and the transversus abdominis. One of its branches is the anterior cutaneous which pierces the internal oblique and becomes subcutaneous piercing also the aponeurosis of the external oblique approximately 2.5 cm above the superficial inguinal ring;

In the posterior area, it has already been mentioned, can be found lateral femorocutaneous, the femoral branch of the genito-femoral nerve, and the femoral nerve, the latter being located in proximity of the limit between the triangle of pain and doom deep under the psoas fascia.

Tips The main cause of postoperative chronic pain is direct nerve entrapment in a suture, or in tacks as outlined by several published studies. It is important to avoid complications the correct nerve identification, since it has been shown clearly that an intentional sacrifice of the nerve is less dangerous than an inadvertent lesion of the fibers in terms of postoperative pain occurrence.

2.2.4 Semilunar Line of Spigel

The aponeurotical fibers of the transversus abdominis concur to the creation of the semilunar line of Spigel which runs from the IX rib to the pubic tubercle. The weakest portion of this structure is represented by the area limited by spino-iliac line of Monro, the bispino-iliac line and the arcuate line of Douglas, the semilunar line, and the lateral border of the rectus muscle. At this level, the fibers of both the internal oblique and transverse muscle run horizontally and parallely, and thus every small gap in this aponeurotic structure can give rise to lateral abdominal wall hernias.

Tips The so-called line of Spigel is a weak point of the lateral abdominal wall that should never be interrupted, in particular during anterior component separation, in order to avoid lateral incisional hernias in complex midline abdominal wall reconstructions.

2.2.5 Triangle of Petit

This area was first described by the French surgeon Jean Louis Petit in 1774, as originally outlined this is an inferior triangular weak point in the posterior abdominal wall. The boundaries of this area are the iliac crest inferiorly, the medial edge of the external oblique muscle laterally and the lateral edge of the latissimus dorsi medially.

According to various descriptions, the floor of the triangle has been shown as formed by the thoracolumbar fascia alone or in association with internal oblique or transversus abdominis. Its dimension and presence are variable (80% of cases), and the absence of this structure is connected to the presence of the external oblique muscle aponeurosis as a roof to the triangle.

2.2.6 Triangle of Grynfeltt

This triangle has been described as a site of a primitive hernia by Grynfeltt in 1886, and it is located superiorly to the triangle of Petit with its apex directed inferiorly. The limits are represented by the posterior border of the internal oblique muscle anteriorly, the anterior border of the sacrospinalis muscle posteriorly, the base is 12th rib and the serratus posterior inferior, the external oblique and latissimus dorsi are the roof, and the aponeurosis of the transversus abdominis represents its floor. The real weak area of the Grynfeltt triangle is represented by the entry of the neurovascular bundle immediately under the 12th rib where the unprotected transversalis fascia is perforated and not protected by the external oblique muscle.

Suggested Reading

Askar OM. Surgical anatomy of the aponeurotic expansions of the anterior abdominal wall. Ann R Coll Surg Engl. 1977;59:313.

Axer H, Keyserlingk DG, Prescher A. Collagen fibers in linea alba and rectus sheaths. I. General scheme and morphological aspects. J Surg Res. 2001;96(1):127–34.

Bendavid R. The space of Bogros and the deep inguinal venous circulation. Surg Gynecol Obstet. 1992;174:355.

Condon RE. Surgical anatomy of the transversus abdominis. Ann Surg. 1971;173:1.

Cooper A. The anatomy and surgical treatment of abdominal hernia. Philadelphia, PA: Lea & Blanchard; 1804.

Fathi L. Surgical anatomy and morphologic variations of umbilical structures. Am Surg. 2012;78(5):540–4.

Fruchaud H. Anatomie Chirurgicale Des Hernies De L'aine. Paris: G. Doin; 1956.

Lau H, Patil NG. Umbilical hernia in adults. Surg Endosc. 2003;17:2016–20.

Loukas M, El-Zammar D, Shoja MM, Tubbs RS, Zhan L, Protyniak B, Krutoshinskaya Y. The clinical anatomy of the triangle of Grynfeltt. Hernia. 2008;12(3):227–31.

Loukas M, Tubbs RS, El-Sedfy A, Jester A, Polepalli S, Kinsela C, Wu S. The clinical anatomy of the triangle of Petit. Hernia. 2007;11(5):441–4.

Macchi V, Porzionato A, Morra A, Picardi EEE, Stecco C, Loukas M, Tubbs RS, De Caro R. The triangles of Grynfeltt and Petit and the lumbar tunnel: an anatomo-radiologic study. Hernia. 2017;21(3):369–76.

Ndiaye A, Diop M, Ndoye JM, Konaté I, Ndiaye AI, Mané L, Nazarian S, Dia A. Anatomical basis of neuropathies and damage to the ilioinguinal nerve during repairs of groin hernias (about 100 dissections). Surg Radiol Anat. 2007;29(8):675–81.

Punekar IRA, Khouri JS, Catanzaro M, Shaikh AL, Langstein HN. Redefining the rectus sheath: implications for abdominal wall repair. Plast Reconstr Surg. 2018;141(2):473–9.

Rizk NN. A new description of the anterior abdominal wall in man and mammals. J Anat. 1980;131:373.

Skandalakis JE, Skandalakis PN, Skandalakis LJ. Abdominal wall and hernias. In: Surgical anatomy and technique. New York: Springer; 2000. p. 133–5.

Sudrania OP, Agrawal RK, Deb S, Khanna AK. Pubomyoaponeurotic foramen and posterior groin plait for groin hernia. Hernia. 2003;7(4):210–4.

Testut L, Jacob O. Trattato Di Anatomia Topografica, vol. II. Torino: Utet; 1922.

Wijsmuller AR, Lange JF, Kleinrensink GJ, van Geldere D, Simons MP, Huygen FJ, Jeekel J, Lange JF. Nerve-identifying inguinal hernia repair: a surgical anatomical study. World J Surg. 2007;31(2):414–20.

Clusters of Pathology and Interventions

3

Pier Luigi Ipponi and Diego Cuccurullo

3.1 History

The term hernia defines the exit of an organ through the wall of the cavity in which it normally resides, either through an existing or a newly formed orifice.

It is widely used inside the surgical community since it refers to one of the most frequent diseases encountered in daily practice. Nevertheless its etymological origin is still controversial. According to some the term originated from the ancient Greek word *ernos*, which means "branch" or "sucker" given due to its similarity to an abdominal wall germination, while others claim a Latin etymological root from the word *hira*, which means "bowel."

A hernia is one of the oldest recorded afflictions of mankind since numerous references have been already reported in Assyro-Babylonian and Egyptian manuscripts and it is fascinating to observe how, over the centuries [1], the improvement in hernia treatment has gone hand in hand with the cultural evolution of the human race.

The oldest preserved documents in medical science, the Papyrus of Ebers, written during the reign of Amenhotep I (ca 1552 A.D.) but probably dating back to the First Dynasty (ca 3000 A.D.), describes patients suffering from an inguinal hernia and its relationship to coughing [2].

Although, the interpretation of the ancient Egyptian texts is complex and leaves some doubts about the suggested treatment of inguinal hernia. It's still unclear if the heat applied on the groin hernia is recommended to reduce the hernia content or to cauterize, achieving a closure of the hernia defect by scar tissue production.

P. L. Ipponi (✉)
Department of Surgery, Azienda USL Centro Toscana, San Giovanni di Dio Hospital, Florence, Italy
e-mail: pierluigi.ipponi@uslcentro.toscana.it

D. Cuccurullo
Department General, Laparoscopic and Robotic Surgery, AORN dei Colli Monaldi Hospital, Naples, Italy
e-mail: diego.cuccurullo@ospedalideicolli.it

D. P. Greco, E. Borgonovi (eds.), *Abdominal Wall Surgery*,
https://doi.org/10.1007/978-3-030-02426-0_3

However, studies on the mummified remains of the pharaohs Merneptah (ca 1215 A.D.) and Ramses V (ca 1157 A.D.) suggest that both were likely treated for an inguinal hernia aggressively [1].

Later, during the Hellenistic period, numerous treatises testify a deep awareness to hernia pathology. The disciples of Hippocrates argued the rupture of the peritoneum with the stretching of the overlying fascia and muscular tissues as the origin of abdominal hernias.

In De Medicina, the roman encyclopedic writer Cornelio Celso (30–50 A.D.) described an advanced surgical treatment in sedated patients, with hemostatic vascular ligature, hernial sac closure, and preservation of the testis [3].

Anyway, this refined culture was lost during the Middle Ages, ruled by the principle of Ecclesia abhorret a sanguine. At that time, many surgeons were reluctant to perform surgery and castration was the most common practice.

Renaissance surgeons dare more than their predecessors, benefiting from the dawn of printing with the first monographies in treatment of herniation, as Traitè des hernies by Pierre Franco (1500–1561) favored the knowledge and improved their skill all over the Europe [4].

A resumption of the surgical approach was summarized in the work of Ambroise Pare (1510–1590), who acquired the lesson providing an innovative surgical technique: the Golden Thread [5].

Through a groin incision, the hernial sac was loosened from testicular vessels and cremaster muscle and closed with several golden transfixed stitches (Point dorè) and then sutured at the wound edges.

But only in the nineteenth century, a milestone on hernia surgery has been pursued by an Italian surgeon, Edoardo Bassini (1844–1924), who first asserted the strategic role of the posterior inguinal wall in hernia recurrence [6]. Thanks to an improved knowledge in anatomy, anesthesia, and antisepsis, he performed an innovative technique, suturing the conjoined tendon to the inguinal ligament and conferring a strong reinforcement to the inguinal wall. The astonishing results in terms of recurrence and infection paved the way to contemporary hernia surgery.

3.2 Etiology

Beyond the fascinating historical aspects, passing time has also played a key role on the abdominal hernias.

The natural evolution of the terrestrial mammals can be considered the oldest etiological factor in hernia onset. Assuming the erect station they exposed the weakest parts of their body to the negative effects of gravity. In addition to phylogeny, even ontogeny may be involved in some abdominal hernia onset. During the fetal life, some physiological functions may negatively impact on structural strength of the abdomen. The umbilical cord for fetal nutrition and the peritoneal vaginal duct for the descent of the testicle into the scrotum in the inguinal canal are weak areas which usually undergo obliteration after delivery, but an inadequate closure, when engaged by viscera, inevitably leads to a congenital hernia.

Although congenital hernias are typical of childhood, acquired hernias are mainly observed in adults, as an inevitable consequence of the wear and tear of living. Its onset is influenced by favoring and triggering factors, which act simultaneously [7].

Predisposing factors may be divided into acquired (ageing, tobacco smoke, nutritional disorders as lathyrism, surgical scars) or congenital (collagenosis as Marfan and Ehlers-Danlos syndromes), justifying the higher incidence of abdominal hernia in certain familiar lines. They are both able to alter the collagen quality, which normally confers mechanical resistance to the biological tissue.

Trigger factors as pregnancy, chronic obstructive pulmonary disease, prostatic hypertrophy, ascites, obesity, chronic constipation or traumatic events, increasing intra-abdominal pressure for a long time expose the weaker part of the abdominal wall to a chronic mechanical stress. Following the principle of Laplace law, which states that mechanical wall stress is equal to wall tension divided by wall thickness, thin areas, as abdominal midline (linea alba) or inguinal canal, are more prone to a structural failure and hernia onset.

3.3 Epidemiological and Social Aspects

Epidemiological and economical researches attribute to abdominal hernias the definition of social problem. Even if we don't know exactly the scale of the problem worldwide, the prevalence of this pathology in the USA, referred to a population of people who are managing abdominal hernia at any given time, is estimated at 1:60 people, while incidence, referred to the annual diagnosis rate or the number of new cases of an abdominal hernia diagnosed each year, shows a rate of 1:339 people, which corresponds by extrapolations to 800.000 new cases per year, 66.666 per month, equal to 1 per minute!

The projections quoted are confirmed by statistical data, reporting inguinal hernia repair as one of the most common operations performed in general surgery, with rates ranging from 10:100.000 people in the UK to 28:100.000 in the USA [8].

Some factors as age, lifestyle, and gender can influence negatively the incidence, even if in different manners. For example, in inguinal hernia the age of distribution shows a bimodal trend, peaking at early childhood and subsequently in old age (Table 3.1), while the abdominal hernias show a peak between 3rd and 6th decades, with the highest incidence in multipara females (38%).

Lifestyle may impact only slightly on hernia onset, appearing more evident on hernia recurrences and surgical site infections.

Undoubtedly hernia onset can be influenced by gender, with a lifetime risk of 27% for men and 3% for women with a higher incidence of an inguinal hernia in male (ratio of 7–9:1) (Table 3.2) and a higher incidence of an abdominal hernia in female (ratio of 2:1) [9].

Table 3.1 Age and inguinal hernia repair

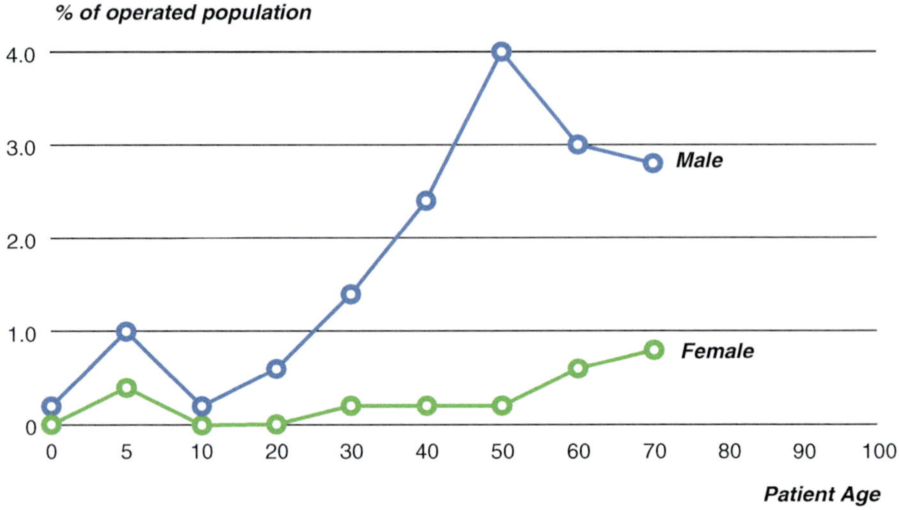

Table 3.2 Cumulative probability of inguinal hernia by sex among adults in the USA

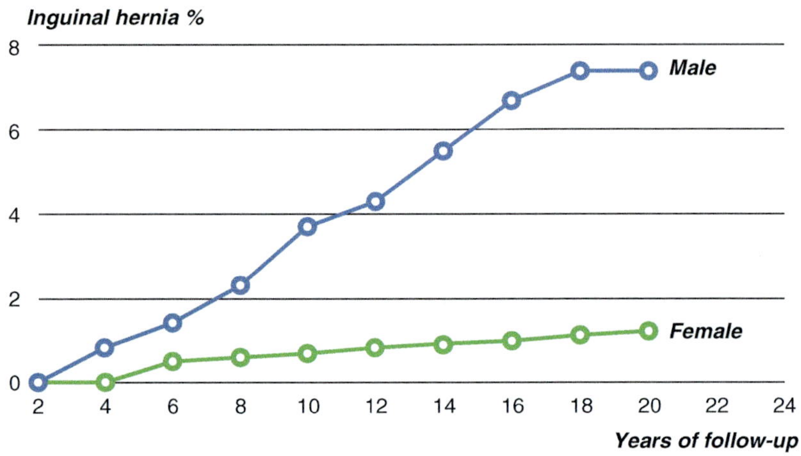

The commitment of human and economic resources involved in hernia care must be assessed not only for surgical activity but extended to health care and social management too.

During the period 2002–2003, in England, hospital consultant episodes were related in 0.67% to an inguinal hernia and in 0.005% to an unspecified abdominal hernia, followed by emergency hospital admission, respectively, in 8% of cases and in 36% of cases, with a mean length of stay in hospital of 2.4 days for an inguinal hernia and 7.7 days for an unspecified abdominal hernia, which required more than 100.000 hospital bed days/year [10].

The extreme variability of clinical forms in which this disease occurs, patients are managed clinically through different care settings, depending on the extent of the disease treated.

Much of the inguinal and the abdominal wall primary pathology is treated as outpatient, providing effective performance at low cost. Fragile patients or patients with severe co-morbidities and major pathological forms require an in-patient setting, with prolonged hospital stays and high costs to the health system.

The social impact may be also guessed by statistic reports, measuring disability and loss of working days per year. In a seminal 1890 publication on his technique, Edoardo Bassini recommended 6 weeks of bed rest followed by an extended period of convalescence [11].

This advice remained the standard of care throughout the forties. Only starting from the sixties, the surgeons led to early mobilization and return to activity immediately after surgery, even after major abdominal surgery [12, 13].

However, because recurrence is a frequent issue after operation, the practice of recommending extended convalescence has persisted long-lasting, despite the research demonstrates that early return to activity has no detrimental effect [14, 15].

Recently, a case-control study performed in Denmark on convalescence, after Lichtenstein procedure defined the gold standard technique in inguinal hernia repair, reported a median length of absence from work of 7 days (4.5 days for sedentary work and 14 days for heavy work), with the pain as the most common cause of delay (60%), followed by wound complications (20%) [8].

The number of days of work lost for hernia pathologies is higher than for any other chronic digestive condition [16]. With a statistical prediction of more than 20 million of surgical procedures performed each year worldwide, it is possible to calculate a 140 million of loss in working days per year, only for inguinal hernia.

3.4 Classification

By a clinical point of view, inguinal and other abdominal hernias can be considered a cluster of pathologies since they are assimilated by nosological and clinical aspects.

Different systems to classify abdominal and inguinal hernia have been proposed over the times, sometimes using more than one, to define better the clinical aspect.

Classifications play important roles in organization and management of the knowledge. They are a useful tool to identify anatomical landmark, plan surgery, and evaluate results in terms of recurrence or postoperative quality of life, degree of disability, and time of convalescence. Through these instruments can be prepared consistent follow-up and statistic studies.

One of the most used classifications is on ontogenic basis, distinguishing between congenital and acquired hernia, when the onset is at or after the birth, as mentioned before. Sometimes it is used as pathogenetic criterion, distinguishing primary, with a spontaneous onset, from secondary hernia following a previous surgical treatment, called also recurrent or incisional hernia.

The reference to the anatomical site is another effective method to classify hernias in daily practice, describing inguinal, femoral, epigastric, umbilical, lumbar, diaphragmatic, or perineal hernia.

In 2007 the European Hernia Society [17] proposed a new systematic classification of groin hernia, still appreciated for its simplicity and completeness. It collects together some primary parameters such as the anatomical district (inguinal or femoral), the site of onset referred to the epigastric vessels which divide the inguinal floor in a medial zone (M for medial hernia) and in a lateral zone (L for lateral hernia) (Pictures 3.1 and 3.2), the size of the defect (<1.5 cm, 1.5–3 cm, >3 cm), and its relation to recurrence with a primary hernia (P) or recurrent hernia (R). X indicates site not investigated by surgeon and 0 no hernia detected (Table 3.3).

Applying the same methodology, the European Hernia Society proposed also a new classification for abdominal wall defects which was simple, reproducible, and internationally accepted on a straight-line basis of topographical, dimensional, and clinical definition [18].

Taking into account the hernia site, the abdominal wall was divided into median (M1–M5) (Picture 3.3) and lateral defects (L1–L4) (Picture 3.4) with a cranio-caudal sectoralization.

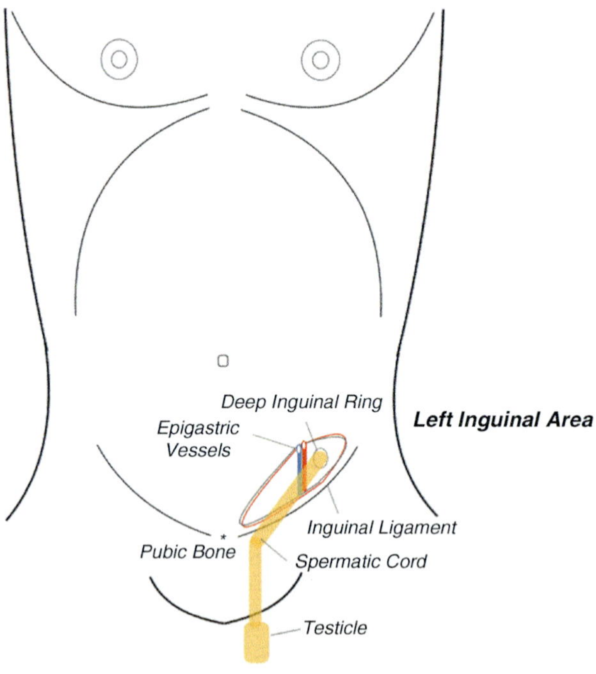

Picture 3.1 Anatomy of inguinal area

Picture 3.2 Site of inguinal hernia

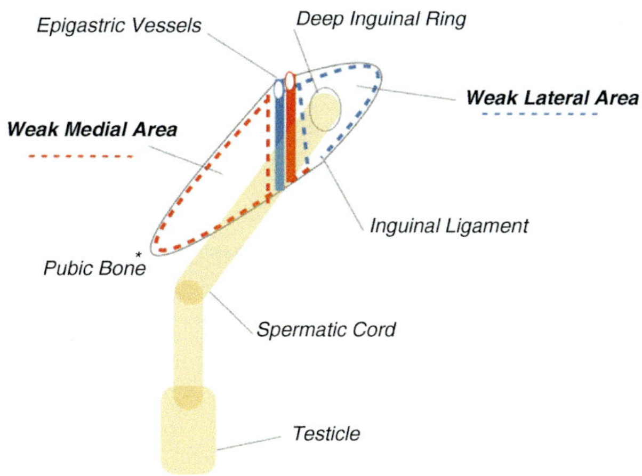

Table 3.3 Schematic European Hernia Society inguinal hernia classification

		P	R		
	0	1	2	3	X
L					
M					
F					

P: Primary Hernia
R: Recurrent Hernia

L : Lateral/Indirect Hernia
M: Medial/Direct Hernia
F : Femoral Hernia

0: No Hernia Detectable
1: < 1,5 cm
2: < 3 cm
3: > 3 cm
X: Not Investigated

European Hernia Society, 2007

The size of hernia measured the width of the defect expressed in linear centimeters (W1 < 4 cm, W2 4–10 cm, W3 > 10 cm). It was considered the relation with recurrence, defining subgroups on the basis of the recurrence times ($R0$, $R1$, $R2$,…Rn).

This method of evaluation is undoubtedly a comprehensive model, but considered "static" since it doesn't take into account two important parameters as patient, with his co-morbidities and wound classification, which may influence the final result.

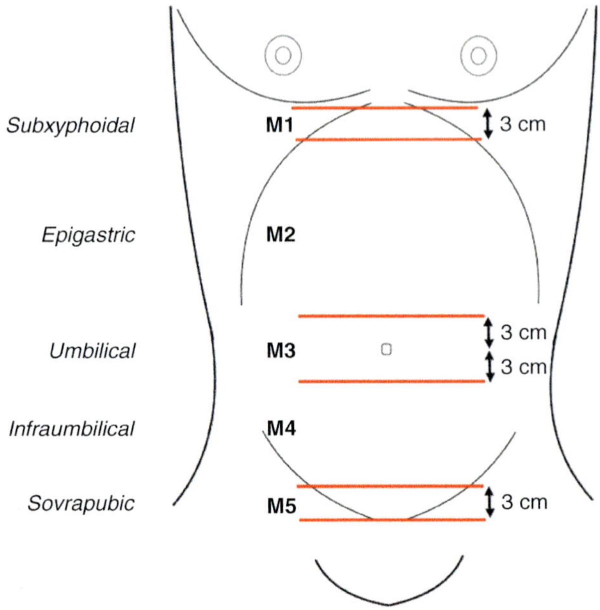

Picture 3.3 Abdomen hernia site—midline. European Hernia Society classification

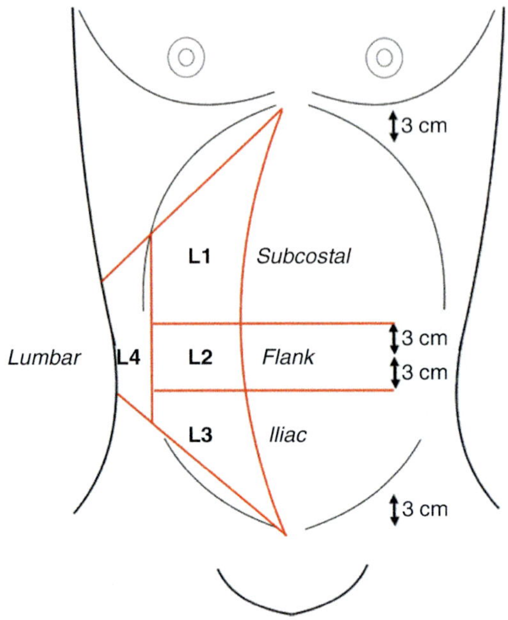

Picture 3.4 Abdomen hernia site—lateral. European Hernia Society classification

The Ventral Hernia Working Group [19], comprising expert surgeons, starting from the literature proposed a three grades classification, based on surgical field contamination and patient co-morbidities (Table 3.4).

The Grade One includes healthy patients and clean surgical field, the Grade Two patients with co-morbidities as diabetes, smoking, obesity, immunosuppression,

Table 3.4 Stratification of risk infection in mesh implantation

SYNTHETIC MESH		*BIOLOGIC MESH*
Grade 1 Low risk	**Grade 2** *Comorbidity*	**Grade 3** Contamination
Low risk of complications No history of wound infection	– Smoker – Obese – Disbetic – COPD – History Wound Infection – Malnutrition	3a. Clean 3b. Contaminated 3c. Active Infection

"The Ventral Hernia Working Group" Surgery 2010.148:544 - 558

and previous wound infection, and the Grade Three distinguished in subgroup a (clean-contaminated field), subgroup b (contaminated field), and subgroup c (active infection). They stated some clinical recommendations on perioperative optimization and surgical approach as the choice of the right mesh. Synthetic meshes are suitable for Class 1 and 2, while biologic or bio-like meshes are indicated for Class 3a and Class 3b. The Class 3c should be downgraded to Class 3b with the negative pressure wound therapy before to implant a non-synthetic mesh during the same period of hospitalization.

In the future we hope a new comprehensive classification which takes into account not only anatomical and dimensional but also clinical criteria, providing a platform for future investigations regarding technique, prosthetic choice, and perioperative optimization [20].

The diagnosis of inguinal and abdominal hernia is often made clinically and frequently associated with a visible bulging (Picture 3.5). However, a certain percentage of patients are asymptomatic and detected during the follow-up for other pathologies.

Pain is the most frequently observed symptomatology in the early stages of hernia pathology increasing after lifting heavy weight, abundant meals, or constipation.

Groin and abdominal hernia patients show some physical limitations in daily activity, while in huge abdominal hernia they usually experience social exclusion with limited ability to work and self-care may be substantially impaired in these patients (Picture 3.6).

In case of reducible hernia content without symptoms a watchful waiting may be a recommended strategy for groin hernia, while a surgical treatment should be planned in incisional hernia, symptomatic hernia, or when the content is not reducible.

Larger abdominal hernias are frequently associated with ischemic sufferance of the skin overlying the hernia sac and with chronic spinal complaints, due to an impairment of the lateral muscles of the abdomen.

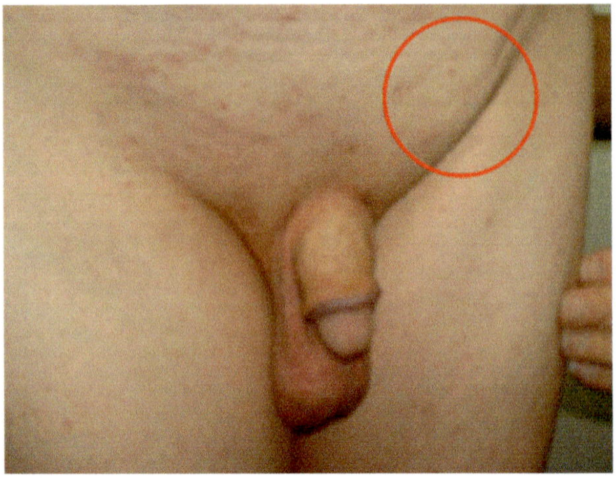

Picture 3.5 Small left inguinal hernia

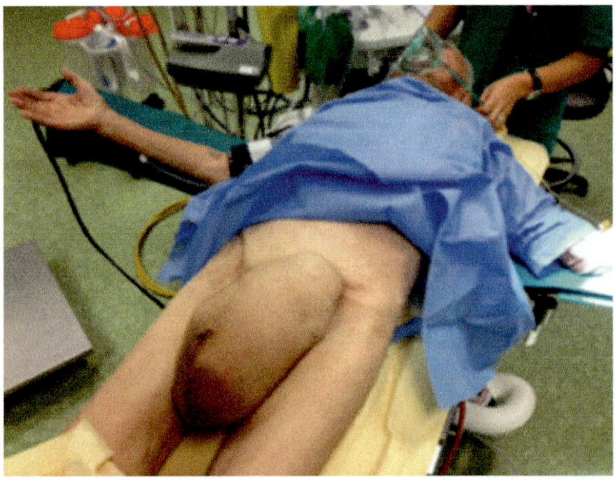

Picture 3.6 Giant inguinal hernia

In non-palpable mass a cough is requested to the patient, to facilitate the outflow of the viscera into the hernial sac, which will be easily evaluated by the exploring finger.

Sometimes in obese patients may be useful a radiological investigation to detect the unknown presence of the hernia. Sonography is a non-invasive method and may be helpful in good hands, but Tc scan gives much more information about the site of herniation, involved viscera, and dimensional evaluation of the defect. This enables to schedule a preoperative and surgical strategy, mandatory for huge abdominal hernia with loss of domain and convenient in most of incisional hernia.

Among the diagnostic investigations executed for inguinodynia, in the absence of clinical evidence of an inguinal hernia, the magnetic resonance may detect muscular impairment, aponeurotic tears, or an enthesopathy as cause of the symptomatic framework.

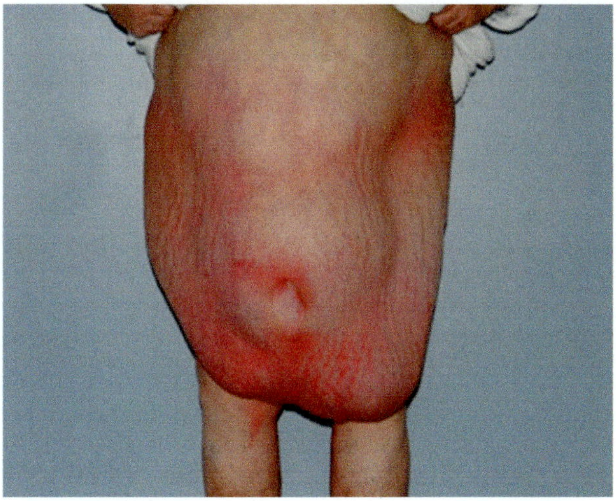

Picture 3.7 Giant ventral hernia (courtesy of Prof. P. Negro and Prof. F. Gossetti, Rome)

Strangulated hernia is a typical emergency hospital presentation with a non-reducible abdominal bulging associated with pain, vomiting, and constipation. It is estimated to affect 3% circa of inguinal and 6–15% of cases of abdominal hernia [21]. Presumably, the number of unreported cases is higher.

It requires an immediate surgical treatment with a complete debridement to avoid the ischemic consequences on the herniated viscera.

In more recent years, significant results in terms of survival, complications and recurrence rates have been achieved in patients affected by huge defects, (Picture 3.7) major co-morbidities, previous abdominal surgical procedures or open abdomen.

3.5 Surgery

Every year 20 million operations of inguinal hernia are performed worldwide and 350.000 and 100.000 ventral hernia procedures in the USA and Germany, respectively.

An important improvement in terms of recurrence rates after inguinal hernia repair has been achieved following the introduction of the meshes.

Also in terms of QOL, length of hospital stay, and postoperative pain, better outcomes have been reported when comparing mesh repair with standard tissue repair.

The majority of hernia surgeries can be performed in an out-patient setting with a classical open anterior mesh repair under local anesthesia. There are several surgical techniques using different mesh devices (Table 3.5). Among these, the Lichtenstein tension free mesh repair is still the most commonly performed. An open hernia repair under local anaesthesia (Table 3.6) lasts on average 45 min and the patient can be dismissed after the surgery, according to ambulatory care setting (Table 3.7).

Table 3.5 Type of meshes related to hernia site

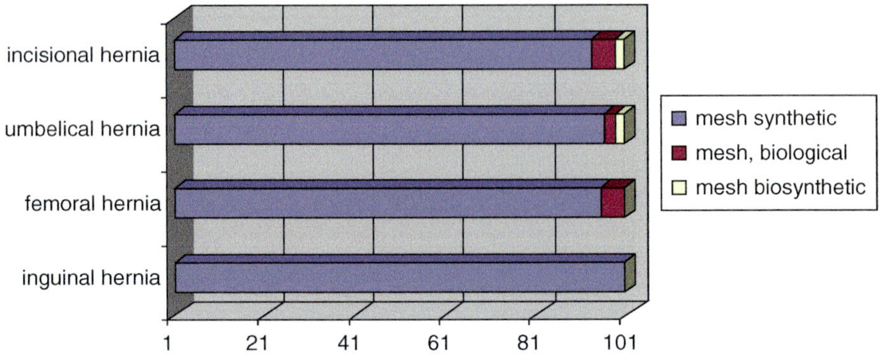

Table 3.6 Site of hernia and type of anesthesia performed

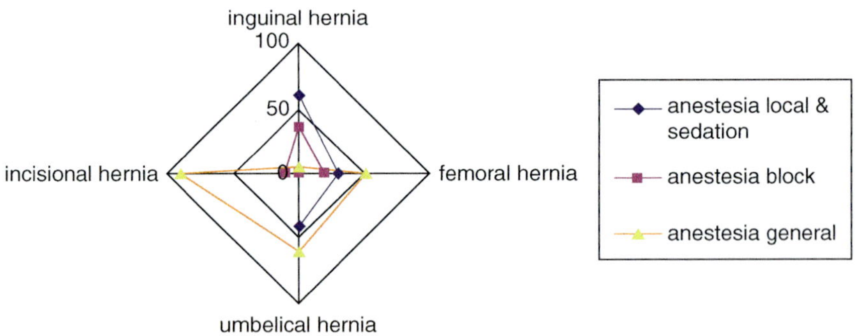

Table 3.7 Type of hernia and clinical settings

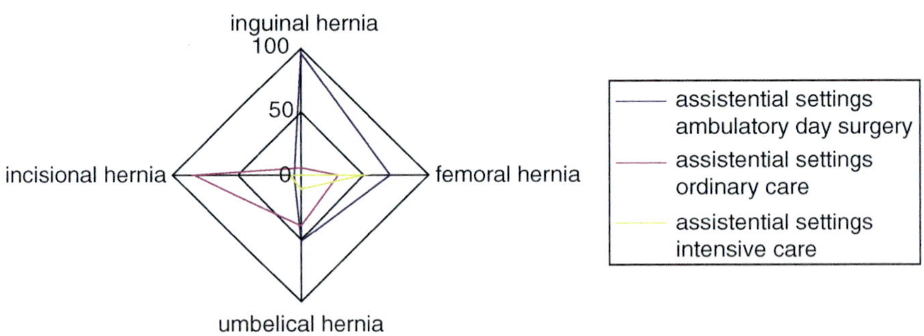

Minimally invasive approach for inguinal hernia repair was first introduced at the beginning of the 1990s. Totally extra-peritoneal (TEP) and transabdominal pre-peritoneal (TAPP) approaches are the two techniques used and the choice depends on the surgeon's preference. Operative time for a TAPP or a TEP procedure varies depending on the experience of the surgical team, the available technologies, the features of the clinical case and it could reach 1 h or more for complex recurrences.

All minimally invasive inguinal hernia repairs are done under general anesthesia, even it has been reported the feasibility of a TEP under spinal anesthesia.

The laparoscopic approach should be preferred to an open one in case of recurrent hernias because it allows avoiding the scar tissue of the previous repair. Bilateral hernia can be a good indication for laparoscopy as it permits the simultaneous treatment of both sides using the same trocar accesses, eliminating the need of a second incision.

Associated abdominal pathology is also considered an indication for the laparoscopic approach, allowing the concomitant minimally invasive treatment of both pathologies in the same session.

Recently, robotic approach has been used for inguinal hernia repair. However, longer operative times and increased costs with no evidence of better outcomes in terms of recurrence rate and hospital stay showed no superiority compared to the laparoscopic approach.

Ventral hernia can occur primarily or postoperatively. Meshes are widely used in ventral hernia repair and are associated with a lower rate of recurrence and better clinical outcomes.

The abdominal wall has to be considered as an organ and therefore its alterations are not only related with local symptoms, but may cause gastrointestinal, cardiovascular, respiratory, postural, and psychological dysfunctions.

Incisional hernia repair can vary widely according to the size and type of the defect. It can range from short procedures for small defects (<5 cm) to much more challenging and long-lasting procedures for complex abdomen requiring high technical skills and higher discomfort for the patient.

The laparoscopic approach can be indicated if the defects are not too large less than 6–7 cm, and mainly if the parietal tension is maintained, so only in case in which the surgeon does not have to reconstruct the abdominal wall.

Recently has been readopted the component separation technique (CST), that was firstly described by a plastic surgeon, Ramirez, in the late 1990s. It has been demonstrated that the CST could be the best option to treat the large and more complex defects of the abdominal wall, especially for the lateral and lumbar ones.

While a laparoscopic ventral hernia repair usually lasts approximately 1 h, for most complex cases approached with an open surgery with CST can be requested even 3 h or more, to 6–8 h.

The robotic technique for the treatment of huge ventral hernia can be considered a good option, as largely confirmed especially by most American surgeons. Nowadays the use of robot is most frequent in the abdominal wall repair than in the other pathologies. The robotic technique is cost and time dependent, but it has the advantage to minimize the dissection of the tissue, reducing the bleeding, the risks of postoperative infections, and fluids collapse.

The length of hospital stay ranges from 1/2 day for laparoscopic procedures to a week or more for more complex clinical scenarios. Some complex ventral hernia requires an intensive care unit bed for the immediate postoperative time, where the patient is transferred intubated and then is awakened very slowly.

There are three kinds of prosthesis used for ventral hernia repair: synthetic, biological, and biosynthetic. Biological and biosynthetic are reabsorbable and act as a biological scaffold for tissue regrowth and are indicated in selected cases belonging to Group 2 and 3 according to Ventral Hernia Working Group Classification.

References

1. Skandalakis JE, Colborn GL, Skandalakis LJ, McClusky DA III. Historic aspects of groin hernia repair. In: Fitzgibbons RJ, Greenburg AG, editors. Nyhus and Condon's hernia. Philadelphia, PA: Lippincott Williams and Wilkins; 2002. p. 29–44.
2. Lyons A, Petrucelli RJ. Geschiedenis van de Geneeskunde ('History of Medicine'/Dutch edition). Antwerpen, Amsterdam: Standaard Uitgeverij; 1981.
3. Celsus AC. De Medicina. Book VII Capitula XVIII to XXI.
4. Franco P. Traité des Hernies, contenant une ample declaration de toutes leurs especes, & autres excellentes parties de la Chirurgie. Lyon: Thibauld Payan; 1561.
5. Paré A. Les Oeuvres. Lyon: Pierre Valfray; 1685.
6. Read RC. The centenary of Bassini's contribution to inguinal herniorrhaphy. Am J Surg. 1987;153(3):324–6.
7. Lau H, Fang C, Yuen WK, Patil NG. Risk factors for inguinal hernia in adult males: a case-control study. Surgery. 2007;141(2):262–6.
8. Jenkins JT, O'Dwyer PJ. Inguinal hernias. BMJ. 2008;336(7638):269–72.
9. Ruhl CE, Everhart JE. Risk factors for inguinal hernia among adults in the US population. Am J Epidemiol. 2007;165(10):1154–61.
10. NHS. Hospital Episode Statistics, Admitted Patient Care—England, 2002–03 [Internet]. NHS Digital. https://digital.nhs.uk/data- and-information/publications/statistical/hospital-admitted-patient-care activity/hospital-episode-statistics-admitted-patient-care-england-2002-03. Cited 3 July 2018.
11. Bassini E. Ueber die behandlung des leistenbruches. Arch Klin Chir. 1890;40:429–76.
12. Lichtenstein IL, Herzikoff S, Shore JM, Jiron MW, Stuart S, Mizuno L. The dynamics of wound healing. Surg Gynecol Obstet. 1970;130(4):685–90.
13. Olsén MF, Wennberg E. Fast-track concepts in major open upper abdominal and thoracoabdominal surgery: a review. World J Surg. 2011;35(12):2586–93.
14. Bourke JB, Lear PA, Taylor M. Effect of early return to work after elective repair of inguinal hernia: clinical and financial consequences at one year and three years. Lancet Lond Engl. 1981;2(8247):623–5.
15. Taylor EW, Dewar EP. Early return to work after repair of a unilateral inguinal hernia. Br J Surg. 1983;70(10):599–600.
16. Everhart JE. Abdominal wall hernia. In: Everhart JE, editor. The burden of diseases in the United States. Washington, DC: US Department of Health and Human Services, Public Health Service, National Institutes of Health, National Institute of Diabetes and Digestive and Kidney Diseases, US Government Printing Office; 2008;. NIH Publication No 09-6443. p. 93–6.
17. Miserez M, Alexandre JH, Campanelli G, Corcione F, Cuccurullo D, Pascual MH, et al. The European hernia society groin hernia classification: simple and easy to remember. Hernia. 2007;11(2):113–6.

18. Muysoms FE, Miserez M, Berrevoet F, Campanelli G, Champault GG, Chelala E, et al. Classification of primary and incisional abdominal wall hernias. Hernia. 2009;13(4):407–14.
19. Ventral Hernia Working Group, Breuing K, Butler CE, Ferzoco S, Franz M, Hultman CS, et al. Incisional ventral hernias: review of the literature and regarding and technique of repair. Surgery. 2010;148(3):544–58.
20. Petro CC, Novitsky YW. Classification of hernias. In: Novitsky YW, editor. Hernia surgery: current principles. Berlin: Springer. p. 15–22.
21. Dietz UA, Menzel S, Lock J, Wiegering A. The treatment of incisional hernia. Dtsch Arztebl Int. 2018;115(3):31–7.

Unit of Wall Surgery

4

Francesco Gossetti, Linda D'Amore, Francesca Ceci,
Lucia Bambi, Elena Annesi, and Paolo Negro

4.1 Introduction

Hernia operations are among the most common general surgery procedures, with some 20 million inguinal hernias performed worldwide and 350,000 abdominal wall repairs (AWRs) executed each year for abdominal wall hernias occurring in 2 million patients undergoing abdominal surgery, only in the USA [1]. These repairs have become more and more difficult due to the introduction of laparoscopic approach but also to the variety of surgical techniques and innovative devices, continuously put on the market by the industry.

Moreover, the attention of surgeons toward herniorrhaphy has dramatically changed, focusing their interests on the consideration not only of recurrence and chronic pain but also of indications, choice of materials and devices, postoperative management, and patient's and operator's satisfaction. "The realm of greater understanding of abdominal wall problems and their repairs has improved patient outcomes and delivered this form of surgery to a true specialty" [2].

Patient centered surgery, the so-called tailored approach, has become largely adopted implying the need of a wide knowledge of the topic, including also quality of life measures, functional outcomes, and satisfaction scores.

This is particularly real if we narrow the field to abdominal wall repair. In fact, risk factors are particularly frequent in these patients, thus leading to a high rate of postoperative complications, such as surgical site occurrence (SSO) and surgical site infection (SSI), prolonged hospital stay, frequent readmissions, and therefore

F. Gossetti (✉) · L. D'Amore · F. Ceci · P. Negro
Department of Surgery, Abdominal Wall Surgery Unit, Sapienza University of Rome, Rome, Italy
e-mail: gossetti@tiscalinet.it; linda.damore@uniroma1.it

L. Bambi · E. Annesi
Graduate School in General Surgery, Sapienza University of Rome, Rome, Italy

D. P. Greco, E. Borgonovi (eds.), *Abdominal Wall Surgery*,
https://doi.org/10.1007/978-3-030-02426-0_4

higher cost of care. On the basis of the Cochrane database, the number of AWRs performed worldwide is huge, 350,000 in the USA and 450,000 in Europe [1]. In Italy this rate is about 40,000 AWRs/year, with an estimated cost of 200 million of euro, while in the USA it has been evaluated around 3.2 billion US$/year, with a reported recurrence rate ranging from 24% to 43%. There is a significant added cost to recurrent repair. In fact, it has been calculated a cost saving of US $32 million dollars for each 1% reduction in reoperation rate [1]. Furthermore, the recurrence of incisional hernia may increase morbidity and consequently the cost. These findings reinforce and underline the importance of durable first repair.

Some variables are able to influence the clinical course of the patient and may predict late complications, hospital readmissions, and recurrence, such as demographics, medical history, operative data, and ASA score. Medical history is one of the criteria classifying an abdominal hernia as "complex." The main variable considered as risk factors for a complicated course consists in the recurrence of abdominal hernia. In fact, recurrence rate ranges from 24% after the first repair to 39% after the third one [3]. Other patient-related risk factors are all those conditions impacting on wound healing, as smoking, diabetes, obesity, poor nutritional status, and steroid use.

The definition "complex" is also strictly connected to other conditions, as defect size and location, such as large-sized, parastomal, lumbar, lateral, subcostal locations, more than 20% of loss of intra-abdominal domain, contamination of the wound environment, namely class III and IV, according to Ventral Hernia Working Group (VHWG) classification, conditions of the soft tissue, as significant loss of skin, the presence of a laparostomy covered with skin graft, battle-scarred abdomen, loss of myofascial tissue, and similar.

The clinical scenario also plays a significant role: an emergency hernia operation including a bowel resection has to be considered "complex" as well as the presence of entero-cutaneous fistulas, a previously placed mesh or when a primary closure is not feasible [4].

The classification of a hernia in simple or complex obviously affects the clinical course and therefore the cost for single patient.

An analysis of perioperative factors influencing cost in AWRs, performed by the University Hospital of Pennsylvania in 2014, assessed a charge of 35,000 US$ for each complex AWR, with improved expenses in case of preoperative risk factors, as each increase of ASA score (US$ 35,000) or diabetes (US$ 30,000); extra costs were documented also in case of trauma (US$ 32,000) or concurrent intra-abdominal occurrence (US$ 2500) or if a biological implant is used (US$ 23,000). SSI and mesh infection are responsible of extra costs equivalent to US$ 65,000 and US$ 82,000, respectively [5].

4.2 Which Surgeron?

The high number of inguinal and abdominal wall repairs performed yearly, with over 20 million meshes implanted, together with the great amount of failures has raised the question if surgeons must specialize in abdominal wall surgery to achieve the maximum benefit for patients with the minimum cost for the community [6]. It is actually difficult to argue that AWR does not require a specialization. The treatment of complex incisional hernia is clearly not a minor procedure. It is a major surgery, requiring long operative times, skilled surgeons with high volume experience in complex cases, a multidisciplinary approach, and risk stratification models to reduce complications, mortality rates, and cost [7, 8].

The attention has been particularly focused on the surgical volume–outcome relationship, with the aim of reducing both morbidity/mortality rates and health care cost. Recently Aquina et al. found a solid relationship between individual surgeon incisional hernia repair volume and patient outcome and cost of the procedure [9]. The perception of such correlation was already expressed in 1979 by Luft et al. that showed there was an association between hospital volume and mortality for complex procedures as open heart surgery or coronary by-pass [10]. This relationship was subsequently enlarged to other major surgical techniques but only few studies investigated if a correlation volume–outcome does exist in AWR. The study by Aquina et al. was based on data derived from the Statewide Planning and Research Cooperative System (SPARCS), a database of the New York Department of Health. Authors were able to demonstrate that very high (>35 operations/year) and high (24–35 operations/year) volume surgeons had significantly lower hernia reoperation rates when compared to low volume surgeons, over the 5-year time period (6.0%, 8.7%, and 10.3%, respectively). Moreover, every increase of surgeon volume of ten cases per year led to an 8% reduction in hernia reoperation and this potentially decreased in the same way cost for the community. This study did not include laparoscopic ventral hernia repair or more complex open AWR with component separation or abdominal wall repair. For these cases, further revisions are needed.

If there is a volume–outcome relationship, there should be a trend toward the regionalization and formation of centers of excellence as well as the implementation of continuing medical education courses. Actually there are many institutions specifically dedicated to treat abdominal wall hernias, both hospital-affiliated (44.5%) or independent and their number has been increasing over time. The characteristics of these centers vary greatly and there are no clear protocols to certify their activities and results, also because only a small part of them (44.5%) have published at least one paper on abdominal wall hernias indexed by PubMed [11]. This involves a shortage in sharing results with particular regard to complications and outcomes. One of the main duties of a hernia center should be the education, having as target the improvement of surgeons' specific knowledge also through publication of scientific papers. Moreover an accurate analysis of results may lead to a progress in the management of patients with subsequent increase of their satisfaction. Recently, the Americas Hernia Society established a multi-institutional task force, the Americas Hernia Society Quality Collaborative (AHSQC) with the aim to utilize and develop the concepts of continuous quality improvement [12]. It represents a further effort to maximize value in hernia care delivered to patients built on previous experiences. Quality improvements priorities for the AHSQC are represented by the identification of factors contributing to recurrence (and its mechanism) and mesh infection, the assessment of the quality of life after hernia repair, the reduction of SSI and perioperative pain, the validation of hernia classification system, the evaluation of the impact of hernia characteristics on outcomes, and the choice of the optimal method of mesh fixation, through data outcome-related collected in a standard disease-based registry.

4.3 Certification

Actually there is any institution or board certifying the excellence of a hernia center and the majority of them use this definition not for scientific but only for marketing purposes. "A basic requirement for a credible certification process for hernia centers involves definition of requirements and their verification by hernia societies and/or non-profit organizations that are interested in assuring the best possible quality of hernia surgery. Besides, the treatment quality actually achieved by the certified center must be ascertained through obligatory participation in a quality assurance program or registry involving follow-up of patients" [13]. Until now, there are only two systems for accreditation of hernia centers and hernia surgeons, the Surgical Review Corporation (SRC), a non-profit organization and, in Europe, the German Hernia Society (DHG) with the German Society of General and Visceral Surgery (DGAV). Both these systems issue the accreditation by programs based on volume of surgery, facilities, and outcomes.

The Italian Society of Hernia and Abdominal Wall Surgery (ISHAWS), National Chapter of the European Hernia Society (EHS) has recently proposed a certification program, based on three different levels, addressed both to hernia centers and hernia surgeons. The first level (FLC) certifies a single surgeon, with a particular interest in hernia surgery and who has sufficient skill to deal with inguinal/abdominal hernia patients; the second and the third identify National Referral and High Specialization Centers for Abdominal Wall Surgery.

Every day surgical hernia practice demonstrates that the individual surgeon does impact the outcome quality [14]. This is the reason why FLC certification process takes into account a minimum number of procedures to complete the learning curve for open and laparoscopic inguinal/abdominal hernia repair for a single surgeon. It is given under request in provisory form once the programmed learning curve has been completed; FLC is then confirmed after the report of individual surgeon's annual volume of operations (for inguinal and abdominal hernias, both laparoscopic and open) and the relative results. It is mandatory that these values agree with the standards, previously established by the ISHAWS Commission.

The second (ISHAWS Referral Centers for Abdominal Wall Surgery) and the third (ISHAWS High Specialization Centers for Abdominal Wall Surgery) level of certification have been thought to create facilities with the same surgical and organizational standards, but different tasks: in fact, while ISHAWS Referral Centers are more dedicated to clinical and surgical activity, the attention of High Specialization Centers is directed also to scientific activity, such as promoting studies and publishing results, and referral for complex patients. Moreover, in our opinion, educational training programs for young surgeons should be included among the targets of each center.

References

1. Poulose BK, Shelton J, Phillips S, Moore D, Nealon W, Penson D, Beck W, Holzman MD. Epidemiology and cost of ventral hernia repair: making the case for hernia research. Hernia. 2012;16:179–83.
2. Roll A. A global vision for hernia repair improvement. Gen Surg Laparosc News. 2012;39:1.
3. Flum DR, Horvath K, Koepsell T. Have outcomes of incisional hernia repairs improved with times? A population-based analysis. Ann Surg. 2003;237:129–35.
4. Slater NJ, Montgomery A, Berrevoet F, Carbonell AM, Chang A, Franklin M, Kercher KW, Lammers BJ, Parra-Davilla E, Roll S, Towfigh S, van Geffen E, Conze J, van Goor H. Criteria for definition of a complex abdominal wall hernia. Hernia. 2014;18:7–17.
5. Fischer JP, Wes AM, Wink JD, Nelson JA, Rohrbach JI, Braslow BM, Kovasch SJ. Analysis of perioperative factors associated with increased cost following abdominal wall reconstruction (AWR). Hernia. 2014;18:617–24.
6. Sanders DL, Kingsnorth AN, Windsor AC. Is there a role for hernia subspecialist? Or is this a step too far? Hernia. 2016;20:637–40.
7. Berry MF, Paisley F, Low DW, Rosato EF. Repair of large complex recurrent incisional hernias with retromuscular mesh and panniculectomy. Am J Surg. 2007;194:199–204.
8. Gossetti F, D'Amore L, Ceci F, Grimaldi MR, Negro P. Abdominal wall reconstruction (AWR): The need to identify the hospital units and referral centers entitled to perform it. Updat Surg. 2017;69:289–90. https://doi.org/10.1007/s13304-017-0428-x.
9. Aquina CT, Kelly KN, Probst CP, Iannuzzi JC, Noyes K, Langstein HN, Monson JR, Fleming FJ. Surgeon volume plays a significant role in outcomes and cost following open incisional hernia repair. J Gastrointest Surg. 2015;19:100–10. https://doi.org/10.1007/s11605-014-2627-9.
10. Luft HS, Bunker JP, Enthoven AC. Should operations be regionalized? The empirical relation between surgical volume and mortality. New Engl J Med. 1979;301:1364–9.
11. Kalacoglu H, Oztuna D. Current status of hernia centres around the globe. Indian J Surg. 2015;77(Suppl 3):S1023–6. https://doi.org/10.1007/s12262-014-1115-5.
12. Poulose BK, Roll S, Murphy JW, Mattews BD, Todd Heniford B, Voeller G, Hope WW, Goldblatt MI, Adrales GL, Rosen MJ. Design and implementation of the Americas Hernia Society Quality Collaborative (AHSQC): improving value in hernia care. Hernia. 2016;20:177–89. https://doi.org/10.1007/s10029-016-1477-7.
13. Kockerling F, Berger D, Jost JO. What is a certified hernia center? The example of the German Hernia Society and German Society of General and Visceral Surgery. Front Surg. 2014;1:1–4. https://doi.org/10.3389/fsurg.2014.00026.
14. Lorenz R, Stechemesser B, Reinpold W, Fortenly R, Mayer F, Schroeder W, Kockerling F. Development of a standardized curriculum concept for continuing training in hernia surgery: German Hernia School. Hernia. 2017;21:153–62. https://doi.org/10.1007/s10029-016-1566-7.

Organization and Certification of Abdominal Wall Surgery

5

Carla Rognoni

5.1 Introduction

Hernia surgery has become increasingly complex over the last 25 years due to the introduction of new techniques and a plethora of new medical devices. The use of the different techniques in hernia surgery has been adopted as a personalized approach program which requires intense commitment and extensive experience throughout the field, highlighting the need for specialized hernia centers. In these centers surgery is performed by specifically accredited hernia surgeons that, as far as possible, dominate all the surgical techniques and play an active role in training and continuing education [1].

A study showed that, regardless of the surgical technique, the recurrence rate is significantly higher for general surgeons who are not hernia specialists compared with hernia specialists [2]. Each recurrence after primary hernia repair represents an additional economic burden for the healthcare system and can lead to considerable complications for the patient.

A fundamental requirement for a reliable certification process for hernia centers involves defining requirements and their verification by bodies like hernia societies and/or non-profit organizations interested in ensuring the best possible quality of this kind of surgery. In addition, the treatment quality actually achieved by the certified centers must be determined through mandatory participation in quality assurance programs or registries that include also patient monitoring. Currently, there are two processes for certification of hernia centers [3, 4]:

C. Rognoni (✉)
Centre for Research on Health and Social Care Management (CERGAS), SDA Bocconi School of Management, Bocconi University, Milan, Italy
e-mail: carla.rognoni@unibocconi.it

D. P. Greco, E. Borgonovi (eds.), *Abdominal Wall Surgery*,
https://doi.org/10.1007/978-3-030-02426-0_5

1. Certified Center of Excellence in Hernia Surgery (COEHS) by the non-profit organization Surgical Review Corporation (SRC): the SRC applies an integrated approach by combining a rigorous program and a central database for outcomes monitoring.
2. Certified Hernia Center of the German Hernia Society (DHG) and the German Society of General and Visceral Surgery (DGAV). Three certification levels exist:
   Level 1: DHG (German Hernia Society)—seal of quality assurance in hernia surgery;
   Level 2: Competence Center for Hernia Surgery;
   Level 3: Reference Center for Hernia Surgery.

For each level, hernia centers need to meet a number of requirements, for example, registration and follow-up of patients, minimum operation numbers, and involvement of science and training. In particular, the total complication rate for inguinal hernia surgery must be less than 5%, reoperation rate for inguinal hernia surgery must be less than 2%, reoperation rate for incisional hernia surgery must be less than 10%, infection/revision rate after open incisional hernia surgery must be less than 10%, and infection/revision rate after laparoscopic incisional hernia surgery must be less than 3%. For a Center of Competence and a Center of Reference it is required a case load of 200 and 250 hernias per year, respectively. As regards the follow-up, a rate of at least 60% must be accomplished.

5.2 The Spanish Example

The Spanish hospital network includes more than 800 hospitals, which are classified into three levels according to the complexity of medical care they provide [5]. Anyway, these levels are not related specifically to abdominal wall surgery. For this reason, in Spain there are specialized abdominal wall surgery units in hospitals of different levels of surgical complexity. So the complexity level of a hospital is not always related with the abdominal wall surgery units.

In Spain there is no centralized specific registry of abdominal wall activity. It depends exclusively on surgeons, services, and hospitals. The only available registry is the "Spanish Register of Incisional Hernia" (EVEREG), but not all the hospitals that are operating on incisional hernias are involved, so not all repairs are registered. There are no other types of registries except personal, services, or hospital databases. EVEREG is an online prospective database which has been functioning since July 2012 in which operations for incisional hernia are anonymously recorded. Main data are related to pre-operation period, anatomical considerations, operating time, defect closure, and registration of concomitant abdominal surgery. The database keeps also track of complications, as intraoperative wound contamination or intraoperative/postoperative complications, mesh infection/removal, pain experienced in hospital, and post-surgical patient death. Patients are observed in the follow-up after 1 month, 6 months, 1 year, and 2 years. The follow-up achievement is more than 35% [6].

The average length of the waiting list for surgery is not available for the entire state. Data are variable between Autonomic Communities. In Catalonia in the first semester of 2017 the length of the waiting list for inguinal hernia was 119 days; for umbilical, incisional, and other types of hernia it was 177 days.

Data from 2005 on procedures performed in Day-Hospital show that 38.3% of them are for inguinal hernia, while the remaining 59.7% are for primary ventral hernia. The percentage of private surgery on the total hernia surgeries is unknown because there is no information available about private surgery.

The total number of hernia repairs provided by the Ministry of Health in 2015 was 68,268 (inguinal 52.10%; primary ventral 17.10%; incisional about 30.70%). The mean hospitalization duration for inguinal hernia in 2008 was 1.95 days. The mean time for surgery (operating theatre) is estimated to be about 44 min for both inguinal hernia (open surgery) and umbilical hernia.

The choice of prostheses for hernia repair is mainly based on economic aspects. Data extracted from the incisional hernia register between 2012 and 2015 (not included all the performed repairs in Spain) show that in about 98% of cases synthetic meshes are preferred; 1% utilization rate is reported for both biologic and biosynthetic meshes. The use of custom packs for hernia surgery, generally containing sutures and a hernia mesh, depends on the choice of the Hospital and the Autonomic Community.

As regards the hospital reimbursement, the DRG 162 (2237€ in 2008) is applied for unilateral inguinal hernia [7].

5.3 The Eastern Europe Example (Poland)

In Poland about 30% of hospitals are I level centers, 40% are II level centers, and the remaining 30% represents III level centers. The system is under construction, and the new National Healthcare Service (NHS) will complete the so-called hospital net stratified into three levels during 2018.

As regards clinical data related to patients undergoing hernia surgery, they are collected through local databases but the collection is not mandatory and is performed in a minority of the hospitals. Data regarding accessibility are not shared directly by the NHS, but are in general presented at hernia congresses for the NHS patients. These data show an average length of the waiting list for surgery of 90–120 days for inguinal and umbilical hernia and 90–220 days for incisional hernia.

Although private centers do not belong to the NHS, the percent of private hernia surgery is supposed to be less than 5% of the total hernia surgeries.

Hernia interventions are performed in Day-Hospital in less than 2% of cases, while the remaining 98% of cases are performed on hospitalized patients; these interventions are 60% for inguinal hernia, 15% for umbilical hernia, and 25% for incisional hernia, with a mean hospitalization duration of 3 days.

The surgical intervention in general lasts from 40 to 120 min for inguinal hernia; longer times, from 45 to 240 min, are reported for incisional hernia interventions.

In this setting, the choice of prostheses for hernia repair is mainly based on economic aspects (in the tenders organized in the hospitals 100% of mesh value is price). For incisional hernia repair, in 99% of cases a synthetic mesh is used, while in the remaining cases biologic and biosynthetic meshes are equidistributed.

Concerning the hospital reimbursement, for large incisional hernias few centers apply the DRG code F42 (abdominal cavity adhesiolysis) with a reimbursement of 1457€. For the other types of hernia surgery (inguinal hernia—laparoscopic or open surgery, umbilical hernia, incisional hernia) the DRG code F72 is used, which has a reimbursement of 561€. Custom packs for hernia surgery are not used in the clinical practice.

5.4 The Italian Example

In Italy there is not a specific organization for abdominal wall surgery in centers with different levels. The Italian Society of Hernia and Abdominal Wall Surgery (ISHAWS), National Chapter of European Hernia Society, has just proposed a new method for the certification for both hernia surgeons and hernia centers according to parameters to receive and maintain certification derived from a systematic review of the literature [8]. Hernia centers should offer high standards of care to the patients apart from their level of certification. Therefore, the ISHAWS commission chose to develop a common methodology to define high quality of cure. The process of certification for surgeons and centers has been developed considering the following criteria: learning curve, volume of procedures, and surgical outcomes (morbidity, mortality, surgical site infections, recurrence, and chronic pain). Systematic literature reviews have been performed in order to define the minimum requirements for each criterion (e.g., the number of interventions required to master every single procedure). In case of lack of data from the literature, the criterion was fixed through a commission discussion. Table 5.1 reports a summary of minimum requirements for each criterion.

The Commission defined a certification process including:

1. *First level certification: ISHAWS First Level Certification (FLC) restricted to the single surgeon.* The applicant surgeon should have performed 120 inguinal hernia repairs (60 by open approach, 60 laparo/endoscopic, optional open preperitoneal) and 40 abdominal wall repairs (20 open, 20 laparoscopic) and provide a volume of 50 inguinal hernia repairs (25 open, 25 laparo/endoscopic) and 50 incisional hernia repairs (25 open and 25 laparoscopic) per year.
2. *Second level certification: ISHAWS Referral Center for Abdominal Wall Surgery.* The center should present the following facilities: weekly dedicated outpatient clinic, possibility of admitting emergency patients, surgeon on call 24/7 and anesthesiologist on call 24/7, intensive care unit on site or in network, laboratory testing on site, CT scan available on site or in network, and transfusion center on site. Strict surgical requirements are requested according to the type of procedures offered, the year volumes, and the surgical approaches [8]. The

Table 5.1 List of minimum requirements for each criterion for the different surgical procedures

	Minimally invasive inguinal hernia repair	Open inguinal hernia repair	Laparoscopic abdominal wall reconstruction	Open abdominal wall reconstruction
Learning curve (minimum number of procedures)	60	60	20	20
Volume of procedures (volume/year/surgeon)	25	25	25	25
Mortality	Below 0.5% within 30 days postoperatively		SAWR below 1%; CAWR below 5% within 30 days postoperatively	
Overall morbidity	Below 10% within 30 days postoperatively		SAWR below 30%; CAWR below 50% within 30 days postoperatively	
Surgical site infection	Below 3% within 30 days postoperatively		SAWR below 10%; CAWR below 30% within 30 days postoperatively	
Chronic postoperative pain	Below 15% at 3 months follow-up		–	
Recurrence	Below 2% at 1 year follow-up with any diagnostic technique		SAWR below 5% at 1 year follow-up, and 15% at 3 years follow-up; CAWR below 10% at 1 year follow-up, and 20% at 3 years follow-up; any diagnostic technique	

SAWR simple abdominal wall repair, *CAWR* complex abdominal wall repair

commission requires as mandatory a multidisciplinary approach and the use of adequate follow-up and tools for outcome. Moreover, the Referral Center should serve as a training site for the Italian School providing cases and occasion to learn for surgeons who want to specialize in abdominal wall surgery.

3. *Third level certification: ISHAWS High Specialization Center for Abdominal Wall Surgery.* It is a public or private structure managed by at least three surgeons, members of ISHAWS. Facilities, surgical requirements, follow-up evaluations, and surgical outcomes are the same as those required for Referral Centers, with the addition of 150 procedures for inguinal hernia repair and 50 abdominal wall repair procedures. The Center should serve as a training site for the Italian School and must organize a course or workshop yearly.

All certified hernia surgeons as well as the leading surgeons of a certified hernia center must be members of the Italian Society of Hernia and Abdominal Wall Surgery (Italian Chapter of the European Hernia Society) at the moment of the application.

The design of different kinds of hernia centers does not imply offering different standards of care to the patients. This means creating different entities which offer the same surgical quality with separate missions: the Referral Centers being more dedicated to surgical and clinical activity while High Specialization Centers being more directed to the management of complex cases and to scientific activities.

In order to evaluate surgeons and centers according to the pre-specified criteria, it is fundamental to collect and monitor clinical data in a prospective way through registries/databases. In Italy there isn't a centralized registry of abdominal wall surgeries and patient's data are in general collected through local databases. Data from these sources show that the average length of the waiting list for surgery is about 1 year for inguinal and umbilical hernia and about 300 days for incisional hernia. The majority of hernia surgeries (60%) are performed in a Day-Hospital setting. About 3% of all the interventions are performed through private surgery. In total, 75% of interventions are inguinal hernia repairs, while the remaining are distributed between umbilical (15%) and incisional hernia (10%) repairs. The mean duration of the hospitalization is quite low, in general less than 1 day for inguinal hernia and ranging from 1–3 to 3–10 days for umbilical and incisional hernia, respectively.

The mean time for the operating theater for inguinal hernia is 50 min in open surgery and 90 min in laparoscopic surgery, while for umbilical hernia is about 50 min and for incisional hernia this time may range from 120 to 300 min.

The criteria for the selection of the prosthesis for hernia repair depend on the quality of the surgical field (clean, clean-contaminated, contaminated, dirty); the most used meshes are synthetic.

As regards the reimbursements, an inguinal hernia performed in open surgery with hospitalization less than 1 day is classified with the DRG code 162 with a reimbursement of 1280€. The same inguinal hernia performed with laparoscopic surgery (hospitalization > 1 day) is classified with the same DRG code but with a reimbursement of 1168€. Other types of hernia (e.g., umbilical hernia) are reimbursed through the DRG code 160 but with different tariffs: 1523€ in case of hospitalization less than 1 day and 1371€ in case of longer hospitalizations. DRG code 160 is also applied for the reimbursement for incisional hernia (1523€). Data of the Italian DRG system do not allow to draw any difference about procedures (laparoscopic or open), non-inguinal hernia and post-incisional hernia, or the use of anesthesia.

5.5 Conclusions

The term "specialized hernia center" is often undefined or poorly defined and rarely based on scientific standards of excellence. Hernia specialists should be assessed according to objective parameters of expertise, annual case load, outcomes, and contributions to education and science.

In order to improve hernia surgery outcomes, a quality control should be performed continuously. This implies that outcomes data on all patients who undergo hernia surgery procedures should be collected in a prospective way through registries/databases, consistent with patient privacy and confidentiality regulations.

Thriving outcomes can be assured in hernia surgery only through reliable implementation of quality requirements. In Europe, Germany has already implemented certified programs for hernia centers but other countries show a non-homogeneous modality to classify hernia surgery units. For example, in Spain hospitals are classified into three levels according to the complexity of medical care they provide but these levels are not related specifically to abdominal wall surgery; in Poland the framework is under construction with a foreseen accomplishment of the new stratification of hernia centers into three levels within 2018, while in Italy the implementation of a specific organization for abdominal wall surgery in centers with different levels has just started.

All centers performing hernia surgery should face up to this challenge and become certified. To this end, hernia societies worldwide should implement certification programs to ensure surgery high quality standards.

Acknowledgments The author would like to thank Dr. Cesare Stabilini for having provided updated information on the process for the certification of hernia centers in Italy. The author would also acknowledge with gratitude the clinical experts who gave information about the organization and certification of hernia surgery in the different countries: Dr. Pierluigi Ipponi and Dr. Dalila Patrizia Greco (Italy), Dr. José A. Pereira (Spain), and Dr. Maciej Smietansky (Poland).

References

1. Köckerling F, Berger D, Jost JO. What is a Certified Hernia Center? The Example of the German Hernia Society and German Society of General and Visceral Surgery. Front Surg. 2014;1:26.
2. Gilbert AI, Graham MF, Young J, Patel BG, Shaw K. Closer to an ideal solution for inguinal hernia repair: comparison between general surgeons and hernia specialists. Hernia. 2006;10:162–8.
3. Köckerling F. How to build up specialized hernia centers and is benefits for the patients, surgeons and health care. Hernia. 2016;20(Suppl 2):S152.
4. Van Ramshorst GH, Bonjer HJ, Cuccurullo D, Bittner R, Tran H. Hernia surge guidelines: specialised hernia centers. Hernia. 2016;20(Suppl 2):S153.
5. Trias M, Targarona EM, Moral A, Pera C. Surgery in Spain. Arch Surg. 1998;133(2):218–22.
6. Kyle-Leinhase I, Köckerling F, Jørgensen LN, Montgomery A, Gillion JF, Rodriguez JAP, Hope W, Muysoms F. Comparison of hernia registries: the CORE project. Hernia. 2018;22(4):561–75.
7. Serdén L, O'Reilly J. Patient classification and hospital reimbursement for inguinal hernia repair: a comparison across 11 European countries. Hernia. 2014;18(2):273–81.
8. Stabilini C, Cavallaro G, Bocchi P, et al. Defining the characteristics of certified hernia centers in Italy: the Italian society of hernia and abdominal wall surgery workgroup consensus on systematic reviews of the best available evidences. Int J Surg. 2018;54(Pt A):222–35.

Biomaterials in Abdominal Wall Surgery

6

Dalila Patrizia Greco and Claudia Abbati

6.1 History of Prosthetics in Hernia Surgery

"If we could artificially produce tissues of the density and toughness of fascia and tendon the secret of the radical cure of hernia would be discovered" appeared in the classic Beitrage zur Chirurgie (1878) from Czerny, quoting Billroth [1].

In the early 1900s Witzel and Goepel in Germany produced the first metal prosthesis, from silver filigrees [2, 3]. In 1935 Nylon, the trade name for Polyamide, was discovered; it was the first polymer synthesized. The first reports in which Nylon was used as a prosthetic are by Aquaviva and Bounet of Marseille in 1944 [4] and Moloney et al. in 1948 [5].

The original logic behind using a mesh was very simple, at that time: to reinforce the abdominal wall with the composition of scar tissue. For this reason, it was expected that the best meshes would be those made of very strong material and able to induce the most fibrosis [6]. Unfortunately, this fibrotic reaction led to pain and movement restriction.

Nylon became replaced by other plastics because, over time, it lost its tensile strength from hydrolysis and denaturation. In 1941, polyethylene terephthalate (PET), also known by its brand name, Dacron, was patented in the United Kingdom [7], and the first polyethylene mesh was introduced by Francis Usher.

Soon after, in 1954, the Italian chemist Giulio Natta, and his German colleague, Karl Ziegler, discovered polypropylene (PP), the discovery of which won the two

D. P. Greco (✉)
Day&Week Surgery Unit, Ospedale Niguarda Ca' Granda, Milano, Italy
e-mail: dalilapatriziagreco@gmail.com

C. Abbati
Department of Surgery, Niguarda Hospital, Milan, Italy

University of Milan, Milan, Italy

D. P. Greco, E. Borgonovi (eds.), *Abdominal Wall Surgery*,
https://doi.org/10.1007/978-3-030-02426-0_6

researchers the Nobel Prize in Chemistry in 1961. Polypropylene was introduced as a mesh in 1963, and it became in few times the most popular prosthetic mesh. It was knitted, could be autoclaved, had firm borders, so it could be cut without fraying, and was rapidly incorporated [2]. Plastic meshes made it possible for surgeons to repair hernias by bridging tissue gaps rather than subjecting them to high tension suture closures, resulting in a decrease in recurrences [8].

The benefits of meshes were accepted for many years, but the need for evidence-based medicine led to several trials designed to quantify their advantages [6]. In 2002, the EU trialist collaboration [9] analyzed 58 randomized controlled trials and found that the use of mesh was superior to other techniques, at least in terms of recurrences and persistent pain.

In the late 1990s, the number of companies offering prosthetics increased, and they began to produce many different kinds of products, most of which were made of PP. At the turn of the twenty-first century, surgeons realized that it would be better if they reduce the weight of the prosthetic, which would leave less foreign material in the body [7]. Lightweight meshes were first introduced in 1998 (Vypro), and their superiority over the heavyweight meshes is now widely accepted [6, 10, 11].

In 2006 non-conventional mesh as "mosquito net" [12], whose use was reserved for developing countries with low economic resources as a cheaper alternative to commercial mesh, was firstly investigated. Several studies in the following years confirmed that the material and mechanical properties of the mosquito net are substantially equivalent to those of commonly used lightweight commercial meshes [13, 14]. There is still some concern about the long-term effect that the elements of degradation of mosquito net mesh may potentially produce, since the material is PP, but it has not been produced for implantation in humans.

In the last years the improvements in new techniques, as laparoscopic surgery which needs intra-abdominal mesh, the attention to infections, and post-operative pain, have induced industries to develop new materials such as partially absorbable, combined, biological, and coated meshes.

6.2 Mesh

6.2.1 Classification

Before selecting any mesh or device, it is important to know its features and characteristics. Classifications aim to favor this approach.

In recent years several meshes have come in and out of commerce. In the presence of such a large number of choices, it has become necessary to classify the products. Any grouping should focus on relevant major differences.

The classification may be based, for instance, on porosity (Table 6.1), on weight (Table 6.2), on product category (Table 6.3), or on an association of different parameter (Table 6.4). In this latter classification it is highlighted how the presence of mixed or coated meshes makes classification even more complex, as it becomes difficult to estimate the host's response to the mix of the two materials.

Table 6.1 P. K. Amid's classification based on dimension of pore [15]

Type	Quality	Pore size
I	Totally macroporous	>75 μm
II	Totally microporous	<10 μm
III	Macroporous with multifilamentous or microporous	–
IV	Not referred	Submicronic pore

Table 6.2 Classification from A. Coda et al. based on weight [7]

Classes	Definition	Weight
1	Ultra-light	<35 g/m^2
2	Light	≥35 < 70 g/m^2
3	Standard	≥70 < 140 g/m^2
4	Heavy	≥140 g/m^2

Table 6.3 Modified classification from C. R. Deeken and S. Kalaba based on product category [16]

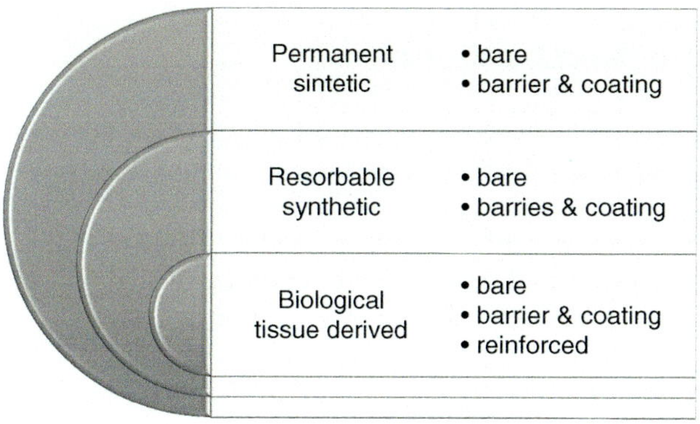

Table 6.4 U. Klinge and B. Klosterhalfen's classification based on weight and biomaterial [17]

Class	Definition	Subgroup
1	With large pore porosity >60%[a]	Monofilament
		Multifilament
		Mixed or polymer
2	With small pore porosity <60%	Monofilament
		Multifilament
		Mixed or polymer
3	With special features[b]	For example, with barriers and coatings
4	With film[c]	–
5	3D mesh[d]	–
6	Biological	Non-cross-linked
		Cross-linked
		Special features

[a]Porosity is intended as the percentage of area, which is not covered by filaments, and then reflecting the textile porosity
[b]Porous mesh with special features as to prevent adhesion
[c]Submicronic pore size or secondarily excised pores
[d]Separated from flat mesh, as is not well known how the geometry can affect the degradation of the mesh and the integration with the host

Any attempt to implement a classification of meshes for hernia surgery has to explain its right to exist [17]. For example, Klinge and Klosterhalfen's classification is made up of 6 classes, in order to include the largest part of products available on the market.

We need it for our own quality control, to learn whether a new device is equivalent or improved compared to a previous similar device, at least in terms of safety and effectiveness; moreover, some devices may be related to more adverse events than others. There is an ongoing discussion about new regulations for the approval of medical devices, stressing the necessity for an intensified pre- and post-market surveillance [18].

Moreover, the possibility to group different implanted meshes into comparable cohorts through a classification allows the comparison among devices, supporting the surgeons during decision on the best approach for each patient and in each situation.

6.2.2 How to Describe Meshes

Since it is essential to understand the characteristics of the hernia repair materials prior to implantation, we should be able to make comparison among them through tests or laboratory investigations.

Many parameters to describe a mesh are currently available. Each company can choose independently which test to use to describe their products. We can summarise standards and methodologies of investigation as follows:

- Biomechanical characterization [6, 16, 19] as elasticity, strength, and stiffness
  - suture retention,
  - tear resistance,
  - uniaxial and biaxial tensile testing, ball burst,
- Porosity, pore size [20]
  - from *very large* (>2000 μm) to *microporous* (<100 μm)
- Weight, prosthetic density [20]
  - heavyweight (>90 g/m^2)
  - lightweight
  - ultra-lightweight (<35 g/m^2)
- Texture
  - monofilament, multifilament, mixed structure, or polymer
  - knitted or woven
- Shape
  - flat
  - pre-shaped, 2D/3D structure
- Structural mesh component
  - permanent
  - absorbable synthetic
  - biological tissue-derived

- Biomaterial [7]
  - simple: made of one pure biomaterial
  - composite: made of two or more different layers, one of which is simple, while the other(s) are non-resorbable or resorbable
  - combined: made of two materials knitted or woven together; both materials may be non-resorbable, or with only one filament resorbable
  - coated: with extracellular matrix, antibacterial substances, metals, nitric oxide
  - biological: non-cross-linked or cross-linked

6.2.3 How to Study Meshes

During preclinical studies, meshes are studied on animal models, considering the mechanical environment and function of the animal abdominal wall in different species.

Studies can be conducted on intact abdominal wall or in models, where a lesion similar to a hernia had previously been created. Of course, there are a number of limitations which should be considered when interpreting results and conclusions from the studies that have utilized animal model to examine abdominal wall mechanics.

Among in vivo experimental models to study infection or microbiological studies to investigate bacterial adherence [21], SEM (scanning electron microscope) is the most employed method.

Imaging is an essential tool to study the mesh/host interface in each phase of the process, both before implantation, after surgery while the mesh is part of the abdominal wall, and also post-explantation. It is particularly useful for defining the degradation of the polymer over time (Fig. 6.1), especially in the case of explants, through various techniques:

- Observation with the electron microscope,
- Traditional pathology
- Radiology, MRI for coated meshes

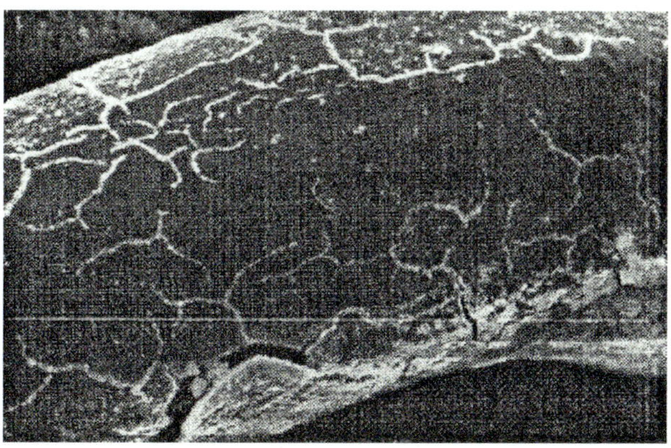

Fig. 6.1 SEM scan 0.1 mm 30.0 KV 1.63E2: corrosion of polypropylene fiber after contact with bacteria. From Greco DP, Forti D. Le protesi nella chirurgia erniaria moderna [19]. [Reproduction authorized by Dr D. P. Greco]

The technique of mesh implants visualization with MRI has been recently introduced [22]; the combination of iron-loaded meshes with MRI gives the possibility to delineate the mesh implant in detail. This might help to improve hernia treatment in two ways: on the one hand, potential mesh-related complications can be assessed accurately and adequate treatment can be initiated, on the other hand, surgeons can learn about regular postsurgical mesh behavior and characteristics. This mesh is made of polyvinylidenfluoride monofilaments and, to provide MR visibility, tiny iron particles have been embedded into the base material, resulting in a mesh concentration of 99% polyvinylidenfluoride and 1% Fe_3O_4.

The most important experience on explanted mesh from human is by Klinge and Klosterhalfen's [17] (Table 6.4). Their studies have also been the basis of one of the most up-to-date classifications. Together with the German Medical Technology Association, they planned to provide this classification on the webpages of the hernia societies.

The introduction and use of a shared and worldwide adopted classification may permit to identify common standards for mesh characterization, and to tailor patients therapy.

Moreover, the constitution of national or international registries for abdominal wall hernia surgery, which of course has to include information about the type of mesh, will account also for quality control of these devices, more than classification. Few examples already exist in some countries [23] and is still under development an international online platform for registration and outcome measurement of ventral abdominal wall hernia repair, EuraHS [24].

6.3 Host and Mesh

6.3.1 Implant and Inflammatory Reaction

The intensity and duration of host mesh reaction depend on type and quantity of the material being used. Primary response is the formation of a layer of palmitic proteins such as albumin, IgG, and fibrinogen around the mesh material, immediately after implantation. Around a week after implantation, the population of mononuclear phagocytic cells differentiates into macrophages. These cells secrete a wide number of effectors which help to modulate the biological response. The inflammatory reaction seals the foreign body in an epithelioid granuloma. In the presence of indigestible prosthetic material, the macrophages coalesce into foreign-body giant cells. The final stage of the biological response is the synthesis of connective tissue. A collagen network is produced for around 21 days. As a consequence of this remodeling, its mechanical strength increases progressively until ~6 months after performing the surgical wound (see Table 6.5). However, at the end of this period, the newly formed tissue only has 80% of the normal mechanical strength of the skin or fascia. Other properties, such as its elasticity or energy absorption capacity, will be even lower [25].

Table 6.5 Inflammatory phases, mesh/host interface

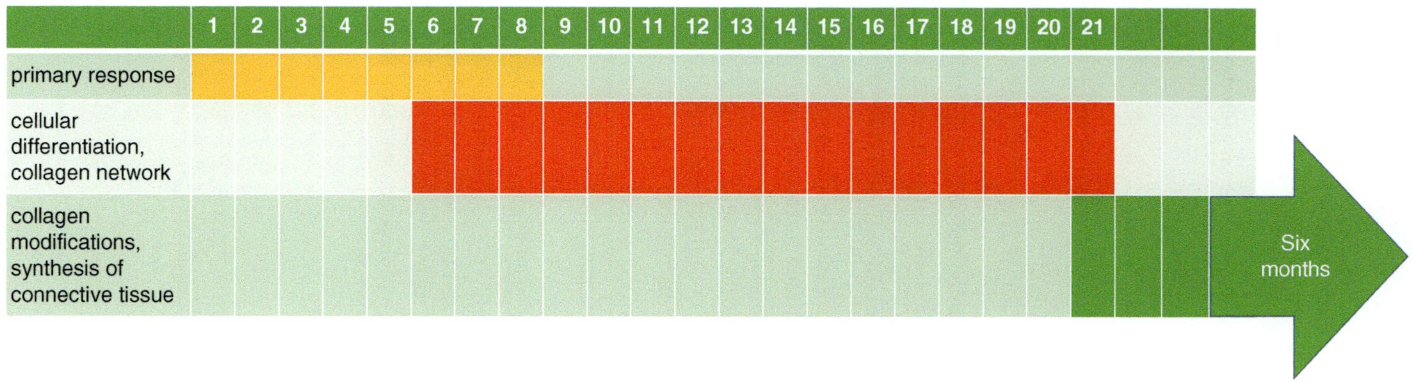

Table 6.6 Distribution of complications over time

	Short term	Long term
Seroma	×	
Shrinkage		×
Fibrotic bridging		×
Recurrence		×
Pain	×	×
Infection	×	×
Fistula		×
Degradation		×
Adhesion		×

6.3.2 Complications and Undesirable Effects

A wide variety of complications or undesirable effects may occur after hernia repair. The abdominal wall is a complex system, and not always after an intervention it is possible to restore the elasticity and total function [11, 21, 26]. The mesh implant has reduced recurrences, but some outcomes can be qualified as direct complications of the mesh. Modern meshes belong to the class of biomaterial, physically and chemically inert and stable, nonimmunogenic and nontoxic. In contradiction to their features, the biomaterials trigger a wide range of adverse response in vivo. The response depends both from the biomaterials and from the host.

We can differentiate between short- and long-term complications [11, 15], as shown in Table 6.6. Many of the recent technological innovations have been developed trying to prevent these complications, in particular related to infections, in the attempt to preserve mesh grafts without removing it [27–30].

6.4 Conclusions

How to choose the correct mesh? The large number of products available makes it clear that none of them is an ideal fit. EBM indicates that the surgeon has to look for a lightweight mesh, with large pores and minimal surface area [11, 31, 32]. Ideally, it should be a monofilament, as for inguinal hernia. For incisional hernia instead, the choice is still more difficult and depends on many factors as:

- Surgical technique
  - Open
  - Laparoscopic
- Host infection risk
  - Low
  - Medium
  - High
- Surgical field
  - Clean
  - Contaminated
  - Infected
- Budget [33]

Table 6.7 Mesh costs in Italy

Description	Dimensions	U.M. (item)	Range Min. – Max. (€)	
Non-absorbable macroporous mesh for inguinal and incisional hernia and abdominal wall reconstruction	6.5 × 11/13 cm	1	220	290
	7.5 × 15 cm	1	280	370
	10/11 × 15 cm	1	290	390
	15 × 15 cm	1	290	390
	20 × 30 cm	1	680	900
IPOM-like composite mesh for laparoscopy	7–8 × 12–15 cm	1	270	350
	10–11 × 14–15 cm	1	380	500
	14–15 × 18–20 cm	1	680	900
	18–20 × 23–25 cm	1	750	1000
	20–25 × 30–33 cm	1	1350	1800
Non-absorbable lightweight macroporous mesh for inguinal and incisional hernia	5–6 × 10–11 cm	1	23	30
	8–10 × 15 cm	1	26	35
	15 × 15 cm	1	38	50
	30 × 30 cm	1	75	100

Table 6.7 presents data from a competitive tender held in Italy. It shows that sometimes there appears to be no correlation between price and complexity of a mesh. Critical budget restricts the choice to few products, making it difficult to customize and tailor treatments according to the risk factors both of the patient and of the procedure.

Some open questions remain:

- The absence of a classification universally recognized, also by the manufacturers, to describe in the same manner so different meshes
- The difficulty of understanding the host–mesh interface of covered or complex meshes, which can vary greatly depending on different clinical situations
- The lack of strong evidence to support the choice of a certain mesh among so many in each specific situation; this often leads to self-making decisions.

Regarding decision making, it is mandatory for future development to collect clinical data through Registries, as indicated by the European Commission's Recommendation 2013/172/EU [34]. This effort will help to combine different experiences, in particular concerning complex meshes (covered, combined, coated), that are not part of routine surgery of individual operating units with specific indications.

The introduction of registries will provide a network among several institutions and hospitals, supporting the surgeons to select the best prosthetics, and the companies to select satisfying research plans.

The choice of material is critical to success in hernia repair. It is necessary for the development of novel materials or coatings. Ideally, fully biodegradable hernia meshes possessing improved host interactions will become commonplace in the future. Today the search for this ideal biomaterial has to start from real data to be collected in a short time from several centers and from a correct information on implanted material. Furthermore, it requires multidisciplinarity, both in terms of analysis and of approach, which includes the incorporation of new emerging disciplines, such as nanoengineering or microinformatics, for the design and development of intelligent devices [27, 35]. The problem of sustainability remains, and we wonder if these products will manage to be safe for the patient and compatible with the budget at the same time.

References

1. Czerny V. Beiträge zur operativen Chirurgie. Stuttgart: Verlag Von Verdinand Enke; 1878.
2. Read RC. Milestones in the history of hernia surgery: prosthetic repair. Hernia. 2004;8(1):8–14.
3. Goepel R. Uber die verschliessung von bruchpforten durch einheilung geflocuhtener fertiger silberdrahtnetze. Verh Dtsch Ges Chir. 1900;9:174–9.
4. Aquaviva D, Bounet P. Cure d'une volumineuse eventration par plaque de Crinofil. Extr. Bull. Soc. Chir. Marseille. 1944; as cited by Zagdoun J, Sordinas A, L'utilisation des plaques de nylon dans la chirurgie des hernies inguinales, Academie de Chirurgie, Se`ance du 1959;25:747–54.
5. Moloney GE, Gill WG, Barclay RC. Operations for hernia; technique of nylon darn. Lancet Lond Engl. 1948;2(6515):45–8.
6. Brown CN, Finch JG. Which mesh for hernia repair? Ann R Coll Surg Engl. 2010;92(4):272–8.
7. Coda A, Lamberti R, Martorana S. Classification of prosthetics used in hernia repair based on weight and biomaterial. Hernia. 2012;16(1):9–20.
8. DeBord JR. The historical development of prosthetics in hernia surgery. Surg Clin North Am. 1998;78(6):973–1006.. vi.
9. EU Hernia Trialists Collaboration. Repair of groin hernia with synthetic mesh: meta-analysis of randomized controlled trials. Ann Surg. 2002;235(3):322–32.
10. Klinge U, Klosterhalfen B, Schumpelick V. Vypro (R): a new generation of polypropylene mesh. In: Bendavid R, et al., editors. Abdominal wall hernias: principles and management. New York: Springer; 2001. p. 286–91.
11. Klosterhalfen B, Junge K, Klinge U. The lightweight and large porous mesh concept for hernia repair. Expert Rev Med Devices. 2005;2(1):103–17.
12. Freudenberg S, Sano D, Ouangré E, Weiss C, Wilhelm TJ. Commercial mesh versus Nylon mosquito net for hernia repair. A randomized double-blind study in Burkina Faso. World J Surg. 2006;30(10):1784–9.. discussion 1790.
13. Sørensen CG, Rosenberg J. The use of sterilized mosquito nets for hernioplasty: a systematic review. Hernia. 2012;16(6):621–5.
14. Sanders DL, Kingsnorth AN, Stephenson BM. Mosquito net mesh for abdominal wall hernioplasty: a comparison of material characteristics with commercial prosthetics. World J Surg. 2013;37(4):737–45.
15. Amid PK. Classification of biomaterials and their related complications in abdominal wall hernia surgery. Hernia. 1997;1(1):15–21.
16. Deeken CR, Lake SP. Mechanical properties of the abdominal wall and biomaterials utilized for hernia repair. J Mech Behav Biomed Mater. 2017;74:411–27.
17. Klinge U, Klosterhalfen B. Modified classification of surgical meshes for hernia repair based on the analyses of 1,000 explanted meshes. Hernia. 2012;16(3):251–8.
18. Challoner DR, Vodra WW. Medical devices and health--creating a new regulatory framework for moderate-risk devices. N Engl J Med. 2011;365(11):977–9.
19. Greco DP. Valutazione Morfologica. In: Greco DP, Forti D, editors. Le protesi nella chirurgia erniaria moderna. Milano: Medical Economics; 1996. p. 23–8.

20. Kalaba S, Gerhard E, Winder JS, Pauli EM, Haluck RS, Yang J. Design strategies and applications of biomaterials and devices for hernia repair. Bioact Mater. 2016;1(1):2–17.
21. Junge K, Binnebösel M, Rosch R, Jansen M, Kämmer D, Otto J, et al. Adhesion formation of a polyvinylidenfluoride/polypropylene mesh for intra-abdominal placement in a rodent animal model. Surg Endosc. 2009;23(2):327–33.
22. Hansen NL, Barabasch A, Distelmaier M, Ciritsis A, Kuehnert N, Otto J, et al. First in-human magnetic resonance visualization of surgical mesh implants for inguinal hernia treatment. Investig Radiol. 2013;48(11):770–8.
23. Kyle-Leinhase I, Köckerling F, Jørgensen LN, Montgomery A, Gillion JF, Rodriguez JAP, et al. Comparison of hernia registries: the CORE project. Hernia. 2018;22(4):561–75.
24. EuraHS. European Registry of abdominal wall hernias [Internet]. http://www.eurahs.eu. Cited 9 July 2018.
25. Elango S, Perumalsamy S, Ramachandran K, Vadodaria K. Mesh materials and hernia repair. Biomedicine. 2017;7(3):16.
26. Klinge U, Klosterhalfen B, Ottinger AP, Junge K, Schumpelick V. PVDF as a new polymer for the construction of surgical meshes. Biomaterials. 2002;23(16):3487–93.
27. Pérez-Köhler B, Bayon Y, Bellón JM. Mesh infection and hernia repair: a review. Surg Infect. 2016;17(2):124–37.
28. Carbonell AM, Cobb WS. Safety of prosthetic mesh hernia repair in contaminated fields. Surg Clin North Am. 2013;93(5):1227–39.
29. Novitsky YW. Biology of biological meshes used in hernia repair. Surg Clin North Am. 2013;93(5):1211–5.
30. Stremitzer S, Bachleitner-Hofmann T, Gradl B, Gruenbeck M, Bachleitner-Hofmann B, Mittlboeck M, et al. Mesh graft infection following abdominal hernia repair: risk factor evaluation and strategies of mesh graft preservation. A retrospective analysis of 476 operations. World J Surg. 2010;34(7):1702–9.
31. Uzzaman MM, Ratnasingham K, Ashraf N. Meta-analysis of randomized controlled trials comparing lightweight and heavyweight mesh for Lichtenstein inguinal hernia repair. Hernia. 2012;16(5):505–18.
32. Rutegård M, Gümüşçü R, Stylianidis G, Nordin P, Nilsson E, Haapamäki MM. Chronic pain, discomfort, quality of life and impact on sex life after open inguinal hernia mesh repair: an expertise-based randomized clinical trial comparing lightweight and heavyweight mesh. Hernia. 2018;22(3):411–8.
33. Bower C, Roth JS. Economics of abdominal wall reconstruction. Surg Clin North Am. 2013;93(5):1241–53.
34. 2013/172/EU: Commission Recommendation of 5 April 2013 on a common Framework for a unique device identification system of medical devices in the Union Text with EEA relevance [Internet]. 2013. Report No.: 32013H0172. http://data.europa.eu/eli/reco/2013/172/oj/eng. Cited 9 July 2018.
35. Ehrlich G, Hu F, Lin Q. Intelligent implants to battle biofilms. ASM News. 2004;70(3):127–33.

Care Settings

7

Dalila Patrizia Greco and Claudia Abbati

7.1 Introduction

Care settings are defined as the organizational modalities through which health care services are delivered.

Different features characterize each level of care:

- Minutes of care per head (nurse-to-patient ratio)
- Length of stay
- Care delivery methods

There is an increasing need for health care services, not reducible nor foreseeable, determined both by the ageing population and the advent of chronicity [1].

Whatever health model is adopted, Beveridge, Bismarck or mixed models, the financial contribution remains the same or can slightly increase in time, being related to GDP [2].

The recent global economic crisis has highlighted the economic pressure on welfare choices even in the G8 countries.

Concern about limited economic resources has driven towards an evolution of conventional hospital stay, involving pre- and post-operative time, introducing new regimes, including Day Surgery, and new pathways, the so-called fast track and ERAS [3–5]. Evidence-Based Medicine validates these choices [6].

D. P. Greco (✉)
Day&Week Surgery Unit, Ospedale Niguarda Ca' Granda, Milano, Italy
e-mail: dalilapatriziagreco@gmail.com

C. Abbati
Department of Surgery, Niguarda Hospital, Milan, Italy

University of Milan, Milan, Italy

D. P. Greco, E. Borgonovi (eds.), *Abdominal Wall Surgery*,
https://doi.org/10.1007/978-3-030-02426-0_7

At present, the only strategy to increase the number of available medical services, without increasing costs, is by improving organizational policies and procedures. Lean analysis of current clinical pathways allows for this [7].

7.2 Surgical Pathway

Clinical Pathway is a methodology and a complex intervention for the mutual patient-care management and organization of care, for a well-defined group of patients; it is based on EBM guidelines, best practice and patient expectations [8–10].

The surgical pathway nowadays in the majority of countries including Italy has quite eliminated the preoperative hospital stay for elective surgery. This has been replaced by pre-surgical management that, through clinical assessment (clinical evaluation of surgical complications) and careful patient selection, allows to reduce preoperative hospitalization without affecting quality or safety [11, 12].

The adoption of ERAS guidelines and best practice [13, 14] helps to shorten hospital stays and decrease use of expensive care areas, as intensive care units.

Traditionally, British and American Health System (NHS; Medicare, Medicaid) includes these care settings:

- Outpatient surgery
  - Office-based surgery
  - Ambulatory surgery
- Inpatient surgery
  - Conventional hospitalization
  - Intermediate intensive care
  - Intensive care

In Italy, day surgery was introduced for the first time in 1985 (Law No. 595/1985), from the Anglo-Saxon medical culture.

The integration of these models into the Italian framework was conditioned by the wide availability of hospitals across the country. Accordingly, the first Italian experience with day surgery encouraged the development of other forms of hospital care, specific to surgical activities [15]. Table 7.1 shows which models are officially recognized today and differences between them.

The outpatient clinic care can be classified into different organizational structures [16]:

- Hospital-integrated (operates in conjunction with the inpatient business),
- Hospital-separated (operates in the hospital as an independent station),
- Satellite-care (operates as an autonomous business entity on the hospital grounds).

Table 7.1 Care Settings in surgery

Setting	Hospital stay	Place of surgical activity
Office-based surgery	Less than 30 min	Policlinic
Ambulatory surgery/day service	Less than 4–6 h	Operating theatre
Day surgery	Less than 12 h	Operating theatre
One-day surgery	Less than 24 h, overnight stay	Operating theatre
Week surgery	Less than 5 days	Operating theatre
Conventional hospitalization	Equal to the middle hospitalization of the single one DRG	Operating theatre
High care unit	Monitoring without assistance of the anaesthesiologist	Operating theatre
Intermediate intensive care unit	Monitoring with assistance of the anaesthesiologist	Operating theatre
Intensive care unit	Monitoring with assistance of the anaesthesiologist and life support	Operating theatre

The goal of these divisions into different models, organizations and settings is to achieve effectiveness and efficiency [17]. As A. L. Cochrane used to say, if there is no demonstration of efficiency, it is absolutely useless to ask the problem of effectiveness [18].

7.3 Why Abdominal Wall Surgery Has Been Important in the Evolution of Care Models

7.3.1 Which Came First: The Chicken or the Egg?

Inguinal hernia repair has been one of the operations that confirmed the success of day surgery. It has been the engine of further development in Ambulatory Surgery or Day Service, in many Italian regions.

The transition to Ambulatory or Day Service in Italy had the goal of reducing the number of hospital beds to achieve the ratio 3.8/1000 people, less than the rest of Europe.

This drive towards Day Surgery/Day Care Services/Ambulatory Surgery can be attributed to specific clinical reasons.

The need for post-operative stay in bed and post-operative immobilization has been reduced by the use of prosthetic and tension-free hernioplasty. Furthermore, improvements in anaesthesia, including the widespread use of local or peripheral nerve block anaesthesia, for example, TAP block, has allowed to achieve an excellent management of post-operative pain, and an early recovery of function [19–21].

The introduction of laparoscopy surgery, particularly for the treatment of incisional hernias, has reduced the post-operative hospitalization to 3–5 days, for incisional hernias of medium size [22, 23].

Moreover, the introduction of component separation technique, dedicated to complex incisional hernias, allowed the following [24–26]:

- To provide the opportunity to treat patients with large incisional hernias,
- To decrease the indication and the need for a post-operative stay in intensive care unit.

Prior to this, many patients were sent to a follow-up with compression garments reducing the quality of life.

Currently, we do not have evidence on the benefits provided by the introduction of robotic surgery. Presently, this technique is indicated for selected cases, generally those inserted in research programs or specific trials, for inpatient surgery [27–29].

7.4 To What Extent Technology Has Affected the Effectiveness of PDTA (Integrated Care Pathways)

We have previously highlighted how and why the introduction of high-tech surgery (prosthetic, laparoscopic and component separation) can affect both the duration of the post-operative care and the functional recovery of the patients, reducing length of hospital stay, health and social costs.

The current reimbursing system in Italy is DRG related.

The pressure on DRG (Diagnosis-Related Group) reimbursement makes it difficult to preserve the standards today achieved by abdominal wall surgery.

The value of the reimbursement for DRG 161/162 (groin hernia) is fixed at 1280€, while the one related to DRG 159/160 (umbilical and incisional hernia) is 1371€ in uncomplicated patients and 4892€ in complicated patients.

Table 7.2 shows the value of the DRG related to abdominal wall surgery in Italy in 2012 [30].

Table 7.2 DRGs related to abdominal wall surgery and the related reimbursement in Italy

DRG	Pathology	Value of reimbursement			
		Outpatient		Inpatient	
		Day surgery	One-day surgery	Conventional	Out of threshold €/day
159	Not inguinal nor femoral hernia with complication >17aa	1523	1453	4892	190
160	Not inguinal nor femoral hernia without complication >17aa	1523	575	1371	94
161	Inguinal or femoral hernia with complication >17aa	1280	1240	3571	212
162	Inguinal or femoral hernia without complication >17aa	1280	649	1168	137

This value is still related to the preceding models of surgery, before the advent of prosthetic and minimally invasive technologies. It was set evaluating a short hospital stay for groin hernia repair, and 5–8 days for incisional hernia.

The reimbursement fixed for incisional hernia was not sufficient to cover the indirect costs of the hospitals and direct cost of the procedure, trained staff and medical devices.

Abdominal wall surgery is a standardized surgery. Many guidelines are available, some recently validated, and others in progress [31–33].

The success of surgery also depends on the correct and multimodal management of post-operative pain [12]; this can be obtained through:

- A team approach (surgeon, anaesthetist and nursing staff)
- A pharmacological multimethod approach:
  - Local or regional anaesthesia (TAP block) [34–36]
  - Discharge analgesia

This approach allows one to achieve early discharge and a physical and relational quick recovery. In addition, it reduces psychological impact and post-operative cognitive dysfunction in the elderly.

7.5 Is a Future Evolution Possible?

This book is addressed to economists, health managers and surgeons; many of them may be wondering if a future evolution is possible and how long will it take.

One may hypothesize that in a near future 1-day surgery will be safe for patients who are now treated with conventional hospitalization, with a long stay. This has already happened for other specialties, e.g. Interventional Radiology.

Changes in abdominal wall surgery are difficult to achieve quickly, as devices and techniques need to further evolve [37].

A chapter of specific importance in abdominal wall surgery is prevention. Through prevention the incidence of those pathologies leading to surgery can be reduced, by developing new devices and implementing new protocols.

New materials for meshes, for example with antimicrobial properties, may lower the incidence of SSI, thus preventing incisional hernias [38].

For example, nowadays we are witnessing a decrease in mortality and morbidity in open abdomen, or in infectious complications in large eventration in complex patient, thanks to negative-pressure wound therapy (NPWT) [39].

Incisional hernias, diastasis recti and open abdomen are among the pathologies that can benefit from new policies and innovations.

Appropriate care settings, prevention and the introduction of high-tech has changed the management of abdominal wall surgery in these last 20 years.

Sustainability has not yet been achieved.

References

1. Milani RV, Lavie CJ. Health care 2020: reengineering health care delivery to combat chronic disease. Am J Med. 2015;128(4):337–43.
2. Greco DP, Amatucci F, Padula GA. Treatment cost reimbursement from the healthcare systems. In: Inguinal hernia surgery. Milano: Springer; 2017. p. 193–205.. (Updates in Surgery).
3. Ljungqvist O, Scott M, Fearon KC. Enhanced recovery after surgery: a review. JAMA Surg. 2017;152(3):292–8.
4. Roulin D, Donadini A, Gander S, Griesser A-C, Blanc C, Hübner M, et al. Cost-effectiveness of the implementation of an enhanced recovery protocol for colorectal surgery. Br J Surg. 2013;100(8):1108–14.
5. Thiele RH, Rea KM, Turrentine FE, Friel CM, Hassinger TE, McMurry TL, et al. Standardization of care: impact of an enhanced recovery protocol on length of stay, complications, and direct costs after colorectal surgery. J Am Coll Surg. 2015;220(4):430–43.
6. Spanjersberg WR, Reurings J, Keus F, van Laarhoven CJ. Fast track surgery versus conventional recovery strategies for colorectal surgery. Cochrane Database Syst Rev. 2011;2:CD007635.
7. Lawal AK, Rotter T, Kinsman L, Sari N, Harrison L, Jeffery C, et al. Lean management in health care: definition, concepts, methodology and effects reported (systematic review protocol). Syst Rev. 2014;3:103.
8. European Pathway Association. Care pathways [Internet]. Available from: http://e-p-a.org/care-pathways/. Cited 11 Mar 2018.
9. De Bleser L, Depreitere R, De Waele K, Vanhaecht K, Vlayen J, Sermeus W. Defining pathways. J Nurs Manag. 2006;14(7):553–63.
10. de Luc K. Developing care pathways: the handbook. 1st ed. Abingdon: Routledge; 2000. p. 192.
11. Mathis MR, Naughton NN, Shanks AM, Freundlich RE, Pannucci CJ, Chu Y, et al. Patient selection for day case-eligible surgery: identifying those at high risk for major complications. Anesthesiology. 2013;119(6):1310–21.
12. Gandhimani P, Jackson IJB. UK guidelines for day surgery. Surg Oxf. 2006;24(10):346–9.
13. Revell MA. Role of research in best practices. Nurs Clin North Am. 2015;50(1):19–32.
14. Davidson J. Why a column on ambulatory best practices? AORN J. 2014;99(5):612–5.
15. Ferre F, de Belvis AG, Valerio L, Longhi S, Lazzari A, Fattore G, et al. Italy: health system review. Health Syst Transit. 2014;16(4):1–168.
16. Fischer K. Ambulatory operations and day surgery in the hospital--financing from the viewpoint of the hospital. Zentralbl Chir. 1994;119(7):470–6.
17. Greco DP. Dal protocollo alla tariffa: un percorso per affrontare e gestire le problematiche dei costi della sanità. Milan: FrancoAngeli; 2000. p. 196.
18. Cochrane AL. Effectiveness and efficiency: random reflections on health services. Nuffield Provincial Hospitals Trust; 1972. p. 112.
19. Kurzer M, Belsham PA, Kark AE. The Lichtenstein repair. Surg Clin North Am. 1998;78(6):1025–46.
20. Callesen T. Inguinal hernia repair: anaesthesia, pain and convalescence. Dan Med Bull. 2003;50(3):203–18.
21. Spallitta SI, Termine G, Zappulla A, Greco V, Compagno GM, Lo Iacono I, et al. Tension-free hernioplasty in the treatment of inguinal hernia in the adult: our experience with local anesthesia and a review of the literature. Minerva Chir. 1999;54(9):573–89.
22. Sauerland S, Walgenbach M, Habermalz B, Seiler CM, Miserez M. Laparoscopic versus open surgical techniques for ventral or incisional hernia repair. Cochrane Database Syst Rev. 2011;3:CD007781.
23. Barbaros U, Asoglu O, Seven R, Erbil Y, Dinccag A, Deveci U, et al. The comparison of laparoscopic and open ventral hernia repairs: a prospective randomized study. Hernia. 2007;11(1):51–6.
24. Cornette B, De Bacquer D, Berrevoet F. Component separation technique for giant incisional hernia: a systematic review. Am J Surg. 2018;215(4):719–26.

25. Kenchadze G, Pipia I, Demetrashvili Z, Botezatu A, Marakutsa E, Raileanu R, et al. Incisional hernia: plastic aspects, component separation, technical details & pediatrics. Hernia. 2015;19(Suppl. 1):S187–94.
26. Eriksson A, Rosenberg J, Bisgaard T. Surgical treatment for giant incisional hernia: a qualitative systematic review. Hernia. 2014;18(1):31–8.
27. Walker PA, May AC, Mo J, Cherla DV, Santillan MR, Kim S, et al. Multicenter review of robotic versus laparoscopic ventral hernia repair: is there a role for robotics? Surg Endosc. 2018;32(4):1901–5.
28. Arcerito M, Changchien E, Bernal O, Konkoly-Thege A, Moon J. Robotic inguinal hernia repair: technique and early experience. Am Surg. 2016;82(10):1014–7.
29. Allison N, Tieu K, Snyder B, Pigazzi A, Wilson E. Technical feasibility of robot-assisted ventral hernia repair. World J Surg. 2012;36(2):447–52.
30. Decreto Ministero della Salute 18 ottobre 2012. GU Serie Generale n.23 del 28-01-2013—Suppl. Ordinario n.8): http://www.gazzettaufficiale.it/eli/id/2013/01/28/13A00528/sg.
31. Antoniou SA, Agresta F, Garcia Alamino JM, Berger D, Berrevoet F, Brandsma H-T, et al. European Hernia Society guidelines on prevention and treatment of parastomal hernias. Hernia. 2018;22(1):183–98.
32. Muysoms FE, Antoniou SA, Bury K, Campanelli G, Conze J, Cuccurullo D, et al. European Hernia Society Guidelines on the closure of abdominal wall incisions. Hernia. 2015;19(1):1–24.
33. Simons MP, Aufenacker T, Bay-Nielsen M, Bouillot JL, Campanelli G, Conze J, et al. European Hernia Society guidelines on the treatment of inguinal hernia in adult patients. Hernia. 2009;13(4):343–403.
34. Takebayashi K, Matsumura M, Kawai Y, Hoashi T, Katsura N, Fukuda S, et al. Efficacy of transversus abdominis plane block and rectus sheath block in laparoscopic inguinal hernia surgery. Int Surg. 2015;100(4):666–71.
35. Cohen DD, Dillon JB. Anesthesia for outpatient surgery. JAMA. 1966;196(13):1114–6.
36. Capdevila X, Dadure C. Perioperative management for one day hospital admission: regional anesthesia is better than general anesthesia. Acta Anaesthesiol Belg. 2004;55(Suppl):33–6.
37. Stark GB, Horch R, Tánczos E. Biological matrices and tissue reconstruction. Berlin: Springer-Verlag; 1998. p. 328.
38. Pérez-Köhler B, Bayon Y, Bellón JM. Mesh infection and hernia repair: a review. Surg Infect. 2016;17(2):124–37.
39. Bruhin A, Ferreira F, Chariker M, Smith J, Runkel N. Systematic review and evidence based recommendations for the use of negative pressure wound therapy in the open abdomen. Int J Surg Lond Engl. 2014;12(10):1105–14.

Preventing Incisional Hernias: Closure of Abdominal Wall, Follow-Up in Abdominal Surgery

8

Cesare Stabilini, Linda D'Amore, Elena Annesi, Lucia Bambi, Paolo Negro, and Francesco Gossetti

8.1 Epidemiology of Incisional Hernia

Incisional hernia (IH) is a common complication of abdominal surgery with a wide range of incidence, occurring from 5% to 20% in the general population, with a weighted mean rate of 12.8% at 23.8 months in a systematic review and meta-regression study [1]. This value, however, appears to be much higher, up to 30%, in some subgroups of patients, such as those submitted to open abdominal aortic aneurysm or bariatric and colorectal surgery, obese individuals (body mass index, BMI >30 kg/m^2), even if no standardized definition actually exists for these subjects.

Patients with abdominal aortic aneurysm (AAA) are considered at high risk due to an underlying connective tissue disorder, with dysregulation of collagen type 1 and type 3, that plays a primary role, both in aneurysm formation and in pathogenesis of IH [2].

In obese individuals, on the other hand, the intra-abdominal pressure, higher than normal, may cause greater tension on abdominal wall sutures. Moreover, the overweight patients' impaired vascularization leads to local hypoxia with altered synthesis of mature collagen and subsequent wound healing complications. Wound healing, affected also by other well-known risk factors, such as surgical site infection (SSI), diabetes, chronic obstructive pulmonary disease (COPD), smoking, and malignant diseases, plays a significant role in IH formation [3, 4]. IH rate registers up to 40% and more of incidence also in colorectal cancer surgery, especially when routine CT scan is added to clinical examination during follow-up [5].

C. Stabilini
Department of Surgery (DISC), IRCCS Policlinico San Martino, Università degli Studi di Genova, Genoa, Italy

L. D'Amore (✉) · E. Annesi · L. Bambi · P. Negro · F. Gossetti
Department of Surgery, Abdominal Wall Unit, Sapienza University of Rome, Rome, Italy
e-mail: linda.damore@uniroma1.it; gossetti@tiscalinet.it

D. P. Greco, E. Borgonovi (eds.), *Abdominal Wall Surgery*,
https://doi.org/10.1007/978-3-030-02426-0_8

It is well-known that IH damages body image, decreases quality of life, impairs functions, causes pain, and adds morbidity and mortality to the patient [6]. Subsequent hernia repair is associated with significant financial loss for institutions [7]; thus, the optimal care for these patients remains a major public health issue [8]. In fact, despite advances in abdominal wall repair (AWR), recurrence rates remain very high, ranging from 12% to 54%, and even up to 63% for suture repair [6]. Moreover, patients who experienced recurrence are susceptible to a vicious cycle because each subsequent repair presents greater technical challenges with longer operative duration, compounds costs, and carries an increased risk for complications, particularly SSI and recurrence. In Holihan's multicenter study, 37% of primary ventral hernias, 64% of first recurrence, and 73% of third recurrence have relapsed at 140-month follow-up [9].

8.2 Prevention

8.2.1 Guidelines

Despite these discouraging data, hernia prevention is still vague, whereas patient reported outcome and adequate follow-up should be carefully assessed to evaluate any progress of care delivery as suitable tools predicting an individual's risk. In this direction, Goodenough et al. developed a simple risk stratification score to predict IH following abdominal surgery (HERNIAscore), based on surgical approach (open laparotomy/hand-assisted laparoscopy/laparoscopy), BMI and COPD. These indicators were found to be independently associated with IH formation, while other factors, such as ASA score, history of SSI, diabetes, anemia, were significant on univariate analysis but not on the final Cox regression multivariate analysis [10]. The risk assessment may offer both surgeons and patients a starting point to discuss surgical implications and preventive solutions.

The frequency of IH and its sequelae has made mandatory to build evidence-based guidelines. The European Hernia Society moved in this direction, publishing in 2015 the Guidelines on the Closure of Abdominal Wall Incisions, with the aim to promote IH prevention: "Maybe we should first learn and teach how to prevent incisional hernias, rather than how to treat them." Guidelines consider patients submitted to any abdominal surgery, including both open and laparoscopic procedures. Members of the Guidelines Development Group formulated Key Questions, then evaluated related systematic review and/or meta-analysis, choosing only high-quality papers, and finally formulated a recommendation for each Key Question. Three levels of recommendation were assessed, strong/weak/no recommendation, depending on the level of evidence [11].

With regard to the most suitable diagnostic modality to detect incisional hernias, dynamic ultrasounds and CT scan are strongly recommended to integrate clinical examination during follow-up in prospective studies having IH as primary outcome. For these trials, a minimum of 24-month follow-up (preferably 36 months) is strongly advised [11].

A Key Question was specifically addressed to the type of abdominal wall incision and its possible influence on the incidence of IH or burst abdomen. A higher incidence of IH, in fact, has been reported for midline opening, when compared to other type of laparotomy [12–15]. Thus, guidelines strongly recommend to perform a non-midline laparotomy whenever possible [11]. It is important to consider, however, that the midline incision is still the favored approach to the abdominal cavity, because it is adaptable to all surgical eventualities. In these cases, other variables have to be taken into account, as the closure technique and the suture material.

In his careful systematic review and meta-analysis, Hodgson wrote: "The ideal suture for closing abdominal fascia has yet to be determined. Surgical tradition, prejudice, familiarity, and personal conviction tend to dictate surgical procedures rather than evidence-based medicine" [16].

Data from literature are very heterogeneous and there is no high-quality evidence available concerning the best suture material and technique to reduce the incidence of IH after midline laparotomy.

8.2.2 Incision and Suture Techniques

Results from the MATCH meta-analysis indicate that the best closure for midline incision is the small bites suture technique, using a 2–0 slowly absorbable suture (PDS) and including the aponeurosis only, in a suture-to-wound length ratio of at least 4:1 [17]. The superiority of slowly absorbable sutures, when closing fascia, may depend on the biology of healing. Though the abdominal fascia takes somewhere between half a year to several years to completely heal, it needs at least 14 days to partially regain its strength after surgery. Since the half-life tensile strength of absorbable sutures is around 2–3 weeks compared to the 6-week length of slowly absorbable PDS sutures, better results should be expected with the latter material, although this observation is not actually supported by high-quality data [17, 18].

SSI is considered a risk factor for the development of IH, so the use of suture material coated by a bacteriostatic agent for fascial closure has also been investigated. Based on the results from the TRISTAN review, the use of triclosan-coated PDS does not seem to influence the incidence of SSI, while the same triclosan has demonstrated to be effective in reducing SSI rate when Vycril sutures are used [19].

Besides using slowly absorbable sutures, better results may be achieved closing fascia by the continuous running technique [17, 20–22]. This procedure, moreover, is much faster than the interrupted suture and can reduce the length of surgery. This is the reason why a strong level recommendation in EHS guidelines has been formulated [11].

Also the size of suture bites plays a role in IH prevention. A recently published RCT demonstrated, in fact, a significant less IH formation in the small bite group of patients compared to the large-bite group, at 1-year follow-up [23]. EHS guidelines, however, provide only a weak recommendation for the small bites suture technique; an updated systematic review is still requested for a stronger recommendation [11].

Harries et al. designed a prospective, randomized controlled trial to compare two suture techniques (Hughes repair versus standard mass closure) for the closure of midline incisions in colorectal cancer surgery, to reduce the incidence of IH. The Hughes repair, also known as the "far and near" or Cardiff repair, combines a standard mass closure with a series of horizontal and two vertical mattress sutures within a single suture, theoretically distributing the load along and across the incision length [24]. The HART trial, including 28 centers throughout the United Kingdom, have finished recruiting 800 both elective and emergency patients, in which colorectal open surgery, using a midline incision of more than 5 cm, was planned; results are expected in the near future [25].

Due to lack of sufficient data, in EHS guidelines, no recommendation is actually given on the type or the size of the needle to close a laparotomy, on suture material and suturing technique to be used, in non-midline incisions and in emergency surgery. The routine placement of subcutaneous drains has also been investigated to find if there is any benefit in reducing surgical site complications but results failed to show any significant difference [11].

8.2.3 Prophylactic Mesh Placement

Despite the continuous research and advances to optimize abdominal fascia closure, the greater opportunity to decrease IH rates lies in preventing hernia with mesh implantation at the time of primary abdominal surgery. Prophylactic mesh placement (PMP), in fact, provides a biomechanical reinforcement of the closure, unloading the transverse strain from intra-abdominal forces off of the incision, to minimize early fascial separation during the wound healing phase. After this period, the abdominal wall tissue is strong enough to withstand intra-abdominal pressure [8]. It has been stressed that 12 mm of fascial separation, detected by CT scan 1 month after surgery, can be predictive of IH [26]. Playforth et al. previously measured by X-rays this gap, inserting three to five pairs of stainless steel hemostatic clips to the sutured edges of the anterior aponeurosis. A slit >10 mm 1 month after surgery was predictive of IH. According to the author, a possible explanation lies in the early weak fibrous tissue filling the gap between the two flaps that would allow the later protrusion of a hernia [27].

Although the majority of data from the literature was positive, in 2015 the Guidelines Development Group made only a weak recommendation on the use of PMP in patients at high risk for IH, due to great variability of the quality of the studies with heterogeneity among characteristics of patients, position and type of implanted meshes, and length of follow-up [11].

The effects of PMP at the time of initial abdominal aponeurosis closure consist in providing a load-sharing mechanism that helps to restore the native tensile strength of the abdominal wall, thus improving its biomechanical resistance after surgery [28]. However, it is essential to assess proper indications, target patients who can be candidates for PMP, and identify the most suitable mesh and its best position.

Based on currently available studies, patients undergoing midline laparotomy, especially if older than 45 years, including those submitted to open AAA repair, bariatric surgery or other surgery in overweight patients (with a BMI >27 kg/m^2), and colorectal surgery, could be suitable for PMP [3, 8, 19–31]. To date, insufficient evidences are available on PMP in abdominal incisions different from midline, though, in 2016, Blazquez Hernando et al. published positive results at 24-month follow-up, with the implant of prophylactic self-gripping polypropylene mesh in bilateral subcostal laparotomy [32]. There is also a lack of data concerning IH prevention in patients undergoing emergency abdominal surgery. Argudo et al., in a retrospective study, hypothesized that the use of a synthetic mesh in these patients could be safe. At a median 16.7-month follow-up, in fact, onlay PMP showed a decreased IH rate by 80% compared to primary slowly absorbable running suture closure, without an increase in postoperative complications, except more frequent seroma in the mesh group [33].

The next step is to assess the best site of implant for the mesh. The existing body of literature seems to support the use of PMP as technique to reduce IH independently of mesh location [3, 29, 34]. No comparative studies have been published until now comparing different mesh position with the exception of the PRIMA (PRImary Mesh Closure of Abdominal Midline Wound) trial. This multicenter, double-blind RCT, involving high-risk patients with either AAA open repair or BMI >27, investigated the onlay and the retromuscular site of implant as the best location to place the mesh, compared to primary suture closure [3]. The study showed that both techniques significantly decreased the incidence of IH when compared to primary suture, though the percentage of patients who developed IH was not different between the two mesh groups. Onlay mesh position demonstrated to be faster, without adding significant time to surgery, particularly when the mesh is fixed using glue, and suitable also by surgeons not familiar with AWR techniques. However, it is associated with increased seroma rates and exposure risks. The retro-rectus position, on the other hand, is a complex technique, requiring a learning curve and adding time to operation, though it offers several advantages such as a better tension distribution and intra-abdominal pressure resistance and no cutaneous exposure. A major concern is that this position involves the violation of a space that would be very important if the patient will need an abdominal wall repair in the future [9, 26].

Identification of the most efficacious mesh type is also a debated question. Several mesh types including permanent synthetic, biologic, and bioabsorbable, have been studied [3, 30, 35–38]. Available literature data are often not comparable, due to variety of materials, mesh position, and length of follow-up, frequently too short. Actually, though many materials have demonstrated to be effective, no one type still offers the optimal combination of characteristics and advantages [29].

Permanent synthetics have been extensively used in AWR, and their characteristics are very well-known. They are relatively inexpensive and resistant to mechanical strain but, depending on the site of implant, can be associated with increased seroma and infection rates, exposure risk, adhesions, sinus tract, and chronic pain. In fact these materials, especially polypropylene, elicit a chronic inflammatory response, characterized by foreign-body granulomas surrounding mesh fibers, that is persistent over time and probably impairs normal wound healing and tissue regeneration [39, 40]. Some disadvantages could be overcome using meshes coated by an inert barrier (composite materials). Lightweight materials, mainly polypropylene, actually seem to achieve better performances than heavyweight meshes, with regard to exposure risk and chronic pain, also in clean-contaminated and contaminated setting. Anyway the level of evidence on the efficacy of polypropylene to prevent IH after midline incision in high-risk patients is very suggestive [41].

Biologic implants should allow better response to infections and, moreover, they are gradually remodeled by the host, but they show higher rates of bulging, stretching, and recurrence, depending on their structure and time of remodeling, besides to be much more expensive than synthetics. So far, there is no concrete evidence suggesting that a biological implant should be preferred to polypropylene mesh for PMP. The level of evidence on the efficacy of biological implant to prevent IH in high-risk patients after midline laparotomy is very low [11].

An attractive hypothesis is offered by new technologies with the development of bioabsorbable meshes, such as Bio-A, Phasix, and TIGR, in which the scaffold is gradually and slowly degraded by the host while it is replaced by the new generated tissue. Bioabsorbable material is reported to elicit an acute inflammatory host response that declines after 24 months and disappears after 36 months, when a well remodeled, similar to native, durable, and thick layer of connective tissue has completely replaced the mesh [39]. Preclinical and pilot studies on these long-lasting absorbable synthetic polymers seem to appear promising [39, 42, 43]. The PREBIOUS (PREventive midline laparotomy closure with a BIOabsorbable mesh) randomized controlled trial recruited patients undergoing both elective and emergency abdominal surgery. Results are not yet available [42]. Anyway, larger controlled and randomized trials are requested to fully assess long-time effects of these meshes. As for biological implants, actually there is no evidence that they would perform better than polypropylene in preventing IH [41].

In EHS guidelines, the strength of recommendation was greatly influenced from the quality of published studies, often not well comparable on the effectiveness of different techniques and meshes in preventing IH [11]. This was also related to large variation in the length of follow-up. In many studies the follow-up is too short and this can affect results, since it has been documented a growing incidence of IH over time, ranging from 12.6% in the first year to 22.4% at 3 years, with a relative increase of 60% [44].

8.3 Parastomal Hernias

A type of IH that deserves special attention is represented by parastomal hernia (PSH). PSH can be defined as an incisional hernia immediately adjacent and related to an abdominal wall stoma [45]. It is recognized as the most common complication among the stoma-related problems. PSH rates range between 5% and 60%; the use of CT scan may help diagnosis and increase PSH prevalence [46, 47]. Based on data from the literature and relatively to the type of the stoma, its incidence can be summarized as follows: end colostomy 4–48.1% (mean 15.3%), loop colostomy 0–30.8% (mean 4.0%), end ileostomy 1.8–28.3% (mean 6.7%), and loop ileostomy 0–6.2% (mean 1.3%). The number of PSH increases over time, mostly during the 5 years after surgery but also 20 or 30 years later [45, 48, 49]. Goligher stated that some degree of parastomal hernia is inevitable, given enough follow-up time [50].

Its etiology is not well understood, but it is believed that the hernia forms when tangential forces are applied to the circumference of the trans-abdominal hole, with stronger forces correlating to larger openings, continually stretching the abdominal wall defect [51].

At the moment there are five classifications of parastomal hernias, based on clinical examination, perioperative assessment, or clinical imaging. Their use has been very limited, and none of them has been subject to validation [52].

Patient-related risk factors in developing PSH include advanced age (>60 years), obesity (BMI ≥30 kg/m^2 or waist circumference ≥100 cm), COPD, smoking, collagen and metabolism disorders, steroid therapies, female gender, Crohn's disease, malignancies, and the presence of other abdominal wall hernias. Some technical aspects related to stoma creation are matter of discussion, such as the lateral pararectus or transrectus stoma location, the intraperitoneal or extraperitoneal route, the laparoscopic approach, and the ideal size of the fascial aperture. To date, there is insufficient evidence on the comparative risk of PSH, concerning these topics [52, 53].

Diagnosis is currently based on clinical examination in supine and erect position, using the Valsalva maneuver if necessary. In some cases of diagnostic uncertainty, CT scan or intra-stomal 3-D ultrasonography may be helpful [54], though more studies are needed to confirm the role of ultrasonography as routine imaging technique [52].

PSH can progress almost asymptomatically but it can also reduce the quality of life, causing a variety of symptoms, such as discomfort around the stoma, cramping, distention, pain, diarrhea or constipation, leakage from the stoma resulting in skin irritation, and specific more dramatic complications such as bleeding, bowel obstruction, or strangulation [51, 55]. The development of problems due to PSH adds significant costs to an existing emotional distress. In fact, frequent changes of appliances, more expensive custom-fit accessories can greatly increase patient's expenditure for stoma care. Moreover, many of these patients go on disability secondary to activity restrictions and loss of work productivity [55].

In case of mild symptoms, patients can be managed conservatively, with well-made stomal support, skin protective sealants, and regular wound stomal care. Unfortunately, surgery is required when major complications occur. In these cases, regardless of repair technique (simple repair, stoma translocation, mesh repair), emergency has demonstrated to be an independent risk factor for recurrence [56].

High parastomal hernia incidence and the success rate achieved with mesh repair have attracted surgeons' attention on prophylactic mesh placement at the time of primary stoma creation, especially in case of permanent colostomy. Already in 2004, Janes et al. published the results of a randomized trial demonstrating that PMP significantly reduced PSH formation without adding infective complications

[57]. After this, a great number of studies, RCTs, and meta-analysis have been performed to investigate the effect of a preventive mesh in PSH formation, using both synthetic and biologic meshes, in open and laparoscopic approach [58–70]. PMP at the time of stoma formation has been shown to significantly decrease the rates of PSH formation, without increasing wound complications. Only in the prospective multicenter randomized controlled study by Fleshman et al., the sublay placement of non-cross-linked porcine-derived acellular dermal matrix failed to demonstrate any advantage at 24-month follow-up. This study, however, has some limitations, such as the inclusion of both ileostomy and colostomy patients, of open and laparoscopic techniques, and the small number of recruited patients that may impugn results [61].

To date, based on information from comparative studies with high level of evidence, the consistency of outcomes, the low risk of complications, and the low cost of synthetic meshes, the Guidelines Development Group supports the use of a prophylactic synthetic non-absorbable mesh with a strong recommendation, when performing an elective permanent end colostomy. On the contrary, no recommendation can be made either for placing prophylactic mesh when constructing other stoma than end-colostomy or on the best mesh position. Due to insufficient evidence supporting superiority of biological over synthetic meshes, with regard to morbidity and recurrence, no recommendation can be given for the use of bioabsorbable or biological implants in prevention. More studies are necessary to address these subjects [52].

8.4 Trocar Site Hernias

Talking about prevention of hernias following primary abdominal wall incisions, an emerging topic consists on incisional hernias developing at the trocar site (TSIH) after laparoscopic procedures. Its incidence, likely underreported, seems to increase with the length of follow-up, with reported rates ranging from 1% to 6% after 1 year to 26% at 3-year follow-up [71]. It appears that the risk of hernia increases with the size of the trocar, being very low at 5-mm trocar site but significantly greater when trocars $\geq$10 mm are used. A fascial closure is recommended for these latter port sites. Though some authors claim that prosthetic closure of the umbilical trocar site after laparoscopic surgery could become the standard method for preventing TSIH in high-risk patients [72], actually no recommendation has been made by the Guidelines Development Group [52].

8.5 Costs

About the cost-effectiveness of IH prevention, it is important to consider that abdominal wall repair is associated with overall financial losses, especially when biologic implants are used. The high incidence of IH following abdominal incisions makes it a major problem for healthcare costs. These include direct costs, i.e., those directly attributable to a particular patient's care (nursing, technical labor, supplies) and indirect or overhead costs, as facilities, large equipment depreciation, unallocated labor, and management costs [73].

This financial profile of AWR can be even more discouraging if the cost of reoperation is added. It follows that using preventive measures to reduce the incidence of IH after abdominal surgery could result in significant cost saving for the community [74]. Fischer et al. argued about the cost-utility of mesh placement after abdominal incisions and documented that PMP resulted more effective and less costly than primary suture closure in selected high-risk patients [75]. The low incidence of complications and the favorable outcome, also in potentially contaminated and contaminated setting, make PMA effective and safe, though larger trials are needed to express a strong recommendation in the opinion of the Guidelines Development Group. At the moment, only a weak recommendation can be suggested [11].

References

1. Bosanquet D, Aboelrahman T, Ansell J, Cornish J, Davies L, Frewer K, Glasbey J, Harries R, Stimpson A, Russell D, Russell I, Torkington J. Systematic review and meta regression of factors affecting midline incisional hernia rates: an analysis of 14,618 patients. PLoS One. 2015;10(9):e0138745. https://doi.org/10.1371/journal.pone.0138745.
2. Antoniu GA, Georgiadis GS, Antoniu SA, Granderath FA, Giannoukas AD, Lazarides MK. Abdominal aortic aneurysm and abdominal wall hernias manifestations of connective tissue disorder. J Vasc Surg. 2011;54:1175–81. https://doi.org/10.1016/j.jvs.2010.11.053.
3. Jairam AP, Timmermans L, Heker HH, REJGM P, van Klaveren D, Steyerberg EW, Tmman R, van der Ham AC, Dawson I, Charbon JA, Schuhmacher C, Mihaljevic A, Izbicki JR, Fikatas P, Knebel P, Fortelny RH, Kleinrensink GJ, Lange JF, Jeekel HJ, for the PRIMA Trialist Group. Prevention of incisional hernia with prophylactic onlay and sublay mesh reinforcement versus primary suture only in midline laparotomies (PRIMA): 2-year follow-up of a multicentre, double blind, randomized controlled trial. Lancet. 2017;390:567–76. https://doi.org/10.1016/S0140-6736(17)31332-6.
4. Murray BW, Cipher DJ, Pham T, Anthony T. The impact of surgical site infection on the development of incisional hernia and small bowel obstruction in colorectal surgery. Am J Surg. 2011;202:558–60. https://doi.org/10.1016/j.amjsurg.2011.06.014.
5. Claes K, Beckers R, Heindryckx E, Kyle-Leinhase I, Pletinckx P, Claeys D, Muysoms F. Retrospective observational study on the incidence of incisional hernias after colorectal carcinoma resection with follow-up CT scan. Hernia. 2014;18:797–802. https://doi.org/10.1007/s10029-014-1214-z.
6. van Ramshorst GH, Eker HH, Hop WC, Jeekel J, Lange JF. Impact of incisional hernia on health-related quality of life and body image: a prospective cohort study. Am J Surg. 2012;204:144–50. https://doi.org/10.1016/j.amjsurg.2012.01.012.
7. Reynolds D, Davenport DL, Korosec RL, Roth JS. Financial implications of ventral hernia repair: a hospital cost analysis. J Gastrointest Surg. 2013;17:159–66. https://doi.org/10.1007/s11605-012-1999-y.
8. Lanni MA, Tecce MG, Shubinets V, Mirzabeigi MN, Fischer JP. The state of prophylactic mesh augmentation. Am Surg. 2018;54:99–108.
9. Holihan JL, Alawadi Z, Martindale RG, Roth JS, Wray CJ, Ko TC, Kao LS, Liang MK. Adverse events after ventral hernia repair: the vicious cycle of complications. J Am Coll Surg. 2015;221:78–85. https://doi.org/10.1016/j.jamcollsurg.2015.04.026.

10. Goodenough CJ, Tien CK, Kao LS, Nguyen MT, Holihan JL, Alawadi Z, Nguyen DH, Ramon Gonzalez J, Arita NT, Roth JS, Liang MK. Development and validation of a risk stratification score for ventral incisional hernia after abdominal surgery: hernia expectation rates in intra-abdominal surgery (the HERNIA Project). J Am Coll Surg. 2015;220:405–13. https://doi.org/10.1016/j.jamcollsurg.2014.12.027.
11. Muysoms FE, Antoniu SA, Bury K, Campanelli G, Conze J, Cuccurullo D, de Beaux AC, Deerenberg EB, East B, Fortelny RH, Gillion JF, Henriksen NA, Israelsson L, Jairam A, Janes A, Jeekel J, Lopez-Cano M, Miserez M, Morales-Conde S, Sanders DL, Simons MP, Smietanski M, Venclauskas L, Berrevoet F. European Hernia Society guidelines on the closure of the abdominal wall incisions. Hernia. 2015;19:1–24. https://doi.org/10.1007/s10029-014-1342-5.
12. Bickenbach KA, Karanicolas PJ, Ammori JB, Jayaraman S, Winter JM, Fields RC, Govindarajamn A, Nir I, Rocha FG, Brennan MF. Up and down or side to side? A systematic review and meta-analysis examining the impact of incision on outcomes after abdominal surgery. Am J Surg. 2013;206:400–9. https://doi.org/10.1016/j.amjsurg.2012.11.008.
13. Fassiadis N, Roidl M, Henning M, South LM, Andrews SM. Randomized clinical trial of vertical or transverse laparotomy for abdominal aortic aneurysm repair. Br J Surg. 2005;92:1208–11.
14. Grantcharov TP, Rosenberg J. Vertical compared with transverse incisions in abdominal surgery. Eur J Surg. 2001;167:260–7.
15. Proske JM, Zieren J, Muller JM. Transverse versus midline incision for upper abdominal surgery. Surg Today. 2005;35:117–21.
16. Hodgson NC, Malthaner RA, Ostbye T. The search of an ideal method of abdominal fascial closure: a meta-analysis. Ann Surg. 2000;231:436–42.
17. Henriksen NA, Deerenberg EB, Venclauskas L, Fortelny RH, Miserez M, Muysoms FE. Meta-analysis on material and techniques for laparotomy closure: the MATCH review. World J Surg. 2018;42:1666–78. https://doi.org/10.1007/s00268-017-4393-9.
18. Velnar T, Bailey T, Smrkolj V. The wound healing process: an overview of the cellular and molecular mechanisms. J Int Med Res. 2009;37:1528–42.
19. Henriksen NA, Deeremberg EB, Venclauskas L, Fortelny RH, Garcia-Alamino JM, Miserez M, Muysoms FE. Triclosan-coated sutures and surgical site infection in abdominal surgery: the TRISTAN review, meta-analysis and trial sequential analysis. Hernia. 2017;21:833–41. https://doi.org/10.1007/s10029-017-1681-0.
20. Diener MK, Voss S, Jensen K, Buchler MW, Seiler CM. Elective midline laparotomy closure: the inline systematic review and meta-analysis. Ann Surg. 2010;251:843–56. https://doi.org/10.1097/SLA.0b013e3181d973e4.
21. Sajid MS, Parampalli U, Baig MK, McFall MR. A systematic review on the effectiveness of slowly-absorbable versus non-absorbable sutures for abdominal fascial closure following laparotomy. Int J Surg. 2011;9:615–25. https://doi.org/10.1016/j.ijsu.2011.09.006.
22. van't Riet M, Steyerberg EW, Nellensteyn J, Bonjer HJ, Jeekel J. Meta-analysis of techniques for closure of midline abdominal incisions. Br J Surg. 2002;89:1350–6.
23. Deerenberg EB, Harlaar JJ, Steyerberg EW, Lont HE, van Doorn EC, Heisterkamp J, Wijnhoven BPL, Schouten WR, Cense HA, Stockmann HB, Berends FJ, Dijkhuizen PH, Dwarkasing RS, Jairam AP, van Ramshorst GH, Kleinrensink GJ, Jeekel J, Lange JF. Small bites versus large bites for closure of abdominal midline incisions (STITCH): a double-blind, multicentre, randomised controlled trial. Lancet. 2015;386:1254–60. https://doi.org/10.1016/S0140-6736(15)60459-7.
24. Harries RL, Cornish J, Bosanquet D, Rees B, Horwood J, Islam S, Bashir N, Watkins A, Russell IT, Torkington J, on behalf of the HART Trial Management Group. Hughes Abdominal Repair Trial (HART) – abdominal wall closure techniques to reduce the incidence of incisional hernias: feasibility trial for a multicentre, pragmatic, randomised controlled trial. BJM Open. 2017;7:e017235. https://doi.org/10.1136/bmjopen-2017-017235.
25. Cornish J, Harries RL, Bosanquet D, Reees B, Ansell J, Frewer N, Dhruva Rao PK, Parry C, Ellis-Owen R, Philips SM, Morris C, Horwood J, Davies ML, Davies MM, Hargest R, Davies Z, Hilton J, Harris D, Ben-Sassi A, Rajagopal R, Hanratty D, Islam S, Watkins A, Bashir N, Jones S, Russell IR, Torkington J, HART Trial Management Group. Hughes Abdominal

Repair Trial (HART) – Abdominal wall closure techniques to reduce the incidence of incisional hernias: study protocol for a randomised controlled trial. Trials. 2016;17:454. https://doi.org/10.1186/s13063-016-1537-0.

26. Petro CC, Rosen MJ. Repair of ventral abdominal wall hernias. Hamilton: Scientific American Surgery, Decker Intellectual Properties; 2014. p. 1–30.
27. Playforth MJ, Sauven PD, Evans M, Pollock AV. The prediction of incisional hernias by radio-opaque markers. Ann R Coll Surg. 1986;68:82–4.
28. Bellon JM, Lopez-Hervas P, Rodriguez M, Grarcia-Honduvilla N, Pascual G, Bujan J. Midline abdominal wall closure: a new prophylactic mesh concept. J Am Coll Surg. 2006;203:490–7.
29. Borab ZM, Shakir S, Lanni MA, Tecce MG, MacDonald J, Hope WW, Fischer JP. Does Prophylactic mesh placement in elective, midline laparotomy reduce the incidence of incisional hernia? A systematic review and meta-analysis. Surgery. 2017;161:1149–63. https://doi.org/10.1016/j.surg.2016.09.036.
30. Caro-Tarrago A, Olona Casas C, Jimenez Salido A, Duque Guilera E, Moreno Fernandez F, Vicente Guillen V. Prevention of incisional hernia in midline laparotomy with an onlay mesh: a randomized clinical trial. World J Surg. 2014;38:2223–30. https://doi.org/10.1007/s00268-014-2510-6.
31. Garcia-Urena MA, Lopez-Monclus J, Blazquez Hernando LA, Melero Montes D, Valle de Lersundi AR, Castellon Pavon C, Jimenez Ceinos C, Lopez Quindos C. Randomized controlled trial of the use of a large-pore polypropylene mesh to prevent incisional hernia in colorectal surgery. Ann Surg. 2015;261:876–81. https://doi.org/10.1097/SLA.0000000000001116.
32. Blazquez Hernando LA, Garcia-Urena MA, Lopez-Monclus J, Garcia Hernandez S, Valle de Lersundi AR, Cruz Cidoncha A, Melero Montes D, Castellon Pavon C, Gonzalez Gonzalez E, Palencia Garcia N. Prophylactic mesh can be used safely in the prevention of incisional hernia after bilateral subcostal laparotomies. Surgery. 2016;160:1358–66. https://doi.org/10.1016/j.surg.2016.05.010.
33. Argudo N, Pereira JA, Sancho JJ, Membrilla E, Pons MJ, Grande L. Prophylactic synthetic mesh can be safely used to close emergency laparotomies, even in peritonitis. Surgery. 2014;156:1238–44. https://doi.org/10.1016/j.surg.2014.04.035.
34. Muysoms FE, Dietz UA. Prophylactic meshes in the abdominal wall. Chirurg. 2017;88(Suppl 1):S34–41. https://doi.org/10.1007/s00104-016-0229-7.
35. Muysoms FE, Detry O, Vierendeels T, Huyghe M, Miserez M, Ruppert M, Tollens T, Defraigne JO, Berrevoet F. Prevention of incisional hernias by prophylactic mesh-augmented reinforcement of midline laparotomies for abdominal aortic aneurysm treatment: a randomized controlled trial. Ann Surg. 2016;263:638–45. https://doi.org/10.1097/SLA.0000000000001369.
36. Llaguna OH, Avgerinos DV, Nagda P, Elfant D, Leitman IM, Goodman E. Does prophylactic biologic mesh placement protect against the development of incisional hernia in high risk patients? World J Surg. 2011;35:1651–5. https://doi.org/10.1007/s00268-011-1131-6.
37. Sarr MG, Hutcher NE, Snyder S, Hodde J, Carmody B. A prospective, randomized, multicenter trial of Surgisis Gold, a biologic prosthetic, as a sublay reinforcement of the fascial closure after open bariatric surgery. Surgery. 2014;156:902–9. https://doi.org/10.1016/j.surg.2014.06.022.
38. Lopez-Cano M, Armengol M, Quiles MT, Biel A, Velasco J, Huguet P, Mestre A, Delgado LM, Gil FX, Arbos MA. Preventive midline laparotomy closure with a new bioabsorbable mesh: an experimental study. J Surg Res. 2013;181:160–9. https://doi.org/10.1016/j.jss.2012.05.041.
39. Hijort H, Mathisen T, Alves A, Clermont G, Boutrand JP. Three-years results from a preclinical implantation study of a long-term resorbable surgical mesh with time-dependent mechanical characteristics. Hernia. 2012;16:191–7. https://doi.org/10.1007/s10029-011-0885-y.
40. Klinge U, Klosterhalfen B, Muller M, Schumpelick V. Foreign body reactions to meshes used for the repair of abdominal wall hernias. Eur J Surg. 1999;165:665–73.
41. Muysoms FE, Jairam A, Lopez-Cano M, Smietanski M, Woeste G, Kyle-Leinhase I, Antoniu SA, Lockerling F, BioMesh Study Group. Prevention of incisional hernias with biological mesh: review of the literature. Front Surg. 2016;3:53. https://doi.org/10.3389/fsurg.2016.00053.

42. Lopez-Cano M, Pereira JA, Lozoya R, Feliu X, Villalobos R, Navarro S, Arbos MA, Armengol-Carrasco M. PREBIOUS trial: a multicenter randomized controlled trial of PREventive midline laparotomy closure with BIOabsorbable mesh for the prevention of incisional hernia: rationale and design. Contemp Clin Trials. 2014;39:335–41. https://doi.org/10.1016/j.cct.2014.10.009.
43. Soderback H, Mahteme H, Hellman P, Sandblom G. Prophylactic resorbable synthetic mesh to prevent dehiscence and incisional hernia in high high-risk laparotomy: a pilot study of using TIGR Matrix mesh. Front Surg. 2016;3:28. https://doi.org/10.3389/fsurg.2016.00028.
44. Fink C, Baumann P, Wente MN, Knebel P, Bruckner T, Ulrich A, Werner J, Buchler MW, Diener MK. Incisional rates 3 years after midline laparotomy. Br J Surg. 2014;101:51–4. https://doi.org/10.1002/bjs.9364.
45. Pearl RK. Parastomal hernias. World J Surg. 1989;13:569–72.
46. Israelsson LA. Preventing and treating parastomal hernia. World J Surg. 2005;29:1089.
47. Moreno-Matias J, Serra-Aracil X, Darnell-Martin A, Bombardo-Junca J, Mora-Lopez L, Alcantara-Moral M, Rebasa P, Ayguavives-Garnica I, Navarro-Soto S. The prevalence of parastomal hernia after formation of an end colostomy. A new clinic-radiological classification. Colorectal Dis. 2009;11:173–7. https://doi.org/10.1111/j.1463-1318.2008.01564.x.
48. Carne PW, Robertson GM, Frizelle FA. Parastomal hernia. Br J Surg. 2003;90:784–93.
49. Mylonakis E, Scarpa M, Barollo M, Yarnoz C, Keighley MR. Life-table analysis of hernia following end colostomy construction. Colorectal Dis. 2001;3:334–7.
50. Goligher JC, Duthie HL, Nixon HH. Surgery of the anus, rectum and colon. London: Bailliere Tindall; 1984.
51. Gillern S, Bleier J. Parastomal hernia repair and reinforcement: the role of biologic and synthetic materials. Clin Colon Rectal Surg. 2014;27:162–71. https://doi.org/10.1055/s-0034-1394090.
52. Antoniu SA, Agresta F, Garcia Alamino JM, Berger D, Berrevoet F, Brandsma HT, Bury K, Conze J, Cuccurullo D, Dietz UA, Fortelny RH, Frei-Lanter C, Hansson B, Helgstrand F, Hotouras A, Janes A, Kroese LF, Lambrecht JR, Kyle-Leinhase I, Lopez-Cano M, Maggiori L, Mandalà V, Miserez M, Montgomery A, Morales-Conde S, Prudhomme M, Rautio T, Smart N, Smietanski M, Szczepkowski M, Stabilini C, Muysoms FE. European Hernia Society guidelines on prevention and treatment of parastomal hernia. Hernia. 2018;22:183–98. https://doi.org/10.1007/s10029-017-1697-5.
53. Sohn YJ, Moon SM, Shin US, Jee SE. Incidence and risk factors of parastomal hernia. J Korean Sco Coloproctol. 2012;28:241–6. https://doi.org/10.3393/jksc.2012.28.5.241.
54. Nasvall P, Wikner F, Gunnarsson U, Rutegard J, Strigard K. A comparison between intrastomal 3D ultrasonography, CT scanning and findings at surgery in patients with stomal complaints. Int J Colorectal Dis. 2014;29:1263–6. https://doi.org/10.1007/s00384-014-1944-5.
55. Aquina CT, Iannuzzi JC, Probst CP, Kelly KN, Noyes K, Fleming FJ, Monson JRT. Parastomal hernia: a growing problem with new solutions. Dig Surg. 2014;31:366–76. https://doi.org/10.1159/000369279.
56. Helgstrand F, Rosenberg J, Kehelet H, Jorgensen LN, Wara P, Bisgaard T. Risk of morbidity, mortality, and recurrence after parastomal hernia repair: a nationwide study. Dis Colon Rectum. 2013;56:1265–72. https://doi.org/10.1097/DCR.0b013e3182a0e6e2.
57. Janes A, Cengiz Y, Israelsson LA. Randomized clinical trial of the use of a prosthetic mesh to prevent parastomal hernia. Br J Surg. 2004;91:280–2. https://doi.org/10.1002/bjs.4417.
58. Brandsma HT, Hansson BM, Aufenacker TJ, van Geldere D, van Lammeren FM, Mahabier C, Steenvoorde P, de Vries Reilingh TS, Wiezer RJ, de Wilt JH, Bleichrodt RP, Rosman C. Prophylactic mesh placement to prevent parastomal hernia, early results of a prospective multicentre randomized trial. Hernia. 2016;20:535–41. https://doi.org/10.1007/s10029-015-1427-9.
59. Chapman SJ, Wood B, Drake TM, Young N, Jaune DG. Systematic review and meta-analysis of prophylactic mesh during primary stoma formation to prevent parastomal hernia. Dis Colon Rectum. 2017;60:107–15. https://doi.org/10.1097/DCR.0000000000000670.
60. Cornille JB, Pathak S, Daniels IR, Smart NJ. Prophylactic mesh use during primary stoma formation to prevent parastomal hernia. Ann R Coll Surg Engl. 2017;99:2–11. https://doi.org/10.1308/rcsann.2016.0186.

61. Fleshman JW, Beck DE, Hyman N, Wexner SD, Bauer J, George V, PRISM Study Group. A prospective, multicenter, randomized, controlled studi of non-cross-linked porcine acellular dermal matrix fascial sublay for parastomal reinforcement in patients undergoing surgery for permanent abdominal wall ostomies. Dis Colon Rectum. 2014;57:623–31. https://doi.org/10.1079/DCR.0000000000000106.
62. Fortelny RH, Hofmann A, May C, Kockerling F, BioMesh Study Group. Prevention of parastomal hernia by biological mesh reinforcement. Front Surg. 2015;2:53. https://doi.org/10.3389/fsurg.2015.00053.
63. Lambrecht JR, Larsen SG, Reiertsen O, Vaktskjold A, Julsrud L, Flatmark K. Prophylactic mesh at end-colostomy construction reduces parastomal hernia rate: a randomized trial. Colorectal Dis. 2015;17:191–7. https://doi.org/10.1111/codi.13065.
64. Lopez-Cano M, Brandsma HT, Bury K, Hansson B, Kyle-Leinhase I, Alamino JG, Muysoms F. Prophylactic mesh to prevent parastomal hernia after end-colostomy: a meta-analysis and trial sequential analysis. Hernia. 2017;21:177–89. https://doi.org/10.1007/s10029-016-1563-x.
65. Lopez-Cano M, Serra-Aracil X, Mora L, Sanchez-Garcia JL, Jimenez-Gomez LM, Marti M, Vallribera F, Fraccalvieri D, Serracant A, Kreisler E, Biondo S, Espin E, Navarro-Soto S, Armengol-Carrasco M. Preventing parastomal hernia using a modified Sugarbaker technique with composite mesh during laparoscopic abdominoperineal resection: a randomized controlled trial. Ann Surg. 2016;264:923–8. https://doi.org/10.1097/SLA.0000000000001684.
66. Odensten C, Strigard K, Rutegard J, Dahlberg M, Stahle U, Gunnarsson U, Nasvall P. Use a prophylactic mesh when creating a colostomy does not prevent parastomal hernia: a randomized controlled trial- STOMAMESH. Ann Surg. 2017; https://doi.org/10.1097/SLA.0000000000002542.
67. Planka F, Probst P, Keller AV, Saure D, Grummich K, Buchler MW, Diener MK. Prophylactic mesh placement for the PREvention of paraSTOmal hernias: the PRESTO systematic review and meta-analysis. PLoS One. 2017;12(2):e0171548. https://doi.org/10.1371/journal.pone.0171548.
68. Serra-Aracil X, Bombardo-Junca J, Moreno-Matias J, Darnell A, Mora-Lopez L, Alcantara-Moral M, Ayguavives-Garnica I, Navarro-Soto S. Randomized, controlled, prospective trial of a use of a mesh to prevent parastomal hernia. Ann Surg. 2009;249:583–7. https://doi.org/10.1097/SLA.0b013e31819ec809.
69. Vierimaa M, Klintruo K, Biancari F, Victorzon M, Carpelan-Holmstrom M, Kossi J, Kellokumpu I, Rauvala E, Ohtonen P, Makela J, Rautio T. Prospective, randomized study on the use of a prosthetic mesh for prevention of parastomal hernia of permanent colostomy. Dis Colon Rectum. 2015;58:943–9. https://doi.org/10.1097/DCR.0000000000000443.
70. Wang S, Wang W, Zhu B, Song G, Jiang G. Efficacy of prophylactic mesh in end-colostomy construction: a systematic review and meta-analysis of randomized controlled trials. World J Surg. 2016;40:2528–36. https://doi.org/10.1007/s00268-016-3576-0.
71. Comajuncosas J, Hermoso J, Gris P, Jimeno J, Orbeal R, Vallverdú H, López Negre JL, Urgellés J, Estalella L, Parés D. Risk factors for umbilical trocar site incisional hernia in laparoscopic cholecystectomy: a prospective 3-year follow-up study. Am J Surg. 2014;207:1–6. https://doi.org/10.1016/j.amjsurg.2013.05.010.
72. Armañanzas L, Ruiz-Tovar J, Arroyo A, García-Peche P, Armañanzas E, Diez M, Galindo I, Calpena R. Prophylactic mesh vs suture in the closure of the umbilical trocar site after laparoscopic cholecystectomy in high-risk patients for incisional hernia. A randomized clinical trial. J Am Coll Surg. 2014;218:960–8. https://doi.org/10.1016/j.jamcollsurg.2014.01.049.
73. Reynolds D, Davenport DL, Korosec RL, Roth JS. Financial implications of ventral hernia repair: a hospital cost analysis. J Gastrointest Surg. 2013;17:159–67. https://doi.org/10.1007/s11605-012-1999-y.
74. Gillion JF, Sanders D, Miserez M, Muysoms F. The economic burden of incisional ventral hernia repair: a multicentric cost analysis. Hernia. 2016;20:819–30. https://doi.org/10.1007/s10029-016-1480-z.
75. Fischer JP, Basta MN, Wink JD, Krishnan MN, Kovach SJ. Cost-utility analysis of the use of prophylactic mesh augmentation compared with primary fascial suture repair in patients at high risk for incisional hernia. Surgery. 2015;158:700–11. https://doi.org/10.1016/j.surg.2015.02.03.

Part II

Economics

State-of-the-Art of Abdominal Wall Surgery in Italy: Coding, Reimbursement, Hospitalisations and Expenditure for Surgical Meshes

9

Maria Caterina Cavallo, Giuditta Callea, and Rosanna Tarricone

9.1 Introduction

In the mid-nineties, most western countries moved from retrospective payment (i.e. ex post reimbursement of hospitals incurred costs) to prospective payment, where hospitals are reimbursed a predetermined fee for each hospitalisation. Hospitalisations are classified into homogeneous groups called diagnosis-related groups (DRGs) according to patients' characteristics (i.e. age and gender), main reason for admission (i.e. principal diagnosis), comorbidities (i.e. secondary diagnoses), procedures, length of stay and status at discharge (i.e. discharged alive, transferred to other hospital, dead).

DRGs were introduced with the aim of increasing transparency about services provided by the hospitals and enhancing the efficient use of resources (i.e. discouraging the provision of unnecessary services and encouraging the efficient delivery of appropriate care). On the other hand, under DRG-based reimbursement systems, hospitals are encouraged to reduce the cost per hospitalisation, keeping their average costs below the payment rate in order to avoid making losses. This might hinder

The database of Italian regional coding guidelines was funded by the Italian Ministry of Health, Directorate General of Medical Devices and Pharmaceutical Service through an unrestricted grant. The authors are grateful to Francesca Borghetti, Dalila Patrizia Greco and Davide Mozzanica for their helpful comments.

M. C. Cavallo · G. Callea (✉)
Centre for Research on Health and Social Care Management (CeRGAS), SDA Bocconi School of Management, Milan, Italy
e-mail: mariacaterina.cavallo@unibocconi.it; giuditta.callea@unibocconi.it

R. Tarricone
Centre for Research on Health and Social Care Management (CeRGAS), SDA Bocconi School of Management, Milan, Italy

Department of Social and Political Science, Bocconi University, Milan, Italy
e-mail: rosanna.tarricone@unibocconi.it

D. P. Greco, E. Borgonovi (eds.), *Abdominal Wall Surgery*,
https://doi.org/10.1007/978-3-030-02426-0_9

the adoption and use of new cost-increasing technologies at least until the payment system is updated to account for the extra costs.

Ever since the introduction of DRG-based hospital payment systems, there have been concerns that these reimbursement systems may not provide the right set of incentives to encourage the desired level of adoption and use of technological innovations in health care [1]. In general, any time new technologies increase the quality of care but are associated with higher costs, DRG-based hospital payment is not in line with societal objectives. Consequently, several mechanisms have been developed by most countries using DRGs to account for technological innovation in health care [2]. Long-term updating mechanisms ensure that technological innovations are formally incorporated into the reimbursement system, either through patient classification system (PCS) updates or through updates of the payment rate. Short-term payment mechanisms, such as additional payments on top of DRG rate, encourage the use of cost-increasing technological innovations in the transitory period until the system accounts for the technological innovation.

9.2 Patient Classification and Hospital Reimbursement System in Italy

Italy adopts the International Classification of Diseases, 9th revision, Clinical Modification (ICD-9-CM) for diagnoses and procedures. Updates are rare and usually occur at least two years after the release by the National Center for Health Statistics (NCHS) and the Centers for Medicare and Medicaid Services (CMS), the US governmental agencies responsible for overseeing all changes and modifications (Table 9.1). Since 2011, Italy started defining and developing its own classification system, the Italian DRG system (It.DRG), which is supposed to be adopted in the next years.

Hospitalisations are classified into DRGs by a software called DRG Grouper. In the USA, Medicare releases an updated version of the Grouper every year. On the contrary, in Italy updates are irregular as shown in Table 9.2. In the current DRG version, hospitalisations are classified into 538 groups based on 14,232 ICD-9-CM diagnoses and 3,306 procedure codes.

Italy has a decentralised health care system. Regions have a significant power in the management of health care, including the freedom to set own coding guidelines (i.e. to provide indications on how to combine existing ICD-9-CM codes) and to introduce new DRGs or split existing ones, when specific procedures are performed or certain technologies are used [3].

Table 9.1 Updates of ICD-9-CM in Italy

Year of release by HCNS and CMS	Year of introduction in Italy
1997	2000
2002	2006
2006	2009

Table 9.2 Updates of DRG Grouper in Italy

DRG Grouper version	Year of the US release	Year of introduction in Italy
HCFA 10	1992	1995
HCFA 14	1996	2000
CMS 19	2001	2006
CMS 24	2006	2009

Table 9.3 Updates of national DRG tariffs in Italy

National law	Validity
Ministerial Decree 12/14/1994	1995–1996
Ministerial Decree 06/13/1997	1997–2006
Ministerial Decree 09/12/2006	2006–2012
Ministerial Decree 10/18/2012	2013–(still valid)

National DRG-related tariffs were introduced in 1995 based on cost data collected in eight Italian hospitals located in northern and central regions (Table 9.3). Similarly to coding systems, updates are sporadic: in 2018, tariffs approved in 2012 are still valid. National tariffs represent an upper threshold in the level of reimbursement, and regional governments are free to set and update regional DRG rates, which anyhow have to be lower or equal to the national tariffs.

9.3 Technologies for Abdominal Wall Repair

Hernia repair is one of the most frequent surgical procedures performed globally, with over 20 million hernia repair procedures worldwide every year [4]. The number of procedures has been increasing over time and is projected to further increase due to several risk factors such as obesity and prior abdominal surgeries [5].

Based on the weaker points of the abdominal wall, hernias are classified into inguinal (the most frequent form, accounting for 75% of the cases), umbilical (9.5%) and femoral (2.7%) [6]. Less common types are hiatus, epigastric, spigelian, hiatal, muscle and incisional hernias.

Most abdominal hernias can be surgically repaired, either through open surgery or through laparoscopy. The latter reduces the time for recovery after the intervention. Muscle reinforcement techniques often involve synthetic materials, the so-called hernia mesh prosthesis. Many types of meshes are available in the market, with different biological response and handling characteristics and different costs: non-absorbable and synthetic; non-absorbable and synthetic with a barrier; synthetic and partially absorbable; combined; and biological materials. Researchers have investigated metals, composites, polymers and biodegradable biomaterials in the attempt to obtain the ideal surgical mesh and implantation procedure [4]. To date, the evidence remains insufficient to determine whether cost and clinical benefits exist, and clinicians can decide what mesh to use depending on patient case characteristics. Recent literature [7] claims further clinical studies and economic evaluations to ascertain the superiority of a single mesh generation on others [8]. Anyway, a recent Italian study [9] presented a budget impact analysis in the setting of incisional hernia repairs. The analysis has been performed in order to evaluate the changes in the hospital budget considering future scenarios with increased utilisation rates of biosynthetic meshes over synthetic and biologic meshes. The study showed possible savings per patient of about 780€ in a time horizon of 5 years, supporting the use of biosynthetic meshes for complex abdominal wall repairs.

9.4 Classification of Hospitalisations and Coding Guidelines for Abdominal Wall Surgery

9.4.1 Methods

We analysed the patient classification and DRG systems used in Italy, checking whether they were able to appropriately detect different types of hernia repair procedures and/or different types of devices. Moreover, we performed a systematic search of all the coding guidelines published in Italy, at national and regional level, from 2009 (when CMS DRGs version 24 were introduced in the Italian NHS) to 2017 in order to verify whether regional authorities replaced national existing codes. The search was conducted on the following websites and databases: Ministry of Health, Italian National Agency for Regional Health Services (AGENAS), regional healthcare agencies, Italian Official Gazette and search engines (e.g. Google). The following keywords (alone or in combination) were used in the searches: hospital discharge codes, coding guidelines, ICD-9-CM updates, abdominal wall codes, mesh/graft/implant, bioprosthesis, biosynthetic mesh/graft/implant, ventral/incisional hernia and inguinal hernia. All the available national and regional guidelines were collected and analysed, and coding guidelines were extracted.

9.4.2 Results

Table 9.4 shows the ICD-9-CM procedure codes for repair of hernia valid in Italy starting from 1997. The codes with the highest level of detail relate to inguinal and femoral hernia, and allow to distinguish unilateral vs. bilateral, direct vs. indirect hernia, with or without graft or prosthesis.

Hospitalisations for abdominal wall surgery are classified in DRGs 159–163 according to type of hernia (i.e. inguinal or femoral vs. other types), patient's age (0–17 vs. >17 years) and presence of complications (Table 9.5). The classification of DRGs has not been updated since 1995.

Our analysis of national and regional guidelines highlighted that 9 Italian regions out of 21 developed their own coding guidelines (i.e. indications on how to combine existing ICD-9-CM codes when certain technologies are used), 11 adopted the national guidelines approved by the Ministry of Health in 2010, while one region did not explicitly adopt any guidance (Fig. 9.1). Anyhow, it is worth noticing that the guidelines (both national and regional) provide with coding indications for other therapeutic areas but they disregard procedures related to hernia repair.

Table 9.4 ICD-9-CM procedure codes for repair of hernia (versions 1997, 2002 and 2007)

ICD-9-CM code	Description
53.0	*Unilateral repair of inguinal hernia*
53.00	Unilateral repair of inguinal hernia, not otherwise specified, inguinal herniorrhaphy NOS
53.01	Repair of direct inguinal hernia
53.02	Repair of indirect inguinal hernia
53.03	Repair of direct inguinal hernia with graft or prosthesis
53.04	Repair of indirect inguinal hernia with graft or prosthesis
53.05	Repair of inguinal hernia with graft or prosthesis, not otherwise specified
53.1	*Bilateral repair of inguinal hernia*
53.10	Bilateral repair of inguinal hernia, not otherwise specified
53.11	Bilateral repair of direct inguinal hernia
53.12	Bilateral repair of indirect inguinal hernia
53.13	Bilateral repair of inguinal hernia, one direct and one indirect
53.14	Bilateral repair of direct inguinal hernia with graft or prosthesis
53.15	Bilateral repair of indirect inguinal hernia with graft or prosthesis
53.16	Bilateral repair of inguinal hernia, one direct and one indirect, with graft or prosthesis
53.17	Bilateral inguinal hernia repair with graft or prosthesis, not otherwise specified
53.2	*Unilateral repair of femoral hernia*
53.21	Unilateral repair of femoral hernia with graft or prosthesis
53.29	Other unilateral femoral herniorrhaphy
53.3	*Bilateral repair of femoral hernia*
53.31	Bilateral repair of femoral hernia with graft or prosthesis
53.39	Other bilateral femoral herniorrhaphy
53.4	*Repair of umbilical hernia* *Excludes: repair of gastroschisis 54.71*
53.41	Repair of umbilical hernia with prosthesis
53.49	Other umbilical herniorrhaphy
53.5	*Repair of other hernia of anterior abdominal wall (without graft or prosthesis)*
53.51	Incisional hernia repair
53.59	Repair of other hernia of anterior abdominal wall Repair of hernia: epigastric, hypogastric, Spigelian and ventral
53.6	*Repair of other hernia of anterior abdominal wall with graft or prosthesis*
53.61	Incisional hernia repair with prosthesis
53.62	Repair of other hernia of anterior abdominal wall with graft or prosthesis
53.7	*Repair of diaphragmatic hernia, abdominal approach*
53.8	*Repair of diaphragmatic hernia, thoracic approach*
53.80	Repair of diaphragmatic hernia with thoracic approach, not otherwise specified thoracoabdominal repair of diaphragmatic hernia
53.81	Plication of the diaphragm
53.82	Repair of parasternal hernia
53.9	*Other hernia repair*

Table 9.5 DRG codes for repair of hernia (versions 10, 14, 19 and 24)

DRG code	Description
159	Hernia procedures except inguinal and femoral procedures, age >17, w CC
160	Hernia procedures except inguinal and femoral procedures, age >17, w/o CC
161	Inguinal and femoral hernia procedures, age >17, w CC
162	Inguinal and femoral hernia procedures, age >17, w/o CC
163	Hernia procedures, age 0–17

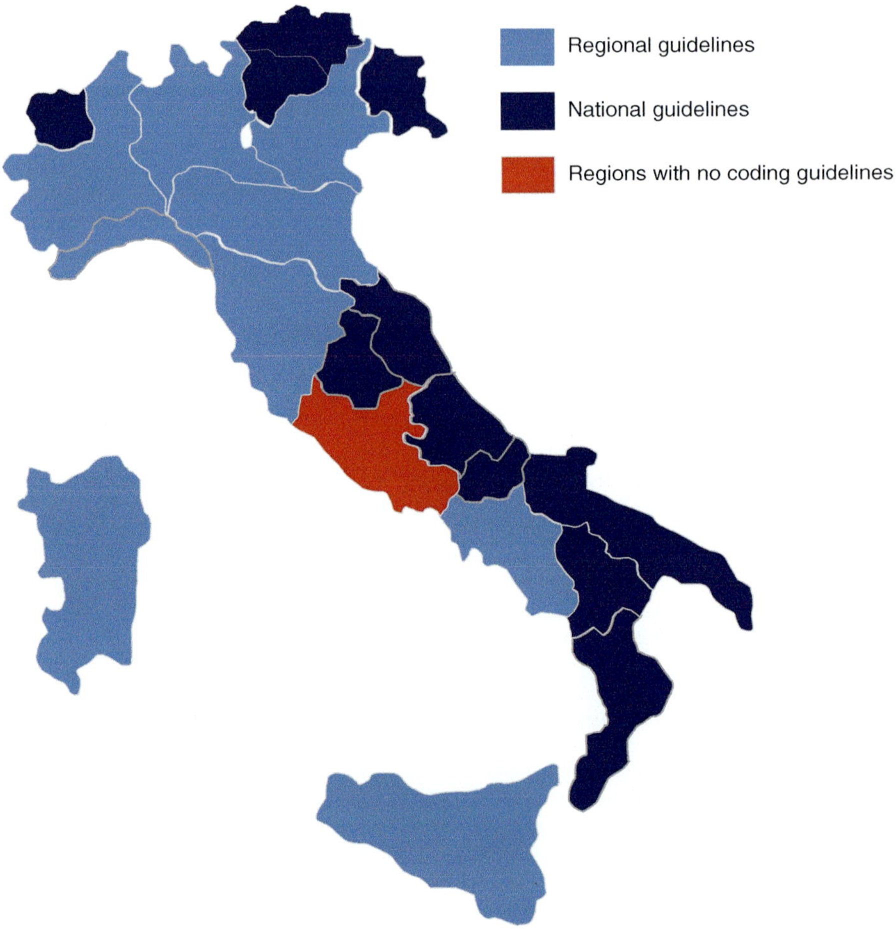

Fig. 9.1 State of adoption of national and regional coding guidelines

9.5 Reimbursement for Abdominal Wall Surgery in Italy

9.5.1 Methods

We searched the Ministry of Health and Italian regions' websites to identify national and regional tariffs for DRGs related to hernia repair and the existence of special funding mechanisms (e.g. supplementary payments on top of DRG rate)

aimed at encouraging the use of innovative, often more expensive, medical devices.

9.5.2 Results

The following figure shows the national tariffs for hospitalisations with hernia repair valid since 2012 in Italy (Fig. 9.2). DRGs 159 and 161 tariffs discourage to treat in day surgery patients with complications, who could probably be treated in a less costly setting according to clinical evaluation. On the contrary, for DRGs 160 and 162 encourage day surgery for cases without complications (i.e. the level of reimbursement is higher compared to inpatient setting).

The majority of Italian regions defined their own tariffs, with huge differences in the level of the reimbursement (Table 9.6). As an example, DRG 159 ranges from a minimum of €1,019 in Campania, Calabria, Sicilia and Sardegna to €3,475 in Lombardia and Veneto till €6,814 in Friuli Venezia Giulia.

From our analyses, it emerged that no regions introduced special payments to encourage the use of innovative devices for hernia repair.

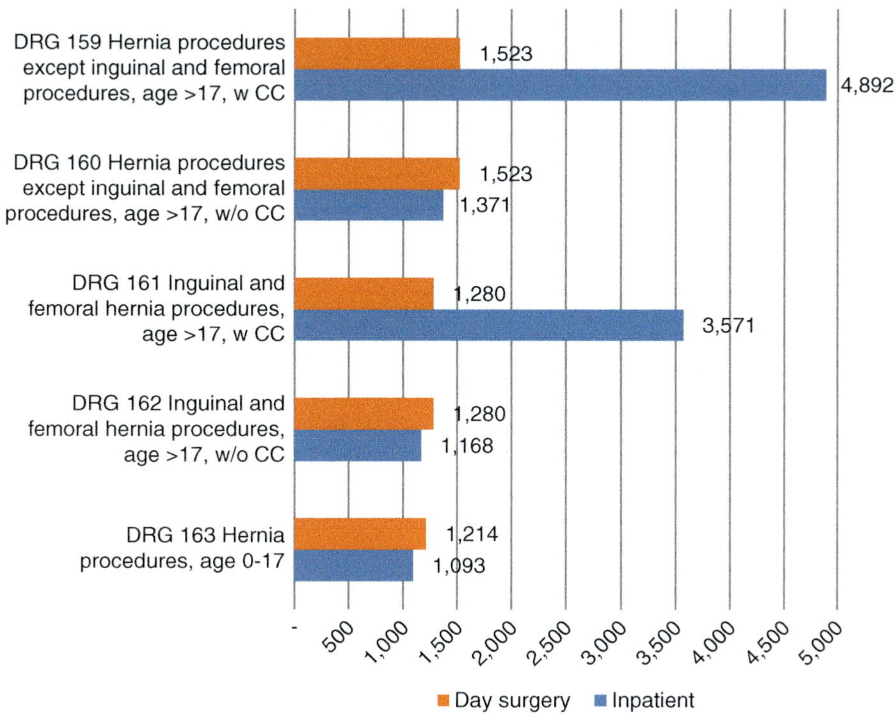

Fig. 9.2 Italian national tariffs for hospitalisations with hernia repair (2012 tariffs still valid in 2018) (source: Italian national tariffs ex Ministerial Decree 10/18/2012)

Table 9.6 National and regional DRG rates for hospitalisations for hernia repair (valid in 2018)

		DRG 159		DRG 160		DRG 161		DRG 162		DRG 163	
Region ID	Region	Inpatient	Day surgery	Inpatient	Day surgery	Inpatient	Day surgery	Inpatient	Day surgery	Inpatient	Day surgery
010	Piemonte	4,892	1,453	1,371	575	3,571	1,240	1,168	649	1,093	603
020	Valle d'Aosta	4,892	1,453	1,371	575	3,571	1,240	1,168	649	1,093	603
030	Lombardia	3,475	1,583	1,583	1,583	2,639	1,180	1,180	1,180	1,112	1,112
041	P.A. Bolzano	4,116	3,665	1,912	1,908	2,400	2,138	1,481	1,477	1,060	1,058
042	P.A. Trento	5,197	1,081	2,396	993	3,031	1,002	1,855	1,027	1,328	1,088
050	Veneto	3,475	3,475	1,704	1,704	2,403	2,403	1,386	1,386	1,755	1,755
060	Friuli Venezia Giulia	6,814	6,814	3,325	3,325	3,974	3,974	2,575	2,575	1,843	1,843
070	Liguria	5,870	1,744	1,645	690	4,285	1,488	1,402	779	1,312	724
080	Emilia Romagna	4,892	1,523	1,371	1,523	3,571	1,280	1,168	1,280	1,093	1,214
090	Toscana	5,214	3,911	2,479	2,479	2,997	2,247	1,229	1,229	1,193	1,193
100	Umbria	4,892	1,453	1,371	575	3,571	1,240	1,168	649	1,093	603
110	Marche	6,124	4,899	1,681	1,867	3,571	2,857	1,301	1,446	981	1,090
120	Lazio	4,892	1,523	1,371	1,523	3,571	1,280	1,168	1,280	1,093	1,214
130	Abruzzo	4,777	1,419	1,338	561	3,487	1,211	1,141	634	1,067	589
140	Molise	4,892	1,453	1,371	575	3,571	1,240	1,168	649	1,093	603
150	Campania	4,900	1,091	2,391	898	2,858	945	1,851	929	1,325	984
160	Puglia	4,892	1,453	1,371	575	3,571	1,240	1,168	649	1,093	603
170	Basilicata	4,892	1,523	1,371	1,523	3,571	1,280	1,168	1,280	1,093	1,214
180	Calabria	4,900	1,019	1,822	898	2,858	945	1,410	929	1,064	984
190	Sicilia	4,900	1,019	2,391	898	2,858	945	1,851	929	1,325	984
200	Sardegna	4,900	1,019	1,984	898	2,858	945	1,488	892	1,183	984
	National tariff	4,892	1,523	1,371	1,523	3,571	1,280	1,168	1,280	1,093	1,214

9.6 Hospitalisations for Abdominal Wall Surgery in Italy

In 2016, 83,427 hospitalisations for hernia repair were performed in Italian hospitals, of which 87% without complications (58% in DRG 162 Inguinal and femoral hernia procedures, age >17, without complications and 29% in DRG 160 hernia procedures except inguinal and femoral procedures, age >17, without complications) (Fig. 9.3). The region with the highest number of cases is Lombardy (12,860, representing 15% of Italian hospitalisations), followed by Piemonte (10,592, 13%) and Campania (8,477, 10%) (Fig. 9.4).

If we focus on DRG 159 hernia procedures, except inguinal and femoral, age >17, with complications, the majority of hospitalisations are characterised by a length of stay (LOS) between 3 and 27 days, the latter being the threshold for DRG 159 (represented by grey bar in Fig. 9.5). The equivalent hospitalisations without complications (i.e. DRG 160) have much shorter LOS, the majority of cases between one and 3 days (sum of blue and orange bars in Fig. 9.5). Inguinal and femoral hernia procedures, in patients aged more than 17, are generally characterised by shorter LOS, both in patients with complications (DRG 161) and without complications (DRG 162) (Fig. 9.6).

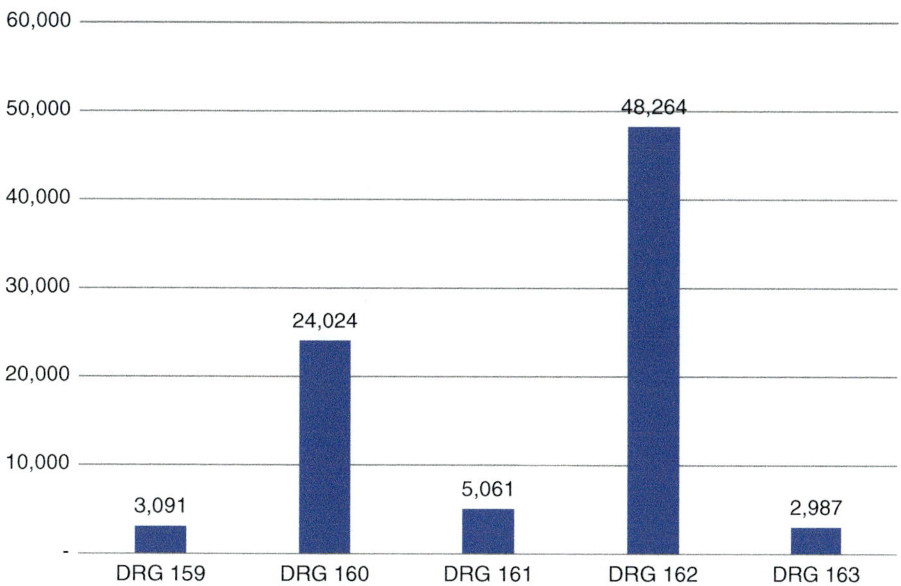

Fig. 9.3 Italian hospitalisations for hernia repair in 2016 (source: Authors' calculations based on [10])

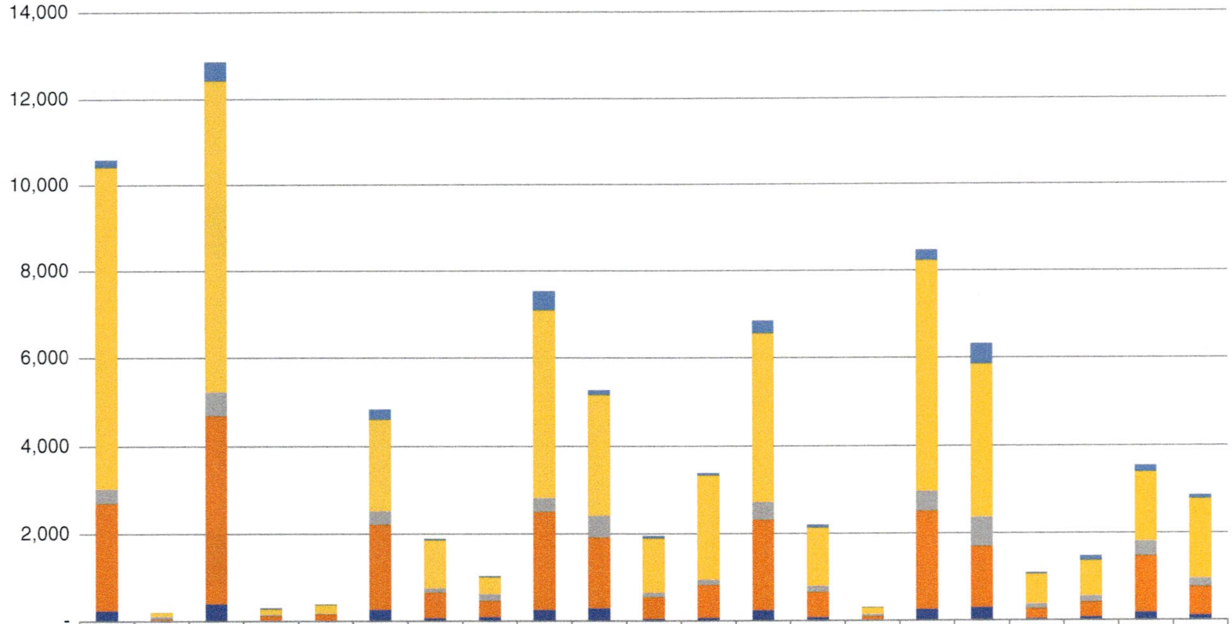

	010	020	030	041	042	050	060	070	080	090	100	110	120	130	140	150	160	170	180	190	200
DRG 163	171	-	429	19	9	225	28	22	437	107	56	54	293	63	2	242	466	30	103	146	85
DRG 162	7,386	83	7,195	130	196	2,096	1,115	397	4,281	2,744	1,246	2,394	3,845	1,341	156	5,267	3,481	683	812	1,588	1,828
DRG 161	333	65	535	26	16	298	91	151	317	495	105	117	400	146	51	452	668	114	145	342	194
DRG 160	2,462	35	4,303	108	151	1,963	585	374	2,249	1,634	495	756	2,076	578	69	2,260	1,409	226	341	1,293	657
DRG 159	240	13	398	18	13	261	76	93	259	294	54	72	247	78	26	256	298	37	72	180	106

DRG 159 DRG 160 DRG 161 DRG 162 DRG 163

Fig. 9.4 Hospitalisations for hernia repair in Italian regions in 2016 (source: Authors' calculations based on [10]) (see Table 9.6 for transcoding region ID)

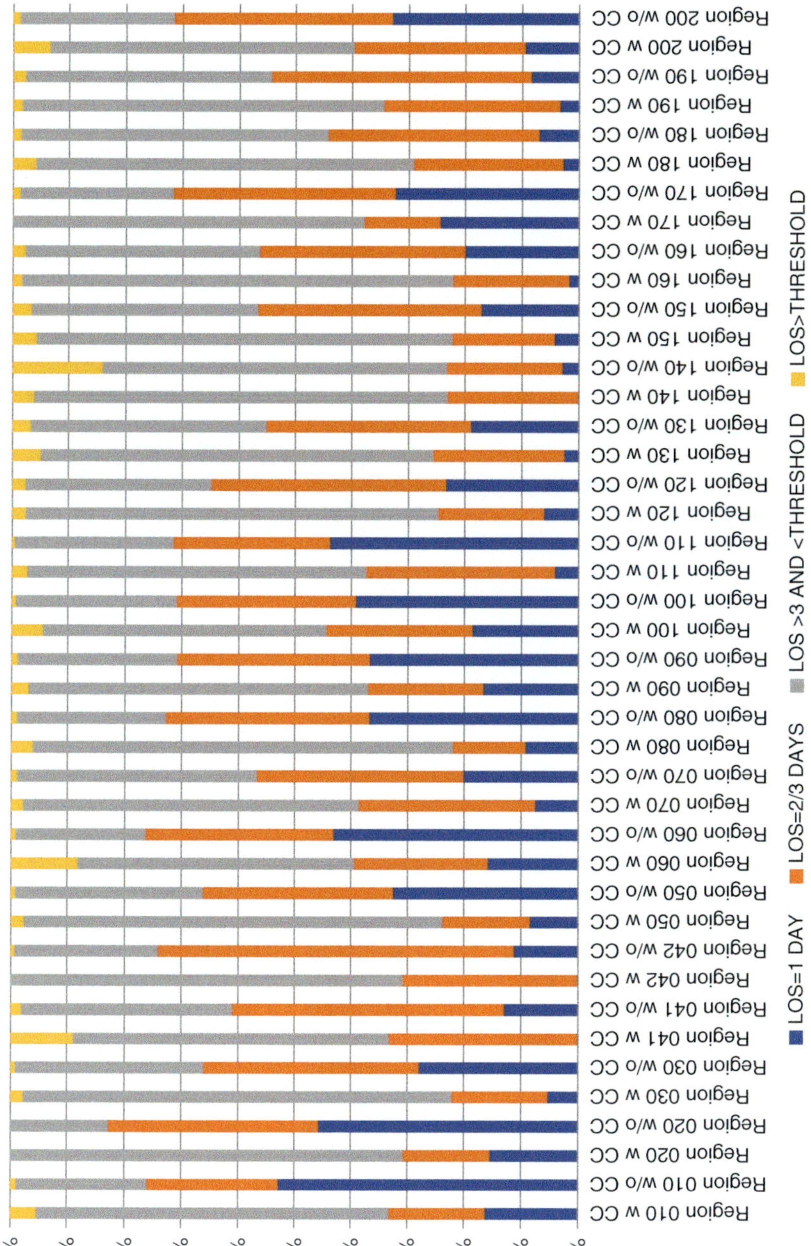

Fig. 9.5 Distribution of hernia procedures (except inguinal and femoral), age >17, with complications (DRG 159) and without complications (DRG 160) per classes of LOS in Italian regions (source: Authors' calculations based on [10]) (see Table 9.6 for transcoding region ID)

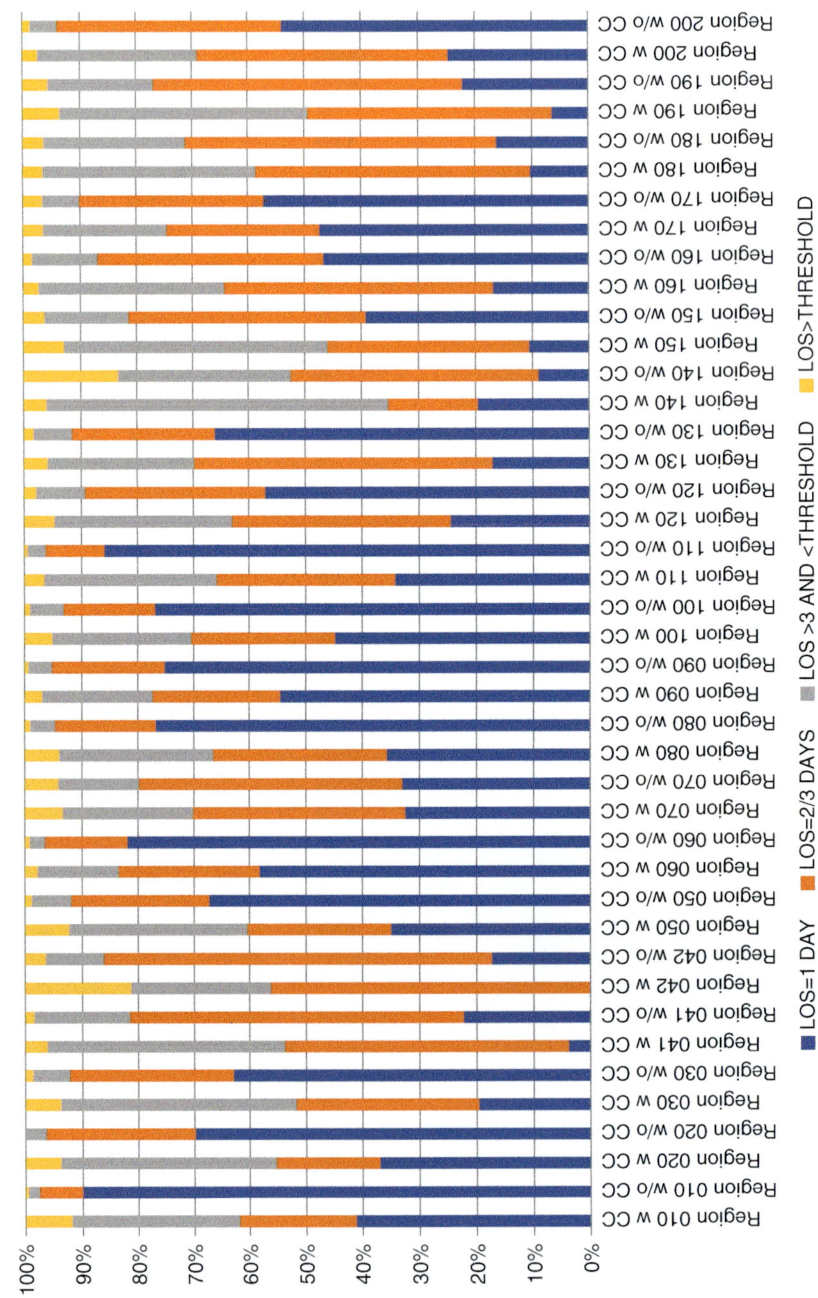

Fig. 9.6 Distribution of inguinal and femoral hernia procedures, age >17, with complications (DRG 161) and without complications (DRG 162) per classes of LOS in Italian regions (source: Authors' calculations based on Italian [10]) (see Table 9.6 for transcoding region ID)

9.7 The Market of Surgical Meshes for Hernia Repair in Italy

The Italian national classification system of medical devices (Classificazione Nazionale dei Dispositivi medici CND) classifies surgical meshes for hernia repair (P9002) according to the materials they are made of, as shown in Table 9.7. Absorbable meshes are classified in the group P900402—Biodegradable devices, filler and reconstructive. In June 2018, 2,251 different meshes were registered in the *Banca Dati e Repertorio dei Dispositivi Medici*, the national repository of the medical devices marketed in the Italian NHS, almost half of which (43%) being surgical meshes in polypropylene (Fig. 9.7).

Table 9.7 Italian national classification system for surgical and biodegradable meshes for hernia repair (source: national classification system of medical devices)

CND code	CND description
P9002	*SURGICAL MESHES*
P900201	SURGICAL MESHES, POLYGLYCOLIC ACID
P900202	SURGICAL MESHES, POLYPROPYLENE
P900203	SURGICAL MESHES, PTFE
P900204	SURGICAL MESHES, MORE THAN ONE COMPONENT
P900205	SURGICAL MESHES, POLYESTER
P900206	SURGICAL MESHES, METALLIC
P900299	SURGICAL MESHES - OTHERS
P9002	*TISSUE MATERIALS, FILLER, SUBSTITUTIVE AND RECONSTRUCTIVE*
P900402	BIODEGRADABLE DEVICES, FILLER AND RECONSTRUCTIVE

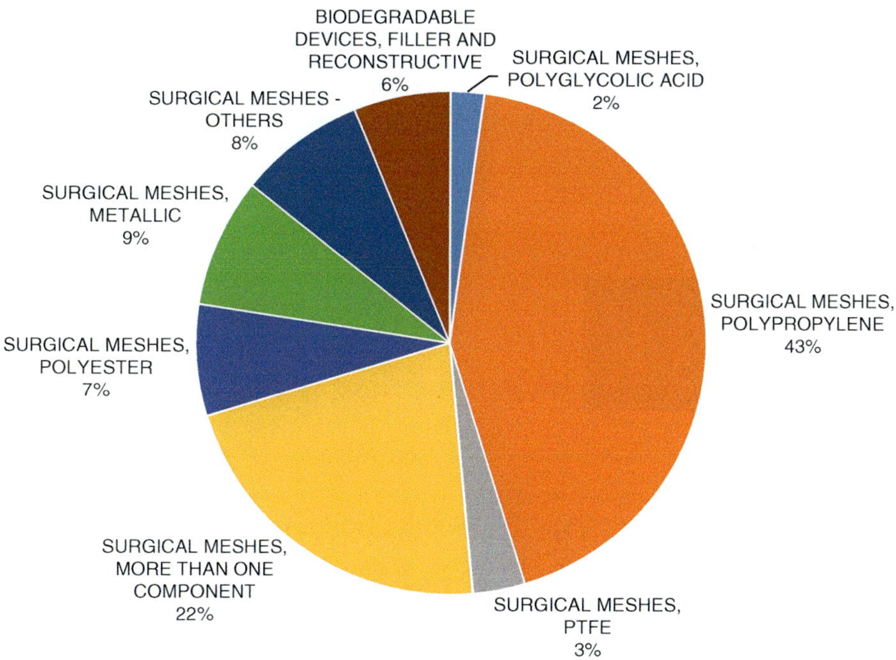

Fig. 9.7 Number of surgical meshes individual products registered in the national repository of the medical devices sold in the Italian NHS (source: Authors' calculations on Italian repository of medical devices sold in the Italian NHS, update 09/06/2018)

Fig. 9.8 Expenditure for surgical meshes in Italian public hospitals (source: Authors' calculations based on appendix of [11])

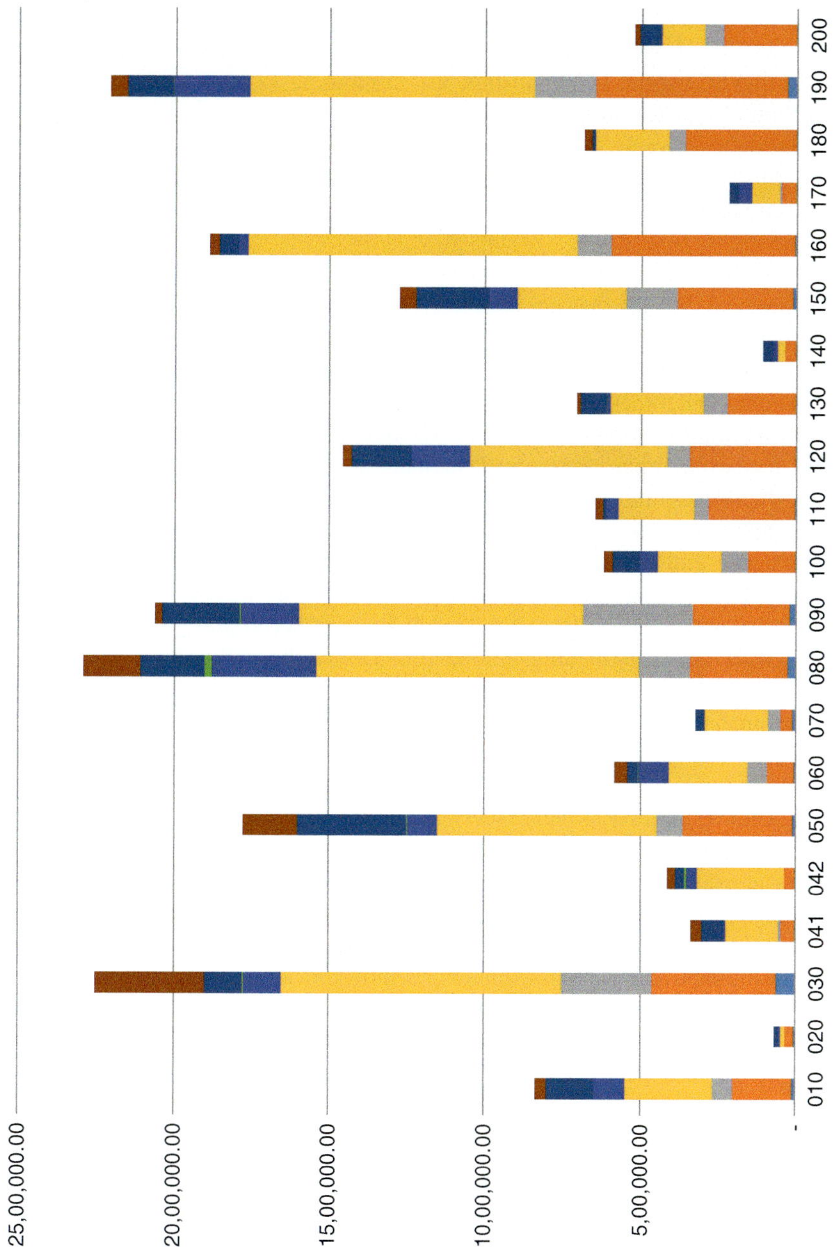

Fig. 9.9 Expenditure for surgical meshes in Italian public hospitals (source: Authors' calculations based on appendix of [10]) (see Table 9.6 for transcoding region ID)

In 2016, the expenditure for surgical meshes, including absorbable devices, by Italian public hospitals was equal to 21,281 million euro, with a 2.0% increase with respect to previous year (Fig. 9.8). On average, surgical meshes with more than one component represent 42% of the overall expenditure, followed by meshes in polypropylene (24%) and others (10%). The regions with the highest level of expenditure are Emilia Romagna (2.29 million €), Lombardia (2.25 million €), Sicilia (2.210 million €) and Toscana (2.06 million €) (Fig. 9.9).

9.8 Discussion

The constant maintenance and frequent updates of classification systems are key issues for medical devices that are characterised by a fast pace of innovation. The lack of updated codes translates into the impossibility to identify the use of new procedures and devices in administrative databases, thus making impossible to monitor patients' outcomes with real-world data [12].

The classification systems currently used in Italy are obsolete and present several challenges for hernia repair. Patients classification is based only on the location of hernia (inguinal/femoral/other), patient's age and presence/absence of complications, but it disregards clinical severity (e.g. hernia size), type of hernia (i.e. monolateral, bilateral and recurrent) and type of intervention (open surgery vs. laparoscopy). Consequently, very different patients are attributed to the same DRG: a single cluster may include procedures such as open hernioplasty with suture or prosthesis (without distinguishing among prosthesis types), posterior or anterior prosthetic open approach, laparoscopic or robotic technologies [13]. Patients heterogeneity translates into heterogeneous resource consumption in terms of personnel, medical devices, consumables related to the different techniques and ultimately into a total cost not recognised by the classification system. Moreover, when several surgical procedures on abdominal viscera are performed in combination, the same DRG includes all of them.

In addition, even though many types of meshes for hernia repair are available in the market, hospital discharge records do not allow to recognise the use of innovative devices and materials, given that ICD-9-CM codes are generic, no codes being available for meshes, and none of the Italian regions provide coding indications.

The consequences are particularly severe nowadays, when governments are starting to rethinking reimbursement systems, moving towards value-based reimbursement schemes, where providers are paid for achieved outcomes instead of delivered outputs. Since outcomes, measured in terms of recurrencies, neuralgies and delayed infections, largely differ among hospitals due to surgeon experience and quality of materials and devices, the adoption of reimbursement schemes that take patients outcomes into consideration would be highly desirable in hernia repair. Unfortunately, at present, due to the Italian coding system obsolescence previously described, the implementation of such a payment system is not feasible. Fortunately, a national working group led by Emilia Romagna is currently working at updating classification systems for abdominal wall surgery in Italy within the IT-DRG project. This makes us confident about the possibility of implementing value-based reimbursement for abdominal wall surgery.

Last, differences in regional tariffs determine different incentives for providers in treating hernia by using available meshes and techniques. A recent Italian study [14] conducted a complete cost analysis of incisional hernia repair with synthetic and biological mesh and compared it with financial reimbursement. Patients were grouped into three levels to determine the complexity of their care, and hence, the costs involved. Group 1 included patients without comorbidities, who underwent a standard incisional hernia repair, with synthetic mesh. Group 2 included patients with comorbidities, who underwent the same surgical procedure. Group 3 included all patients who underwent a complex incisional hernia repair with biological mesh. The direct costs of preoperative and operative phases for groups 1 and 2 were €5,544 and €5,020, respectively, and €16,397 in group 3. The national and regional tariffs related to hernia repair reported in Table 9.6 are insufficient to cover the incurred costs, thus resulting in economic losses for the treatment of complex patients. The economic loss is particularly evident referring to the use of the more costly biological meshes. Hospital costs of €3,822, €7,550 and €3,998 are reported for incisional hernia repair respectively with synthetic, biologic and biosynthetic meshes, in another Italian study [9]. These costs considered the personnel time for visits/exams and surgery, hospital drugs, consumables (mesh included) and the management of main complications in the follow-up (infected mesh removal, superficial infection, deep infection, organ space infection and seroma). The study showed that savings are possible when considering an increased utilisation rate of biosynthetic meshes in place of synthetic or biologic meshes for complex abdominal wall repairs.

9.9 Conclusion

Technological innovation is progressing at such fast pace that no governments can actually catch up. It therefore becomes important to develop and to implement reimbursement policies aimed at selecting and rewarding the most cost-effective technological innovations so to respond to patients' needs by controlling costs. To reach this objective, the use of technological innovation must be tracked, and coding systems need to be constantly updated so to allow a timely analysis of devices' performance and value in terms of health outcomes. Reimbursement schemes would need to encourage healthcare providers to deliver the most cost-effective procedures with the most appropriate devices for each specific subgroup of patients. The IT-DRG project undoubtedly represents an important occasion to do so which we hope the Italian Government wouldn't miss.

References

1. Busse R, Geissler A, Quentin W, Wiley M, editors. Diagnosis-related groups in Europe. New York: McGraw-Hill; 2011.
2. Scheller-Kreinsen D, et al. DRG-based hospital payment systems and technology innovation in 12 European Countries. Value Health. 2011;14:1166–72.
3. Fattore G, Torbica A. Inpatient reimbursement system in Italy: how do tariffs relate to costs? Health Care Manag Sci. 2006;9:251–8. https://doi.org/10.1007/s10729-006-9092-2.

4. Baylon K, et al. Past, present and future of surgical meshes: a review. Membranes. 2017;7:47. https://doi.org/10.3390/membranes7030047.
5. Li X, et al. Characterizing the ex vivo mechanical properties of synthetic polypropylene surgical mesh. J Mech Behav Biomed Mater. 2014;37:48–55.
6. Weber A, Garteiz D, Valencia S. Epidemiology of inguinal hernia: a useful aid for adequate surgical decisions. In: Bendavid R, Abrahamson J, Arregui ME, Flament JB, Phillips EH, editors. Abdominal wall hernias. New York: Springer; 2001.
7. Köckerling F, Alam NN, Antoniou SA, et al. What is the evidence for the use of biologic or biosynthetic meshes in abdominal wall reconstruction? Hernia. 2018;22(2):249–69.
8. Ayson M. Evidence Based Report. Biological mesh for abdominal wall hernia repair. Wellington: Accident Compensation Corporation; 2013.
9. Rognoni C, Bassi UA, Cataldo M, et al. Budget impact analysis of a biosynthetic mesh for incisional hernia repair. Clin Ther. 2018;40(11):1830–44.
10. Italian Ministry of Health. Rapporto sull'attività di ricovero ospedaliero SDO. 2016. Available from http://www.salute.gov.it/portale/temi/p2_6.jsp?id=1237&area=ricoveriOspedalieri&menu=vuoto. Accessed 28 Jun 2018.
11. Italian Ministry of Health. Rapporti sulla spesa per l'acquisto di dispositivi medici nel SSN. 2015/2016. Available from http://www.salute.gov.it/portale/temi/p2_6.jsp?lingua=italiano&id=4652&area=dispositivi-medici&menu=spesa. Accessed 28 Jun 2018.
12. Callea G, Cavallo MC, Tarricone R. Assessment of new medical devices with administrative databases: the need for traceability. Value Health. 2017;20(5):A251. https://doi.org/10.1016/j.jval.2017.05.005.
13. Greco DP, Amatucci F, Padula GA. Treatment cost reimbursement from the healthcare systems. In: Inguinal hernia surgery. Italia S.r.l: Springer; 2017.
14. Rampado S, et al. Cost analysis of incisional hernia repair with synthetic mesh and biological mesh: an Italian study. Updat Surg. 2017;69(3):375–81.

Presurgical Hidden Costs: Imaging, Assessment Clinic

10

Cristiano Sgrazzutti, Ilaria Vicentin, Alessandra Coppola, and Angelo Vanzulli

10.1 Introduction: Role of Imaging

Diagnosis of abdominal hernias is usually made at physical examination.

Sometimes however, the specialist surgeon isn't able to achieve a diagnosis by the only clinical examination.

Usually, radiological support is required for obese patients, in case of abdominal or groin pain without a palpable mass or in case of a mass that expands under impulse, in suspected recurrent groin pain, in patients with mass of uncertain etiology, and in those with suspected bowel obstruction, true in particular for incisional hernias [1].

Imaging provides multiple useful diagnostic tools: primarily, the detection of the presence of hernia, the visualization of its location (i.e., the type of hernia), its content, the size of the hernia neck and of the hernia sack, and the identification of any complications.

Furthermore, imaging permits to distinguish other lesions mimicking hernias, like desmoid tumors in the abdominal wall or hydrocele of the spermatic cord in the groin region.

It is important also after surgery to detect any complication, such as seromas, abscesses, and hematomas, and to follow their evolution [2].

Imaging is also performed for evaluation of multiple concurrent fascial defects, for determination of the correct positioning or dislocation of prior mesh or associated fluid collections, or specification of hernia contents and the degree and type of adhesions (i.e., omentum vs bowel) [1].

C. Sgrazzutti (✉) · A. Vanzulli
Radiology, Niguarda Hospital, Milan, Italy

I. Vicentin · A. Coppola
Radiology, Università degli Studi di Milano, Scuola di Specializzazione in Radiodiagnostica, Milan, Italy
e-mail: ilaria.vicentin@unimi.it; alessandra.coppola@unimi.it

D. P. Greco, E. Borgonovi (eds.), *Abdominal Wall Surgery*,
https://doi.org/10.1007/978-3-030-02426-0_10

Moreover, nowadays the availability of multiple surgical techniques raises the necessity of an accurate diagnosis and characterization of abdominal wall hernias in order to plan the most appropriate procedure for patients to hopefully improve the outcomes.

In this context, the radiologist should assist the surgeon in determining the quality and quantity of the abdominal wall musculature and the integrity of the muscle and fascia. The relative volume of the hernia compared with the intra-abdominal compartment should be estimated, if possible [1].

These information can influence the choice among several operative techniques by the surgeon.

10.2 Imaging Modalities

Different imaging modalities can be used in the assessment of abdominal wall hernias: conventional radiographs, ultrasonography (US), computed tomography (CT), and magnetic resonance (MRI), each with specific areas of utility in the evaluation of abdominal hernia.

10.2.1 Conventional Radiological Techniques

Nowadays, the role of radiography is essentially limited to acute hernia presentation.

In some cases of complicated abdominal wall hernia, indeed (i.e., bowel incarceration or strangulation), conventional radiographs allow detection of signs of mechanical ileus with bowel loops enlargement, thickening of intestinal folds, and air–fluid levels or intra-abdominal free air [3, 4] (Fig. 10.1).

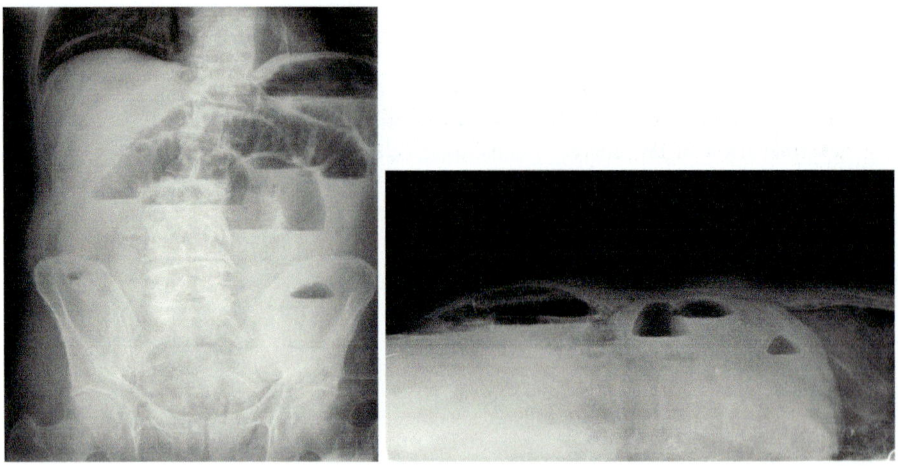

Fig. 10.1 Conventional abdominal radiographs showing air–fluid levels and intra-abdominal free air in erect projection (left) and tangential projection (right)

10.2.2 US Imaging

US is an accurate, non-invasive, and readily available technique [5].

It's the first-line imaging investigation for hernia detection in children [6, 7] and for non-acute adult groin hernia detection, particularly in patients with a palpable swelling or cough impulse or in case of abdominal palpable swelling in the midline [8].

Small hernias could be assessed by a high-frequency linear transducer (10–15 MHz), while larger size hernias with large-sized defect should be assessed by a curvilinear transducer (3.5–7 MHz), given that the diagnostic yield of the ultrasound decreases with large-sized hernias.

Care must be taken not to press too much with the transducer, because this may reduce small hernias [2].

US can help detecting the presence of the hernia, its location, and content and can quantify the size of the hernia neck and of the hernia sack [9] (Fig. 10.2).

According to this, the advantage of ultrasound over other imaging modalities lies mainly in the ability to perform a dynamic scan. In fact, if the sac isn't clear from the beginning of the scan, provocative tests are recommended: the simple use of Valsalva maneuver or examining the patient after a simple standing for 30 s can unmask any occult hernia [2].

Moreover, US can help distinguish hernia from other abdominal wall masses such as cysts, hematomas, neoplasms, or varicoceles.

In case of complications, US may provide information on the herniated organs and repercussions in the peritoneal cavity.

In conclusion, US provides dynamic real-time evaluation in an inexpensive fashion, with no ionizing radiation, being therefore particularly useful to study the pediatric population [1].

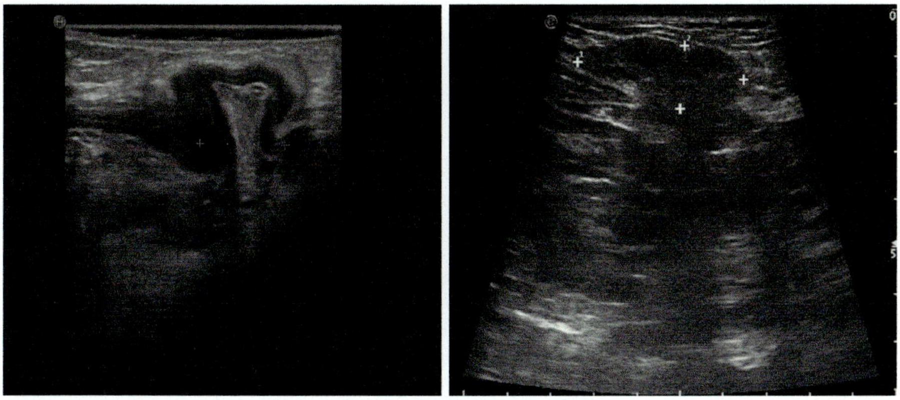

Fig. 10.2 US images showing abdominal wall defects containing small bowel loops (left) and omental fat (right)

Operator dependency, patient physical conformation, and presence of intestinal gas, often prominent in acute patients, are well-known limiting factors.

In some specialized clinics, US is just the first-line exam next to the clinical examination in the clinics specialized in abdominal wall surgery, as already happens for gynecology and urology.

10.2.3 CT Imaging

Allowing an accurate and panoramic view of the abdomen, CT represents the primary modality for the assessment of an adult abdominal hernia in both elective and acute circumstances.

By permitting rapid acquisition of 3D image data sets and exquisite multiplanar reformations, CT precisely delineates hernia type, location, size, and shape [10] (Fig. 10.3).

It's necessary to remind that CT is a technique which employs ionizing radiation: in particular, a complete scan of the abdomen and pelvis brings to an effective radiation dose of 10 mSv that corresponds to 100 chest radiographs, value that rises to 20 mSV in a contrast enhanced CT.

By virtue of its panoramic view, CT can detect any other wall defects, being therefore useful to further advance the preoperative assessment of abdominal hernias (Fig. 10.4).

Furthermore, because of its superior anatomic detail, multi-detector row CT may help detect subtle signs of complication within the hernia sac, including bowel obstruction, incarceration, strangulation, and traumatic wall hernia [10].

CT is also precious in evaluating postsurgical patients after abdominal wall reconstruction during the follow-up.

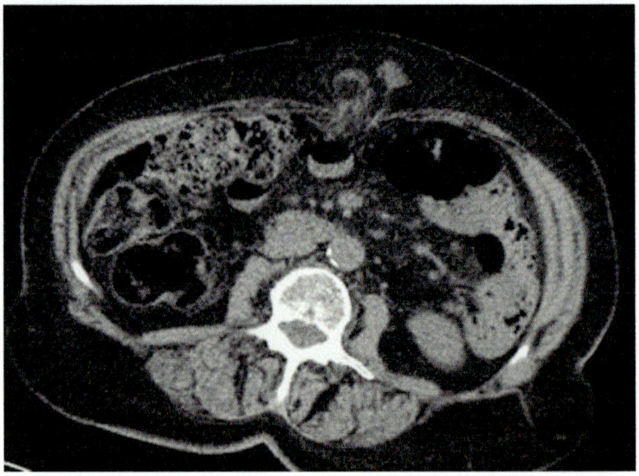

Fig. 10.3 Axial unenhanced CT image showing an epigastric hernia containing small bowel loops and omental fat

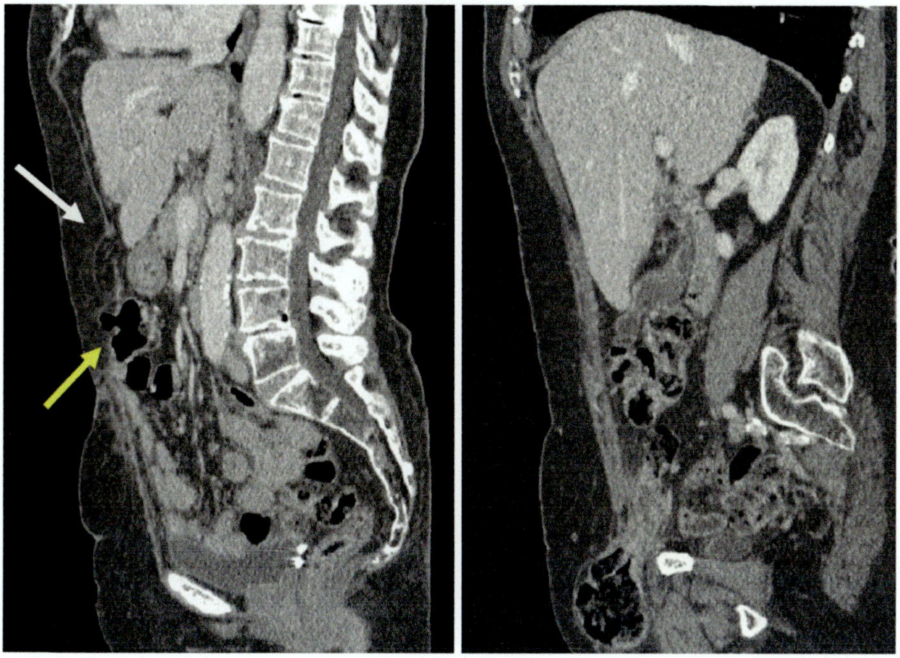

Fig. 10.4 Sagittal view of an enhanced CT of the same patient showing two epigastric hernias (left) containing omental fat (white arrow) and a colic loop (yellow arrow) and one groin hernia (right) containing colic loops

As regards to the technique, a fast helical sequence from the diaphragm to the pubic symphysis is taken in full inspiration, during a single breath-hold, with the patient supine.

Intravenous contrast material is not routinely given but may be administered if other unsuspected abnormalities are detected [11], while it is necessary for characterization of the vascular supply [10].

Dynamic scans may also be performed: postural maneuvers (i.e., prone or lateral decubitus positioning) and maneuvers to increase intra-abdominal pressure (i.e., straining or Valsalva maneuver) can help depict subtle anterior hernias [11] but unlike US, this would increase the patient radiation dose.

Multiplanar reformatted (MPR) images provide important information in addition to that provided by axial images in that they may better delineate the size and shape of the hernia sac and associated complications (Fig. 10.5).

Moreover, displaying the anatomy in a manner more familiar to clinicians may enhance the communication of imaging findings useful to the surgical planning [10].

10.2.4 Magnetic Resonance Imaging

MRI rarely represents the choice exam for the diagnosis of abdominal wall hernias.

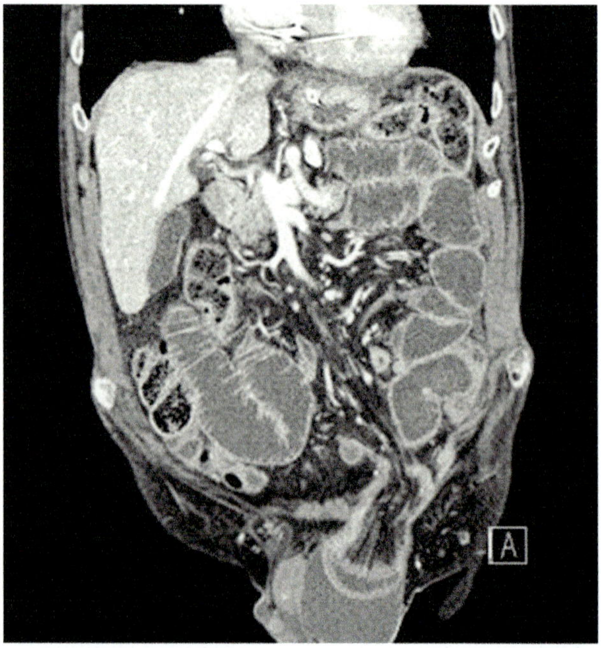

Fig. 10.5 A coronal view of an enhanced CT showing a closed loop obstruction of small bowel and free fluid in a patient with left groin hernia

The main disadvantages are the costs (higher than the other methods), its non-applicability in emergency cases, and the examination time. However, in young patients it may be preferable to other methods.

The advantages of MR are the lack of ionizing radiation, superior soft-tissue contrast resolution (important features for the evaluation of groin hernias), functional evaluation, and particular sensitivity to blood products, helping differentiate hematomas from other causes of abdominal swelling [12].

Possible applications are: operated patients with suspected recurrence or postsurgical complication, discordance objective examination/symptomatology, and atypical hernias (e.g., internal hernias).

Preoperative MRI is very effective in showing the abdominal wall defects, not only in the axial position but also in the sagittal view, allowing an appropriate evaluation of the hernia sac content, especially when the small bowel or colon were included.

The evaluation of the presence and the extent of abdominal adhesions are very useful in surgery planning.

The sagittal view is very useful for the surgeon, not only for the preoperative knowledge of the hernia anatomy but also for the diagnosis of complications and the final result of the procedure [12] (Fig. 10.6).

In the past, the most used sequences in the preoperative and postoperative study of the abdominal wall hernia were T1 sequences, still useful today for anatomical and pathological information of the hernial sac (i.e., possible presence of blood, protein

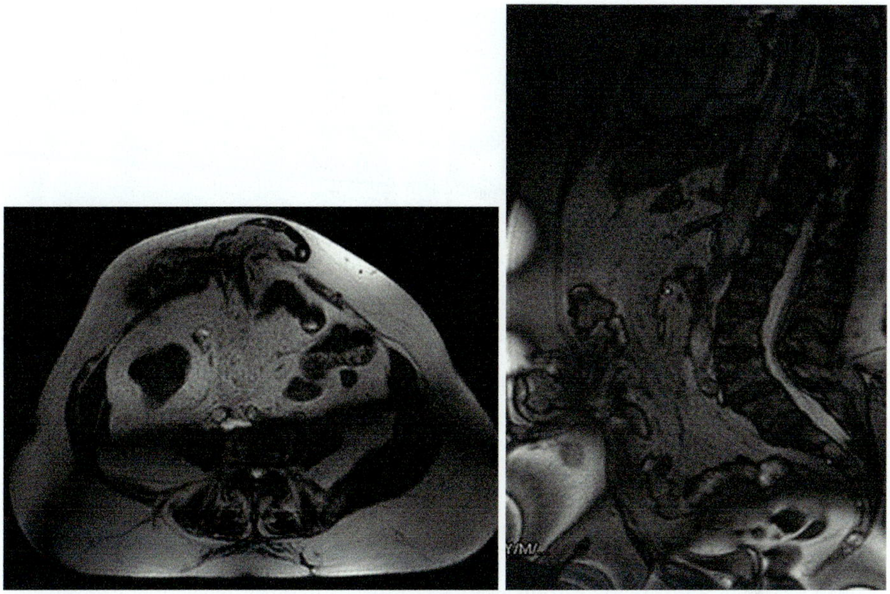

Fig. 10.6 Axial (right) and sagittal (left) balanced fast field echo sequences showing umbilical hernia containing bowel loops and omental fat

Fig. 10.7 Coronal fat saturated T2 image showing a right hydrocele of the canal of Nuck in a female adult

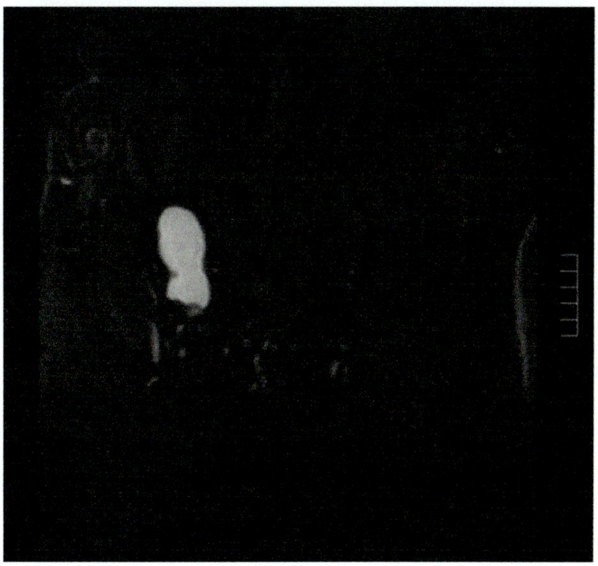

component, or fat component—thanks to the out-of-phase sequences). Nowadays, as a result of their reduced acquisition time, the most used sequences are T2 [13].

T2 sequences can be acquired with *fast spin eco single shot* technique: this allows the acquisition during one apnea. Furthermore, in addition to a low incidence of artifacts, T2 sequences are also acquired with fat suppression: this improves the contrast resolution (Fig. 10.7).

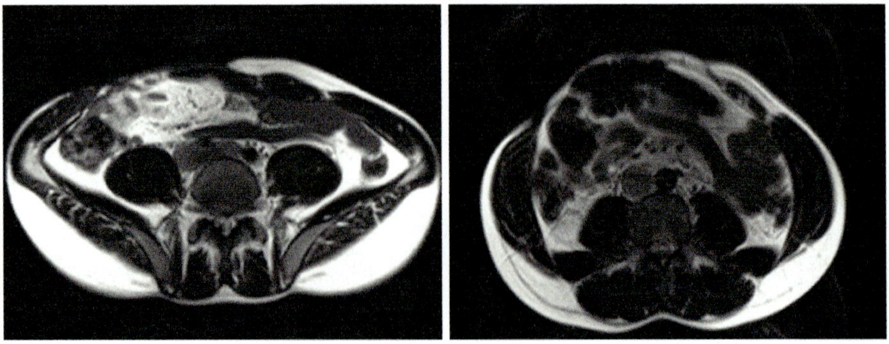

Fig. 10.8 Axial T1 sequence image showing abdominal incisional hernia before (right) and after Valsalva maneuver (left)

The good quality of the images, the space resolution, and the multi-view capacity are features giving important information for the surgeon.

MRI occasionally is used with dynamic cine sequences to evaluate herniation with increased intra-abdominal pressure (i.e., the Valsalva maneuver) [14] (Fig. 10.8).

However, literature data on the use of MRI for hernia care are limited so it cannot be used routinely in all patients because of the costs.

Nowadays, this diagnostic tool should be reserved for complex cases or in young patients.

10.3 Postsurgical Complications

After surgery, the most useful imaging modalities are US and CT.

In the immediate postoperative period after hernia repair, frequent findings are fluid collections, which usually contain serous fluid (seromas) or blood products (hematomas) (Fig. 10.9).

CT helps identify fluid collections, differentiate them from hernia recurrence (which may be difficult at physical examination, especially in obese patients), and confirm their resolution [10].

Also, an ultrasound examination can highlight the depth, volume, and extension of the fluid, and can guide the needle aspiration procedure.

Fluid collections may undergo superinfection [15]: the development of gas or thick septa in a previously "simple" collection, an enhancing rim, or fat stranding in surrounding tissues are suspicious findings for infected fluid collections [10].

Imaging permits to distinguish between superficial and deep fluid collections, allowing the surgeon to choose the correct treatment: superficial collections in fact are managed conservatively, whereas deep infections require interventions such as percutaneous drainage or prosthesis removal.

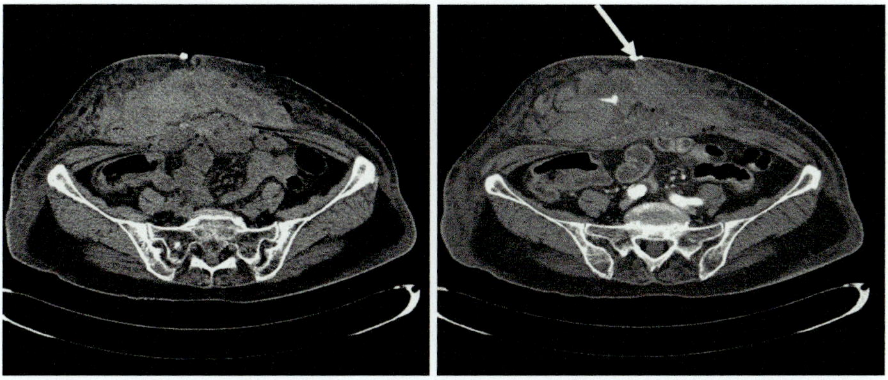

Fig. 10.9 Axial unenhanced CT image showing a large abdominal wall hematoma (right), with evidence of active bleeding after intravenous administration of contrast agent (left)

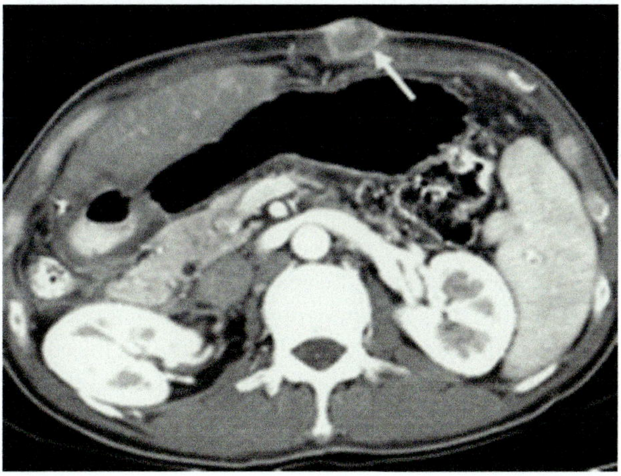

Fig. 10.10 Axial enhanced CT image showing a localization of malignant tumor on abdominal wall

10.4 Differential Diagnosis

Based on physical examination, several abdominal wall disease may be misdiagnosed as hernias; fortunately, differentiation between these diseases and hernias is usually straightforward at multi-detector row CT because hernias are associated with abdominal wall defects, have necks, contain herniated intra-abdominal contents, and may respond to provocative maneuvers [5].

Differential diagnosis includes:

– Benign tumors (e.g., lipomas, hemangiomas, and fibromas), quite common;
– Malignant tumors (metastasis, and primary sarcomas), less common (Fig. 10.10);

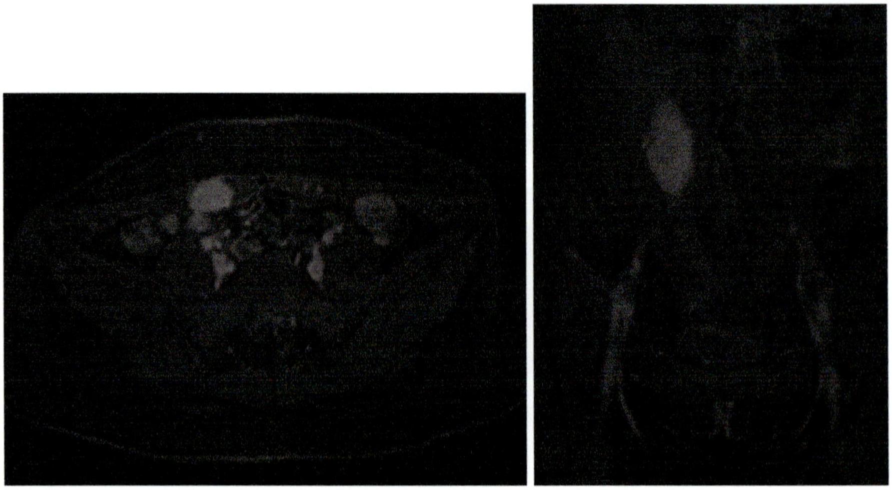

Fig. 10.11 Axial (left) and coronal (right) images of fast GRE T1 weighted sequences showing a desmoid tumor localized in the right abdominal rectus muscle mimicking an internal wall hernia

- Lesions presenting local malignancy as desmoid tumor (Fig. 10.11) or endometriosis (in the suspicion of localization in abdominal wall in young women, also only T1 and T2 weighted sequences of MRI can be resolutive);
- Rectus sheath hematomas that may occur as a result of trauma to the abdominal wall or secondary to disorders of coagulation, blood dyscrasia, or degenerative vascular diseases, in this case, MRI can be resolutive [13];
- Other diseases that may mimic abdominal wall hernias at physical examination include eventration; gas collections within the abdominal wall, which may mimic bowel loops at palpation; enlarged inguinal lymph nodes; an undescended testis; and enlarged vessels in the abdominal wall.

10.5 Costs Analysis

If we consider the Italian National Health System, the rates relating to outpatient specialist assistance services, regarding specifically the imaging modalities previously discussed, are summarized as follows:

– Ultrasound	28,41 €
– CT	
Abdomen and pelvis without contrast	103,68 €
Abdomen and pelvis with and without contrast	158,04 €
– MRI	
Abdomen without contrast	120,08 €
Abdomen with and without contrast	187,13 €
Pelvis without contrast	120,08 €
Pelvis with and without contrast	187,13 € [16]

To discuss the global costs of hernia management, a first difference should be done between costs and reimbursements. The reimbursements exclusively represent the economic contribution of the National Health System to the hospital structure. Regarding costs, it is appropriate to consider the "radiologist time," the presence of the technician and the use of equipment (which includes costs related to the time of the use of scanners, which depends also from amortization costs).

At a first, superficial analysis, it might seem that ultrasound is the "cheapest" diagnostic modality among those described in terms of radiologist time (single operator) and the possibility of performing a dynamic evaluation (Valsalva or standing) without X-rays exposure.

However, in a more general view, the operator dependency makes this imaging modality non-standardizable, leading often to further diagnostic tests, increasing the expense rate.

Moreover, it's not uncommon that, after a first ultrasound exam, a further diagnostic investigation with another imaging modality is required, often CT, since the diagnosis is not certain.

Finally, as previously mentioned, US is not a panoramic technique as it is CT, and therefore often doesn't identify any multiple abdominal wall defects, leading to multiple surgeries, whereas the immediate identification of all the wall defects would allow a single time surgery.

A separate issue has to be reserved to MRI, since the costs of execution, significantly higher than the CT scan, and the availability, less than the CT scan, limit the routine use in the diagnosis of abdominal hernias.

The table below (Table 10.1) shows the strengths and the weaknesses related to the costs of the diagnostic modality used in the hernia management, considering both economic and general features.

In conclusion, the cost analysis in medicine can't be limited to an isolated diagnostic moment, but it should consider an integrated diagnostic–therapeutic pathway, in order to make the most accurate diagnosis and the best treatment.

Table 10.1 Imaging characteristics

Diagnostic modality	Reimbursement	Cost	X-ray exposure	Dynamic evaluation	Use
Sonography	32.70 €	Medium cost (radiologist time)	No	Valsalva or standing	Good for first-line approach (surgeon office)
Computed tomography	105.56 € (unenhanced CT)	Medium cost (radiologist, technician, scanner)	Yes	Not recommended	Use often for postsurgery failure (very good detection of protesis material)
Magnetic resonance	161.55 € (unenhanced MR)	Medium/high cost (radiologist, technician, scanner)	No	Valsalva	Doubtful cases and uncommon locations

References

1. Parikh KR, Al-Hawary M, Millet JD, Burney R, Finks J, Maturen K. Incisional hernia repair: what the radiologist needs to know. AJR Am J Roentgenol. 2017;209(6):1239–46.
2. Bedewi MA, El-sharkawy M. Imaging of hernias, hernia fethi derbel. London: IntechOpen; 2017.
3. Rettenbacher T, Hollerweger A, Macheiner P, et al. Abdominal wall hernias: cross-sectional imaging signs of incarceration determined with sonography. AJR Am J Roentgenol. 2001;177:1061–6.
4. Lassandro F, Iasiello F, Luisa Pizza N, Valente T, Stefano M, Luisa Mangoni di Santo Grassi R, et al. Abdominal hernias: radiological features. World J Gastrointest Endosc. 2011;3(6):110–7.
5. Young J, Gilbert AI, Graham MF. The use of ultrasound in the diagnosis of abdominal wall hernias. Hernia. 2007;11(4):347–51.
6. Munden MM, Trautwein LM. Scrotal pathology in pediatrics with sonographic imaging. Curr Probl Diagn Radiol. 2000;29:185–205.
7. Shadbolt CL, Heinze SB, Dietrich RB. Imaging of groin masses: inguinal anatomy and pathologic conditions revisited. Radiographics. 2001;21:S261–71.
8. Bradley M, Morgan J, Pentlow B, Roe A. The positive predictive value of diagnostic ultrasound for occult herniae. Ann R Coll Surg Engl. 2006;88(2):165–7.
9. Jamadar DA, Jacobson JA, Girish G, Balin J, Brandon CJ, Caoili EM, et al. Abdominal wall hernia mesh repair: sonography of mesh and common complications. J Ultrasound Med. 2008;27:907–17.
10. Aguirre DA, Santosa AC, Casola G, Sirlin CB. Abdominal wall hernias: imaging features, complications, and diagnostic pitfalls at multi–detector row CT. Radiographics. 2005;25:1501–20.
11. Emby DJ, Aoun G. CT technique for suspected anterior abdominal wall hernia. Am J Roentgenol. 2003;181(2):431–3.
12. Olmo JCM, García-vallejo L, Gestal JN, Coello PC, Antona FB, Trincado MT, et al. The usefulness of magnetic resonance imaging in the preoperative study and postoperative control in the laparoscopic treatment of the incisional hernia. Surg Sci. 2015;6:376–82.
13. Salati U, Mansour E, Torreggiani W. True-FISP MRI in diagnosis of postoperative hernia recurrence: a brief report. Hernia. 2014;18(4):597–600.
14. Langbach O, Holmedal SH, Grandal OJ, Røkke O. Adhesions to mesh after ventral hernia mesh repair are detected by MRI but are not a cause of long term chronic abdominal pain. Gastroenterol Res Pract. 2016;2016:2631598.
15. Bendavid R. Complications of groin hernia surgery. Surg Clin North Am. 1998;78(6):1089–103.
16. Nomenclatore dell'assistenza specialistica ambulatoriale [Internet]. Available from: http://www.salute.gov.it/portale/temi/p2_6.jsp?lingua=italiano&id=1767&area=programmazioneSanitariaLea&menu=lea

Post-Surgical Hidden Cost: Neuralgia

11

Paolo Notaro, Paolo Bocchi, Nicola Ladiana, and Claudia Abbati

11.1 Epidemiology

Is Neuralgia a frequent problem? How much does this complication affect the current surgical practice and how much does it cost?

Pain is an unpleasant sensory and emotional experience associated with actual or potential tissue damage or described in terms of such damage [1]. Often, pain acts as a warning symptom of a medical condition or injury. In these cases, treatment of the underlying medical condition is crucial and can resolve the pain. However, pain may persist despite the successful treatment of the condition that initially caused it, becoming itself a disease, also refractory to pharmacological treatments for the phenomena of amplification and modification of conduction and perception of the painful stimulus by the patient.

Chronic pain is the pain that persists or reoccurs for more than 3 months. Such pain often becomes the only or predominant clinical problem in some patients [2]. As such, it can justify a specific diagnostic evaluation, therapy and rehabilitation. Chronic pain is a common condition, affecting about 20% of people worldwide [3, 4].

The same surgery can be the cause of chronic pain called chronic post-surgical pain (CPSP). CPSP is defined as a pain that persists for more than 3 months after surgery and is an important clinical problem [5]. Several risk factors have been identified, including the younger age, the female gender, psychological and genetic

P. Notaro (✉) · N. Ladiana
Pain Management Unit, Niguarda Hospital, Milan, Italy
e-mail: paolo.notaro@ospedaleniguarda.it; nicola.ladiana@ospedaleniguarda.it

P. Bocchi
Valparma hospital, Langhirano, Parma, Italy

C. Abbati
Department of Surgery, Niguarda Hospital, Milan, Italy

University of Milan, Milan, Italy

D. P. Greco, E. Borgonovi (eds.), *Abdominal Wall Surgery*,
https://doi.org/10.1007/978-3-030-02426-0_11

Table 11.1 Incidence of CPSP in some common interventions

Amputations	30–50%
Mastectomy	20–30%
Thoracotomy	30–40%
Inguinal hernia repair	10–30%
Coronary bypass	30–50%
Caesarean section	10%

Table 11.2 Incidence of severe and disabling pain for the same interventions

Amputations	5–10%
Mastectomy	5–10%
Thoracotomy	10%
Inguinal hernia repair	2–4%
Coronary bypass	5–10%
Caesarean section	4%

factors, already occurrence of chronic pain and use of opioids [4, 6, 7]. CPSP is an important problem also in children, even if it is less frequently reported than in adults [8].

Surgery itself is the most important risk factor. Preoperative pain and severe post-operative severe pain are also very consistent risk factors for the development of chronic post-operative pain. An accurate assessment of the patient before the intervention is useful to intercept the potential risk factors to develop CPSP. The aetiopathogenetic mechanisms and the characteristic features of pain, which persist for more than 3 months after surgery, have characteristics very similar to those of a neuropathic pain.

The extent of the problem is summarised by the incidence of chronic post-operative pain in some specific surgical interventions.

In 2006, Lancet published data on the incidence of CPSP in different surgical interventions [9], as shown in Table 11.1.

Table 11.2 shows the incidence of severe and disabling pain for the same interventions.

The European Hernia Society (EHS) Italian Chapter carried on a survey involving 18 Italian centres particularly specialised on abdominal wall surgery. The chapter found, in a sample of 615 operated patients of an average 65 years old, an incidence of "discomfort" in 31%, "pain always present" in 5% and "some sort of physical limitation" in 9.5%.

Schumpelick [10] proposed to abandon prosthetic techniques in routine inguinal hernia repair due to the excessive frequency of chronic post-operative pain, a complication considered intolerable.

11.2 Anatomy

Since chronic pain after incisional hernia repair has the same incidence than chronic pain after general or specialised surgery laparotomy, we will analyse only some anatomical aspects of inguinal canal useful to understand aetiopathogenesis of chronic pain after open or laparoscopic inguinal hernia repair.

It is now well known that the nerves involved in pain after anterior hernioplasty are: the genital branch of the genitofemoral nerve, the iliohypogastric nerve and the ilioinguinal nerve. The lateral femoral cutaneous nerve should also be added in the list.

These sensory nerves present a very important anatomic variability both in terms of positioning and distribution. It is important to remind at least what the most common scenario is:

1. The ilioinguinal nerve runs along the lateral aspect of the cremaster muscle. It is commonly the first to appear at the opening of the aponeurosis of the external oblique muscle.
2. The iliohypogastric nerve runs resting on the internal oblique muscle in a proximal position with respect to the internal inguinal ring.
3. The genital branch of the genitofemoral nerve runs in conjunction with the external sperm vessels, and it exits from the internal inguinal ring and lies on the posterior wall of the inguinal canal of the spermatic cord which is basically covered.

11.3 Pathophysiology

The International Association for the Study of Pain (IASP) defines pain as "an unpleasant sensory and emotional experience associated with actual or potential tissue damage, or described in terms of such damage" [1].

It is an individual and subjective experience, to which purely sensory components converge (nociceptive) related to the transfer of the painful stimulus from the periphery to the central structures, and experiential and affective components, which modulate in an important way what is perceived.

It is important to distinguish pain in broad categories [11, 12]:

1. Inflammatory/Nociceptive pain: Chemical mediators released during an inflammatory response, if not addressed in an adequate and timely manner, have the undesired effect of sensitising and stimulating nociceptors. This may play an important role in the induction and maintenance of chronic pain, modifying conduction plasticity.
2. Neuropathic pain: it occurs in the presence of nerve damage and it derives from the ectopic activation of the neuron in a normally non-receptor portion of it [13]. It can be peripheral or central [14, 15].

The peripheral neuropathic pain is the type of pain arising as a complication of surgery.

Table 11.3 can help to diagnose if the pain is still nociceptive or is shifted to neuropathic.

Table 11.3 Differential diagnosis between nociceptive and neuropathic pain

	Inflammatory (nociceptive)	Neuropathic
Spontaneous pain	Yes	Yes
Hypersensitivity to heat	Yes	No
Hypersensitivity to cold	No	Yes
Hyperpathia	No	Yes
Burning pain	No	Yes
Paroxysms	No	Yes
Loss of sensitivity	No	Yes

11.4 Causes

Although nerve damage appears to be necessary for clinically significant neuropathic pain, in most of the cases of persistent post-operative pain this condition may be not sufficient.

It can certainly be hypothesised that response to pain depends on a combination of genetic, physical and psychological factors [16]. Surely, the surgeon who is repairing an inguinal hernia can impact only on the physical and anatomical factors.

The nerve alteration that produces neuropathic pain can be caused by entrapment (suture point), perineural fibrosis, from a terminal neuroma and a neuroma in the presence of an unamputated (tangential trauma) nerve.

There is no evidence that CPSP incidence depends on the kind of implanted mesh, but there are evidences that the kind of mesh and the mesh fixation technique (glues, sutures, tacks and staples) both affect the intensity and the incidence of post-operative acute pain.

11.5 Prevention

CPSP can be expressed as a combination of different clinical types of pain, such as neuropathic, nociceptive, reported or visceral.

Neuropathic pain is the most common type of CPSP. The use of screening tools (e.g. QLT DN4, painDETECT, NPQ and LANSS), based on verbal pain descriptor alone or combined with a targeted clinical examination, may be useful to identify neuropathic pain as a major or secondary component of CPSP [17].

As with other chronic pain syndromes, CPSP, once entrenched, can be multiform and difficult to reverse. Furthermore, the typical co-morbidities of chronic pain often develop, such as sleep and mood disorders [2].

Prevention remains the key to reducing the health burden of CPSP [9].

We have instruments for preoperatory, intra-operatory and post-operatory prevention.

Preoperatory Phase

Pain assessment in patients with chronic pain (as prostatitis) or inguinodynia not depending only from the presence of inguinal hernia is a good instrument to prevent in the preoperatory phase the onset of CPSP.

Various authors have highlighted several circumstances that can be summarised as follows [18]:

- Operations for recurrences
- High level of preoperative pain
- Preoperative pain originating from other conditions
- Age < 40
- Female gender
- Type of employment

Certainly, in the case of a young person with an almost asymptomatic small hernia, a greater risk of post-operative pain can reasonably be expected. In fact, the EHS's recommendation for the treatment of inguinal hernia reads: "Grade A. In minimally symptomatic or asymptomatic inguinal hernia in men, consider a watchful waiting strategy." [19, 20]

Intra-Operatory Instruments

- Three nerves identification (Campanelli) [21]
- Nerve section, also if in the literature this question is high debated

Many authors have hypothesised some interference between the dissected nerve and the prosthesis [22].

Also, the material used can influence the frequency of onset of chronic post-operative pain. Furthermore, the EHS in its recommendations expresses itself on the type of prosthesis to be used: "Grade A. The use of lightweight/material-reduced/large-pore meshes in open inguinal hernia repair can be considered long-term discomfort, but possibly at the cost of increased recurrence rate." [20] Many studies have shown that the use of fibrin glue to replace the sutures in fixing the prostheses leads to a reduction in post-operative chronic pain even in cases of laparoscopic surgery [23–27].

According to Amid [19, 28], it is recommended to avoid any nerve trauma and in case of sectioning it, the direct contact with the prosthetic material of the nerve abutment should be avoided. However, it appears that the simple identification of the nerve branches during the surgical procedure reduces the occurrence of chronic post-operative pain (Consensus Conference Rome 2008) [19].

All we have explained shows that hernia surgery is a complex surgery, which presupposed dedicated centres of different levels; for inguinal hernia to prevent pain we can think at specialised level 1 centres.

Post-operative Instruments

- Intensive follow-up
- Post-op follow up

In CPSP rise, a multidisciplinary assessment from surgeons and pain specialist is recommended to prevent neuralgia.

11.6 Treatment

11.6.1 Pain Centres

The reference to a multidisciplinary approach program should be considered in selected patients [29]. The multimodal approach to pain management of CPSP is driven rather by the prevailing mechanisms and comorbidities of the person with pain.

The approaches can include the following:

- Patient education and self-management supported
- Pharmacological management [30–33]

Careful periodic evaluation of pain relief and side effects necessary to drive pharmacotherapy.

First-line anti-neuropathic drugs:

- Tricyclic antidepressants
- Inhibitors of serotonin-noradrenaline and gabapentinoid reuptake
- Topical flours with lidocaine and capsaicin

Strong opioids should only be prescribed with great caution after assessing the risk–benefit ratio and monitoring over time.

Pharmacological therapy alone is not always conclusive for refractoriness and it is necessary to intervene with invasive pain techniques.

Among the invasive approaches indicated are targeted injections, radiofrequency, tens, cryoneuromodulation, peridural neurostimulation techniques and ganglion modulation [34].

It is also important to provide rehabilitation programs with physical therapies and any psychologically targeted interventions, such as cognitive behavioural therapy.

Patients with CPSP should be informed that they are at risk for developing new chronic pains after future surgery or trauma. Furthermore, preoperative identification of potential predictors of psycho-social amplification becomes the subject of evaluation and preoperative information.

Specific pain therapy networks have been created in several European countries to control in an appropriate way acute and chronic pain; particularly in Italy, the measurement of acute pain control and the Pain Therapy Network is a statutory obligation [35–38].

11.6.2 Surgical Treatment

It is necessary to proceed with the early re-exploration of the inguinal region only in the case the intensity and permanence of the acute post-operative pain are refractory to common post-operative analgesic therapies. In this case, a nerve could have been involuntarily tied in a suture point (entrapment). Are needed some investigations as an ultrasound that allows the exclusion of non-clinically evident hematomas, the early re-exploration allows to remove the cause of the pain which is usually a suture point.

The necessity of a surgical re-examination has been established in few cases of chronic neuralgia post-ernioplastic because of the refractoriness to other non-invasive therapies. In these cases, the recommendation is the triple neurectomy (ilioinguinal nerve, iliohypogastric nerve and genital branch of the genitofemoral nerve), that is the only intervention that can lead to a satisfactory result in 80% of cases [21].

Recently, it has been found that, after a triple neurectomy, pain could remain in the homolateral testicular [22].

Sometimes, a recurrence that passed undiagnosed it is found in the intervention: in this case, the repair itself may be the cause of the post-operative pain. To prevent this circumstance, it is always important to make accurate diagnostic imaging before surgery (see Chap. 10).

11.7 Costs

It is necessary the compliance to the all pre- and post-operative indications to reduce incidence of CPSP not only for the quality of life but also to reduce costs for the whole sanitary system.

Chronic pain has a negative impact on the daily lives of sick people and on their work abilities, and it is heavy financial burden for all health systems [39–41]. The estimate of the average annual cost per patient amounts to € 4556, 31% of which (€ 1400) is charged to the National Health Service. Of this share, 51% is due to hospitalisation and 6% to the costs of analgesic drugs (mostly NSAID). Indirect costs (€ 3157) are caused by sick leave (31%) and retirement. Based on an estimated prevalence of eight million people with pain in Italy, the impact of direct costs of all forms of chronic pain on public health expenditure is 9.6%, while the incidence of total costs on the product gross domestic product (GDP) is 2.3%, projected on epidemiological evidence with studies from other European countries.

11.8 Conclusions

This summary on post-operative chronic pain in anterior inguinal hernia repair aims to suggest to the surgeons and all the stakeholders that this pathology can give rise to chronic pain.

The only way to minimise this occurrence is to have a correct indication for surgery, to select patients for a preoperative pain assessment, to scrupulously respect the hernia anatomy during surgery, to identify nerves and to use the correct mesh according to guidelines.

References

1. IASP Task Force on Taxonomy. Part III: pain terms, a current list with definitions and notes on usage. 2nd ed. Washington, DC: IASP Press; 1994. p. 209–14. (Classification of Chronic Pain).
2. Macrae WA. Chronic post-surgical pain: 10 years on. Br J Anaesth. 2008;101(1):77–86.
3. Fletcher D, Stamer UM, Pogatzki-Zahn E, Zaslansky R, Tanase NV, Perruchoud C, et al. Chronic postsurgical pain in Europe: an observational study. Eur J Anaesthesiol. 2015;32(10):725–34.
4. Hoofwijk DMN, Fiddelers AAA, Peters ML, Stessel B, Kessels AGH, Joosten EA, et al. Prevalence and predictive factors of chronic postsurgical pain and poor global recovery 1 year after outpatient surgery. Clin J Pain. 2015;31(12):1017–25.
5. Neil MJ, Macrae WA. Post surgical pain- the transition from acute to chronic pain. Rev Pain. 2009;3(2):6–9.
6. Martinez V, Ben Ammar S, Judet T, Bouhassira D, Chauvin M, Fletcher D. Risk factors predictive of chronic postsurgical neuropathic pain: the value of the iliac crest bone harvest model. Pain. 2012;153(7):1478–83.
7. Althaus A, Hinrichs-Rocker A, Chapman R, Arránz Becker O, Lefering R, Simanski C, et al. Development of a risk index for the prediction of chronic post-surgical pain. Eur J Pain. 2012;16(6):901–10.
8. Nikolajsen L, Brix LD. Chronic pain after surgery in children. Curr Opin Anaesthesiol. 2014;27(5):507–12.
9. Kehlet H, Jensen TS, Woolf CJ. Persistent postsurgical pain: risk factors and prevention. Lancet. 2006;367(9522):1618–25.
10. Schumpelick V. Does every hernia demand a mesh repair? A critical review. Hernia. 2001;5(1):5–8.
11. Treede R-D, Rief W, Barke A, Aziz Q, Bennett MI, Benoliel R, et al. A classification of chronic pain for ICD-11. Pain. 2015;156(6):1003–7.
12. Dworkin RH, Jensen MP, Gammaitoni AR, Olaleye DO, Galer BS. Symptom profiles differ in patients with neuropathic versus non-neuropathic pain. J Pain. 2007;8(2):118–26.
13. Gray P. Acute neuropathic pain: diagnosis and treatment. Curr Opin Anaesthesiol. 2008;21(5):590–5.
14. Haroutiunian S, Nikolajsen L, Finnerup NB, Jensen TS. The neuropathic component in persistent postsurgical pain: a systematic literature review. Pain. 2013;154(1):95–102.
15. Dualé C, Ouchchane L, Schoeffler P, Dubray C, EDONIS Investigating Group. Neuropathic aspects of persistent postsurgical pain: a French multicenter survey with a 6-month prospective follow-up. J Pain. 2014;15(1):24.e1–24.e20.
16. Montes A, Roca G, Sabate S, Lao JI, Navarro A, Cantillo J, et al. Genetic and clinical factors associated with chronic postsurgical pain after hernia repair, hysterectomy, and thoracotomy: a two-year multicenter cohort study. Anesthesiology. 2015;122(5):1123–41.

17. Hagelberg N, Haanpää M. Can we prevent pain becoming chronic? Duodecim. 2015;131(3):249–54.
18. VanDenKerkhof EG, Hopman WM, Goldstein DH, Wilson RA, Towheed TE, Lam M, et al. Impact of perioperative pain intensity, pain qualities, and opioid use on chronic pain after surgery: a prospective cohort study. Reg Anesth Pain Med. 2012;37(1):19–27.
19. Alfieri S, Amid PK, Campanelli G, Izard G, Kehlet H, Wijsmuller AR, et al. International guidelines for prevention and management of post-operative chronic pain following inguinal hernia surgery. Hernia. 2011;15(3):239–49.
20. HerniaSurge Group. International guidelines for groin hernia management. Hernia. 2018;22(1):1–165.
21. Campanelli G, Bertocchi V, Cavalli M, Bombini G, Biondi A, Tentorio T, et al. Surgical treatment of chronic pain after inguinal hernia repair. Hernia. 2013;17(3):347–53.
22. Nienhuijs SW, Rosman C, Strobbe LJA, Wolff A, Bleichrodt RP. An overview of the features influencing pain after inguinal hernia repair. Int J Surg. 2008;6(4):351–6.
23. Sun P, Cheng X, Deng S, Hu Q, Sun Y, Zheng Q. Mesh fixation with glue versus suture for chronic pain and recurrence in Lichtenstein inguinal hernioplasty. Cochrane Database Syst Rev. 2017;2:CD010814.
24. Bracale U, Rovani M, Picardo A, Merola G, Pignata G, Sodo M, et al. Beneficial effects of fibrin glue (Quixil) versus Lichtenstein conventional technique in inguinal hernia repair: a randomized clinical trial. Hernia. 2014;18(2):185–92.
25. Negro P, Basile F, Brescia A, Buonanno GM, Campanelli G, Canonico S, et al. Open tension-free Lichtenstein repair of inguinal hernia: use of fibrin glue versus sutures for mesh fixation. Hernia. 2011;15(1):7–14.
26. Tolver MA, Rosenberg J, Juul P, Bisgaard T. Randomized clinical trial of fibrin glue versus tacked fixation in laparoscopic groin hernia repair. Surg Endosc. 2013;27(8):2727–33.
27. Berney CR, Yeo AET. Mesh fixation with fibrin sealant during endoscopic totally extraperitoneal inguinal hernia approach: a review of 640 repairs. Hernia. 2013;17(6):709–17.
28. Chen DC, Amid PK. Prevention of inguinodynia: the need for continuous refinement and quality improvement in inguinal hernia repair. World J Surg. 2014;38(10):2571–3.
29. Chou R, Gordon DB, de Leon-Casasola OA, Rosenberg JM, Bickler S, Brennan T, et al. Management of postoperative pain: a clinical practice guideline from the American Pain Society, the American Society of Regional Anesthesia and Pain Medicine, and the American Society of Anesthesiologists' Committee on Regional Anesthesia, Executive Committee, and Administrative Council. J Pain. 2016;17(2):131–57.
30. Chaparro LE, Smith SA, Moore RA, Wiffen PJ, Gilron I. Pharmacotherapy for the prevention of chronic pain after surgery in adults. Cochrane Database Syst Rev. 2013;7:CD008307.
31. Andreae MH, Andreae DA. Local anaesthetics and regional anaesthesia for preventing chronic pain after surgery. Cochrane Database Syst Rev. 2012;10:CD007105.
32. McNicol ED, Schumann R, Haroutounian S. A systematic review and meta-analysis of ketamine for the prevention of persistent post-surgical pain. Acta Anaesthesiol Scand. 2014;58(10):1199–213.
33. White PF, Sacan O, Tufanogullari B, Eng M, Nuangchamnong N, Ogunnaike B. Effect of short-term postoperative celecoxib administration on patient outcome after outpatient laparoscopic surgery. Can J Anaesth. 2007;54(5):342–8.
34. Markman JD, Philip A. Interventional approaches to pain management. Anesthesiol Clin. 2007;25(4):883–98, viii.
35. Legge 15 marzo 2010 - n° 38 "Disposizioni per garantire l'accesso alle cure palliative e alla terapia del dolore" (G.U. Serie Generale, n. 65 del 19-03-2010).
36. Notaro P, et al. Dolore cronico, Dolore inutile. Strutture di Terapia del Dolore in Italia. Perché un libro bianco [Internet]. 2009. Available from: http://www.nopain.it
37. Notaro P, et al. Dolore cronico, dolore inutile. Strutture di Terapia del dolore in Italia. Perché un aggiornamento del libro bianco [Internet]. 2012. Available from: www.nopain.it
38. NOPAIN, Associazione italiana per la cura della malattia dolore [Internet]. 2007 [cited 2018 Jun 24]. Available from: http://www.nopain.it/

39. Gaskin DJ, Richard P. The economic costs of pain in the United States. J Pain. 2012;13(8):715–24.
40. Tumin D, Drees D, Miller R, Wrona S, Hayes D, Tobias JD, et al. Health care utilization and costs associated with pediatric chronic pain. J Pain. 2018;19(9):973–82.
41. Groenewald CB, Essner BS, Wright D, Fesinmeyer MD, Palermo TM. The economic costs of chronic pain among a cohort of treatment-seeking adolescents in the United States. J Pain. 2014;15(9):925–33.

12 Post-surgical Hidden Costs: Infections

Massimo Puoti, Dalila Patrizia Greco, Marco Merli, and Claudia Abbati

12.1 Introduction

Mesh repair is the most popular technique for treatment of abdominal wall hernia, resulting in a lower recurrence rate than suture repair [1, 2], but unfortunately, as any foreign body, it can a elicit a host's reaction to the implanted material that may cause a series of adverse events, among which infection is the most important and difficult to treat.

The true incidence of this complication is difficult to be determined, because it varies widely in the literature; neither there are evidences in favour of or against different therapeutic strategies.

For example, groin hernia repair is traditionally considered a clean procedure, for which the wound infection rate should be below 2% [3, 4] and antibiotic prophylaxis is not recommended. Nevertheless, it appears to be more frequent than in other clean surgeries, reaching worrying rate (up to 16%) in some follow-up studies [5–7]. A recent survey in the UK showed a high heterogeneity in the use of antimicrobial prophylaxis in inguinal hernia repair, with 44.4% of surgeons reporting routine administration, while 49.4% selective administration and 6.2% no prophylaxis at all [8].

M. Puoti (✉) · M. Merli
Division of Infectious Disease, Niguarda Hospital, Milan, Italy
e-mail: massimo.puoti@fastwebnet.it; marco.merli@ospedaleniguarda.it

D. P. Greco
Day&Week Surgery Unit, Ospedale Niguarda Ca' Granda, Milano, Italy
e-mail: dalilapatriziagreco@gmail.com

C. Abbati
General Surgery Department, Niguarda Hospital, Milan, Italy

University of Milan, Milan, Italy

D. P. Greco, E. Borgonovi (eds.), *Abdominal Wall Surgery*,
https://doi.org/10.1007/978-3-030-02426-0_12

Moreover, little information is available on complication-related resource utilization and costs over time following infection of abdominal wall prosthesis. Despite the low incidence, infections have a severe impact on the patient's life due to extended hospital stay and multiple reoperations, and for the same reasons is also a burden for the health care system, with very elevated social costs [9, 10].

As for all surgical site infections (SSIs), patient's clinical status at the time of surgical intervention mainly determines the risk of infections.

In order to reduce the risk of infection, prosthetic materials need to be accurately selected on the basis of patient's clinical characteristics and type of hernia.

12.2 Pathogenesis

Infection may be limited to the surgical site and/or involve the mesh, which represents a more challenging situation. As for all prosthetic materials, infection frequently occurs at the time of implantation, as a consequence of the entry of even a small amount of microorganisms through surgical wound. The bacteria may be part of the skin flora or carried by the surgical staff or the environment and instruments used in the operation. The ability of bacteria to colonize tissues and the biomaterial, together with the patient's immune status, further determine the rate of infection. After surgery, the damp nature of the environment made of small protein-rich (fibronectin, fibrinogen, collagen, etc.) aqueous film around the mesh, called conditioning film, favours bacterial adhesion, which is a two-stage process: a rapid and reversible interaction between germ and mesh surface mediated by chemical factors followed by an irreversible binding mediated by cellular and molecular factors, the so-called adhesion proteins. The strong interaction between the mesh and different microorganisms stimulates further bacterial proliferation and gives rise to the formation of biofilm, a structure made of polysaccharide, glycolipids, cellular debris, extracellular enzymes, blood products and extracellular matrix proteins produced by bacteria which acts as a protective barrier to external agents (e.g. antibiotics) and to the host's immune system (e.g. immune cells systems and cytokines) [11]. The titration and inactivation of antimicrobial agents by extracellular matrix proteins and the development of an oxygen gradient preventing antibacterial activity of some molecules explain the phenotypic resistance to antibiotic agents observed in this setting [12]. Moreover, bacterial subpopulations called "persister cells" can adapt to a slow growth rate and a low metabolism in order to escape the antimicrobial activity of anti-infective agents. In addition, biofilm may limit the diffusion of antimicrobials given the absence of vessels and its molecular architecture [11, 13].

As for other post-operative infections, the most common causative organisms are *Staphylococcus* species, especially *Staphylococcus aureus* (above 50% of isolated bacteria including methicillin-susceptible and methicillin-resistant ones) followed by coagulase-negative *Staphylococcus* spp. (7–15% of isolates), Gram negative bacilli (mainly *Enterobacteriaceae*), *Streptococcus/Enterococcus* spp. and anaerobic bacteria [14–19]. Polymicrobial infection is reported in a variable number of cases, but it is highly susceptible to the type of sampling performed (e.g. wound swab vs pus collection after debridement) and should be considered with caution. Despite colonization at the time of intervention or at the time of non-infective surgical site occurrence (e.g. seroma) are considered the major route of contamination, a high similarity had been observed between periodontal bacterial flora and mesh flora, suggesting the possibility of haematogenous spread from oral site or, more probably, from the gut [20].

12.3 Epidemiology and Risk Factors

The infection rate after hernia repair has been reported between 0% and 10% depending on the surgical technique, the type of mesh and the patient's co-morbidities.

For open surgery, it has been reported from 1.5% to 4% for inguinal hernia repair [21–23] and 6% to 10% for incisional hernia repair [2, 15, 21], compared to 0.7–1% and 3.6% in laparoscopic operation for inguinal and incisional hernia repair, respectively [24–27]. The lower infection rate after laparoscopic hernia repair may also be a consequence of a deeper site of prosthesis placement (usually intraperitoneally) compared to open surgery, where the prosthesis is usually placed more superficially [26].

A Cochrane Review comparing traditional suture technique and prosthetic repair for inguinal hernia found no significant difference between the two techniques in terms of infection rate, even with the administration of antibiotic prophylaxis [28].

Otherwise, the prevalence of mesh infection is higher and much more complex in incisional hernia [21], and it appears to be related to:

- Intra-operative factors [29]
  - Larger wound
  - Wide dissection
  - Concomitant surgery on the gastrointestinal tract
  - Duration of surgery
- Post-operative factors [30]
  - Seroma or haematoma
  - Drains

A higher infection risk appears to be consequent not only to the procedure but also to the clinical condition in which surgery is performed: urgent surgery, as in the case of incarcerated or strangulated hernia, is burdened by a higher risk of infection (OR 5.1, 95%CI 2.2–8.6; $p < 0.001$), as prolonged operative time [19]. Furthermore, concomitant enterotomy further increases the risk of infection, since bacteria may already be present in the operating field [14, 31].

Finally, post-operative surgical site infection was predictive of deep mesh infection (OR 2.9, CI 1.55 to 4.10; *p* 0.002) [14].

The risk of SSI in hernia procedures may increase further in the presence of generic risk factors, such as an ASA score greater than 2 [23, 32], and care must be taken to the ones which cause reduced perfusion of the skin and subcutaneous tissue or immunosuppression, such as diabetes, obesity, nutritional deficit, smoking, steroid therapy and renal disease [33, 34].

The type of mesh appears to play a role not only in the mechanism of infection, as a consequence of the prosthetic architecture, but also for the need of mesh removal in case of infection: the type of material (synthetic and biological), its structure (laminar, reticular and composite), pore size and yarn configuration contribute to define the risk the biomaterial may be colonized by bacteria (Table 12.1).

Table 12.1 Susceptibility to bacterial contamination of the most relevant material utilized to repair abdominal wall defects

Type of mesh	Most common materials	Susceptibility to material contamination
Synthetic mesh		
Reticular mono-/ multifilament	Non-absorbable Polypropylene (PP) Polyester (PE) Absorbable Poly-lactic acid (PLA) Poly-glycolic acid (PGA)	High-risk adhesion at mesh nodes Higher for – Multifilament – PE – Absorbable Hydrophylic components increase the risk
Laminar Microporous and non-porous	Non-absorbable Polytetrafluoroethylene (PTFE) Expanded PTFE (ePTFE) Absorbable Trimethylene carbonate (TMC)	The wide surface increases the chance of colonization Higher for microporous
Composites	Integrating materials Non-absorbable: PP, PE Barrier Non-absorbable: PTFE-ePTFE Absorbable: poly-ethilen glycol, Hyaluronic acid, cellulose	Barrier components provide a wide surface, with increased risk of colonization Higher risk of adhesion for absorbable barrier

Type of mesh	Matrix degradation	Susceptibility to material contamination
Biologic mesh		
Crosslinked	Slow degradation of collagen matrix	Crosslinking could enhance bacterial adhesion
Non-crosslinked	Rapid degradation of collagen matrix	Bacterial metalloproteases enhance mesh degradation

Adapted from: Perez-Kohler B, Bayon Y, Bellon JM. Mesh infection and hernia repair: a review. Surg Infect (Larchmt) 2016; 17(2):124–137

For a more detailed discussion of this subject, we suggest reading Chap. 6 (Devices and *biomaterials: from chemistry to certification*).

Concerning our issue, in general, absorbable materials have a higher risk of infections compared to non-absorbable ones due to the lower structural support with subsequent higher risk of tissue failure. Regarding the texture, multifilament meshes are more susceptible to bacterial colonization and subsequent infection given the wider contact area compared to monofilament ones. For the same reason, pores increase the risk of colonization and infection. Overall, due to structural advantages, large pore meshes provide ample space to promote tissue growth along with migration of white blood cells and macrophages and are inherently more resistant to infection than firm, smaller pores and heavyweight predecessor meshes [24, 35, 36]. Among non-absorbable materials, polyester appeared less prone to bacterial colonization compared to polypropylene and polyvinylidenfluoride [37]. Biological meshes are made of decellularized and dilapidated tissues rich in collagen, are biodegradable and may be cross-linked, with enhanced bacterial adhesion but higher resistance to matrix metalloproteases, or non-cross-linked. Though higher in terms of cost compared to synthetic meshes, biological meshes are better suited in contaminated surgical fields, given their lower adhesion to bowel and high biocompatibility when implanted, with subsequent reduced inflammation and infection risk [24].

Despite currently available studies did not demonstrate an independent correlation between type of mesh and occurrence of infection, it is probable that an adequate choice of the mesh in different clinical setting may help to reduce infection rate.

12.4 Clinical Presentation

The patient's clinical status, especially the state of immunocompetence, contributes to the chance of developing infection after bacterial colonization. Immunosuppressive therapy, including corticosteroids, and previous post-operative surgical wound infection have found to be strongly associated with the occurrence of mesh infection [14], but other factors as high body mass index and diabetes were also more common in patients who developed mesh infection compared to those who did not [14, 29, 38].

Infections can occur at different time-points after inguinal or abdominal hernia surgery and can vary in terms of involvement of soft tissue layers and the mesh. Some early infections (within 30–45 days) are associated with entero-cutaneous fistula (ECF) or superficial surgical site infection (SSI), not involving the mesh [39]. On the contrary, the great majority of mesh infections after hernia repair with prosthesis presents later after the surgical procedure, with an average of 11 months or more based on available studies [35, 40].

The presentation of mesh infection can range from mild erythema overlying the incision to severe sepsis. Early mesh infection, often presenting as local erythema in the surgical area, needs to be differentiated from surgical site infection, which can usually be managed with systemic antibiotics if no abscess is evident and only cellulitis is present. Considering the wide range of clinical presentation, a clinician should strongly consider the possibility of mesh-related infection in any patient who presents with fever of unknown origin, symptoms or signs of inflammation of the abdominal wall in the area of the mesh or abdominal abscess in the area of the mesh.

The more superficial the prosthetic placement (pre-fascial onlay mesh), the greater the risk that the prosthesis will be contaminated by a simple subcutaneous wound infection. On the contrary, the deeper the prosthetic placement (submuscular and intraperitoneal under-lay repairs), the less the risk of contamination from superficial infection. Given these considerations, even superficial infections need urgent consideration and prompt intervention in order to avoid deeper extension.

12.5 Diagnosis

Imaging techniques, including ultrasound and computerized tomography (CT), are useful for the diagnosis of mesh infection. Such techniques reveal an area of inflammation in the subcutaneous fat or around the mesh, which has different echogenic or density characteristics from other non-suppurative conditions, such as seroma. Moreover, imaging can show the presence of an abscess or can detect flecks of gas, suggesting anaerobic infection or the presence of a communication with the gastrointestinal tract. Nonetheless, imaging data should be interpreted with caution, always considering the clinical context, since fluid surrounding the mesh can be a normal, benign sign [41, 42].

Even though clinical, biochemical and imaging data can support the suspect of mesh infection, definite diagnosis relies on positive deep cultures of the fluid surrounding the mesh or the mesh itself. On the contrary, swabs and culture of wound secretions should be avoided. In the presence of high clinical and/or imaging suspicion of infection, pathogen identification and its antimicrobial susceptibility test (AST) are of cornerstone importance in order to confirm diagnosis and provide adequate antibiotic treatment. Nonetheless, sterile fluid aspiration should be avoided in the absence of other clinical signs of infection, given the possibility of introducing microorganisms during the puncture and transforming as aseptic reaction into an infectious process [41].

12.6 Treatment

Infection after abdominal wall surgery with mesh graft repair is a very serious occurrence, both for surgeon and for patient, and causes an exponential increase in costs, no matter which strategy is followed. Clearly, the best approach to reduce the morbidity associated is to prevent this circumstance, but once infection occurs, the management is challenging and requires an individualized strategy with combined medical and surgical approaches. The extension of the infection defines subsequent management: superficial infections without mesh involvement can be treated with systemic antimicrobial therapy, while deeper infection sometimes requires surgical mesh removal (0.9–1.1%) to reach infection eradication. Anyway, deep infections result in a low risk of mesh removal and in a low rate of recurrence [22, 43, 44]. Nonetheless, clear guidelines on how to manage these patients have not yet been established [17].

Some clinical trials have demonstrated that in certain instances, non-operative strategies with conservative management with local irrigations and systemic antibiotics have been successful for salvaging a mesh [29, 45, 46]. Non-operative strategies are particularly attractive for high-risk patients, who may experience significant morbidity associated with mesh removal, and their success relies on the availability of microbiological diagnosis [47].

The most common risk associated with mesh removal is hernia recurrence, with the need of subsequent reoperations [48, 49].

The use of negative-pressure wound therapy (NPWT) may increase the rate of infection cure with conservative treatment or minimally invasive surgical debridement without mesh removal or lessen the time to recover, especially when early started [50, 51]. Nonetheless, differences have been observed in time to healing with NPWT, with large pore meshes apparently requiring a shorter treatment duration compared to small pore meshes [50, 52].

Considering reported experience and the slow progression of this kind of infections, empiric antimicrobial therapy before pathogen identification is discouraged in the absence of clinical signs of sepsis. Once pathogen has been identified, targeted antibiotic regimen based on susceptibility test should be promptly started. When *Staphylococcus* species is implicated, molecules with activity on biofilm (e.g. daptomycin and rifampicin) should be preferred in a combined regimen in order to optimize pharmacokinetics and to reduce the risk to develop resistance.

Nonetheless, infection eradication is sometimes hard to obtain without mesh removal, as the presence of biofilm limits the effectiveness of antimicrobials [53]. Mesh can be preserved in 30–55% of cases of deep infection [29, 54], and the failure of conservative strategy warrants mesh removal. Complete mesh removal is recommended since partial removal of the mesh is burned by a higher rate of persistent infection, with 50% patients requiring further surgical operation for persistent sinus compared to only 2% in the case of complete mesh removal, despite a lower rate of hernia recurrence and a hospitalization (6.5 vs 9.9 days) [14, 16].

12.7 Economic Impact of Infection

Surgical site infection (SSI) is the most common reason for hospital re-admission after surgical procedures, including hernia repair, which occurs in almost 5–10% patients within 30 days from the first discharge [55]. Even though an SSI not always requires new hospital admission, an increased medical and nursing care is required in terms of additional outpatient visits, blood test sand cultural examinations, imaging tests, wound care supplies and antibiotics. Moreover, an SSI may require additional time of work compared to what expected after the surgical intervention itself. Previous observations showed that SSIs diagnosed within 8 weeks from hospital discharge after surgery were associated with increased resource utilization, such as outpatient visits, emergency room visits, imaging tests and home health care services [56].

Post-surgical hospital costs in hernia repair have been investigated in the USA in a recent report: inpatient post-operative wound complications (2.1% of study sample) were found to be more than tripling total encounter costs. Among these, septic shock and organ/space SSI had the greatest impact in total encounter costs, which were increased more than ten times, followed by sepsis and deep SSI, burdened by an increase of three and five times of total encounter costs, and finally superficial SSI, which—despite the mild entity—almost triplicated total encounter costs. Regarding 90-day post-ventral/inguinal hernia repair discharge costs, the 6.7% patients experiencing wound complication determined a $6700 increase in post-discharge costs. In this setting, deep SSI was burdened by the highest costs, with a $24,800 increase, followed by sepsis ($23,800) and organ/space SSI ($20,700). Superficial SSI showed a moderate increase in post-discharge costs, $5600, although significant given the higher incidence (3.6%) compared to deep SSI (1%) and organ/space SSI (1%). As expected, similar risk factors for increased costs were identified compared to those predicting post-surgical infections, as complex care of multiple comorbidities, elderly patients and/or large ventral hernias requiring long, complex repairs [57].

Concerning the increase in outpatients' resources utilization, it has been observed that any wound complication more than doubled the mean number of visits (+2.3 [95% confidence interval 1.5–3.1] visits), especially in the case of deep SSI (+3.9 [95%CI 1.9–5.9] visits), while superficial SSI determined a mild increase in the number of visits (+1.3 [95%CI 0.4–2.1]) [58].

Apart from health-care service expenses, SSI and wound dehiscence are also associated with social factors, such as potential lost wages and transportation costs associated with increased number of office visits and/or emergency room visit or hospital readmission and the additional healthcare costs associated with home health care.

12.8 Infection Prevention

In order to save costs and reduce patients' discomfort, prevention represents a crucial issue in the infection control in abdominal wall surgery.

In particular, special attention should be given to strict aseptic conditions during mesh preparation and implantation [59], and to peri-operative care [28].

A much-debated issue in prevention is about antibiotic prophylaxis. Several studies have attempted to clarify the effectiveness of prophylaxis in after hernia repair [6, 7, 22, 23], and a Cochrane systematic review specifically related to groin hernia was published in 2012, with a total number of patients included of 7843 [28].

Based on the results of this Cochrane Review, no definitive recommendation can be made in favour of or against the use of prophylactic antibiotics for elective inguinal hernia repair.

The International guidelines for groin hernia management published in 2018 [60] state, with a strong recommendation, that antibiotic prophylaxis in average-risk patients in low-risk environments is not recommended in open surgery, and it is never recommended in laparo-endoscopic repair.

Anyway, it has been suggested to consider the routine use of antibiotic prophylaxis in those clinical settings that report a high rate of wound infection (defined by $a > 5\%$ incidence), or in high-risk patients (recurrence, advanced age, immunosuppressive conditions, expected long operating times and use of drains) [3, 61]. Some authors disagree on this point; Köckerling, for instance, suggests that antibiotic prophylaxis has a substantial impact on avoiding mesh infection in open inguinal repair, thus should be routinely administered [62].

Since an indiscriminate use of antibiotics can lead to the development of bacterial resistance and a consequent increase in costs, the choice of antimicrobial prophylaxis should be carefully evaluated.

Other guidelines in the setting of emergency surgery, as in patients with intestinal incarceration with no evidence of ischemia and no bowel resection, recommend short-term prophylaxis; the antimicrobial regimen should also include Enterobacteriaceae and Enterococcus as possible pathogens. In patients with intestinal strangulation and/or concomitant bowel resection, 48-h antimicrobial prophylaxis is recommended. Antimicrobial therapy is recommended for patients with peritonitis; in the latter case, the antibacterial regimen should also include anaerobes [63]. In any case, the choice of antimicrobial prophylaxis needs to be based on local epidemiology and regularly updated.

Reports showed that topical antibiotics administration can prevent bacterial growth [64]. Nonetheless, no current evidence is available to recommend this approach, given the possibility of selecting antimicrobial resistance. Similarly, the use of rifampin-coated meshes which appear to prevent staphylococcal colonization in animal model [65] is not currently supported by clinical experience and, given the rapid development of rifampin resistance and its potential importance in treated biofilm infections, should be avoided.

Finally, the use of wound drain after incisional hernia repair has not demonstrated to reduce the infection rate and the length of hospital stay, and it can even be the trigger, indeed [30, 66].

What weapons could the surgeon have?

As bacterial adherence and biofilm formation on the biomaterial surface are the most important factors involved in the colonization, a viable strategy might be to improve mesh materials [21].

In the future, this may be pursued with the help of:

- Nanotechnologies, to detect and decrease bacterial colonization [67, 68]
- Artificial intelligence to release drugs only when necessary [67, 69]

These high-tech meshes are not available today for clinical use and will certainly be very expensive, at least in the first phase of application, but these are acceptable costs compared to the burden of infections.

References

1. Burger JWA, Luijendijk RW, Hop WCJ, Halm JA, Verdaasdonk EGG, Jeekel J. Long-term follow-up of a randomized controlled trial of suture versus mesh repair of incisional hernia. Ann Surg. 2004;240(4):578–83; discussion 583-585
2. den Hartog D, Dur AHM, Tuinebreijer WE, Kreis RW. Open surgical procedures for incisional hernias. Cochrane Database Syst Rev. 2008;3:CD006438.
3. Mangram AJ, Horan TC, Pearson ML, Silver LC, Jarvis WR. Guideline for prevention of surgical site infection, 1999. Hospital infection control practices advisory committee. Infect Control Hosp Epidemiol. 1999;20(4):250–78; quiz 279–80
4. Woods RK, Dellinger EP. Current guidelines for antibiotic prophylaxis of surgical wounds. Am Fam Physician. 1998;57(11):2731–40.
5. Juvany M, Hoyuela C, Trias M, Carvajal F, Ardid J, Martrat A. Impact of surgical site infections on elective incisional hernia surgery: a prospective study. Surg Infect. 2018. https://doi.org/10.1089/sur.2017.233.
6. Othman I. Prospective randomized evaluation of prophylactic antibiotic usage in patients undergoing tension free inguinal hernioplasty. Hernia. 2011;15(3):309–13.
7. Shankar VG, Srinivasan K, Sistla SC, Jagdish S. Prophylactic antibiotics in open mesh repair of inguinal hernia—a randomized controlled trial. Int J Surg Lond Engl. 2010;8(6):444–7.
8. MacCormick AP, Akoh JA. Survey of surgeons regarding prophylactic antibiotic use in inguinal hernia repair. Scand J Surg. 2018;107:208–11.
9. Bower C, Roth JS. Economics of abdominal wall reconstruction. Surg Clin North Am. 2013;93(5):1241–53.
10. Totten CF, Davenport DL, Ward ND, Roth JS. Cost of ventral hernia repair using biologic or synthetic mesh. J Surg Res. 2016;203(2):459–65.
11. Römling U, Kjelleberg S, Normark S, Nyman L, Uhlin BE, Åkerlund B. Microbial biofilm formation: a need to act. J Intern Med. 2014;276(2):98–110.
12. Lynch AS, Robertson GT. Bacterial and fungal biofilm infections. Annu Rev Med. 2008;59:415–28.
13. Lewis K. Persister cells. Annu Rev Microbiol. 2010;64:357–72.
14. Bueno-Lledó J, Torregrosa-Gallud A, Sala-Hernandez A, Carbonell-Tatay F, Pastor PG, Diana SB, et al. Predictors of mesh infection and explantation after abdominal wall hernia repair. Am J Surg. 2017;213(1):50–7.
15. Brown RH, Subramanian A, Hwang CS, Chang S, Awad SS. Comparison of infectious complications with synthetic mesh in ventral hernia repair. Am J Surg. 2013;205(2):182–7.
16. Chung L, Tse GH, O'Dwyer PJ. Outcome of patients with chronic mesh infection following abdominal wall hernia repair. Hernia. 2014;18(5):701–4.

17. Shubinets V, Carney MJ, Colen DL, Mirzabeigi MN, Weissler JM, Lanni MA, et al. Management of infected mesh after abdominal hernia repair: systematic review and single-institution experience. Ann Plast Surg. 2018;80(2):145–53.
18. Tolino MJ, Tripoloni DE, Ratto R, Garcia MI. Infections associated with prosthetic repairs of abdominal wall hernias: pathology, management and results. Hernia. 2009;13(6):631–7.
19. Petersen S, Henke G, Freitag M, Faulhaber A, Ludwig K. Deep prosthesis infection in incisional hernia repair: predictive factors and clinical outcome. Eur J Surg. 2001;167(6):453–7.
20. Langbach O, Holmedal SH, Grandal OJ, Røkke O. Adhesions to mesh after ventral hernia mesh repair are detected by MRI but are not a cause of long term chronic abdominal pain. Gastroenterol Res Pract. 2016;2016:2631598.
21. Pérez-Köhler B, Bayon Y, Bellón JM. Mesh infection and hernia repair: a review. Surg Infect. 2016;17(2):124–37.
22. Aufenacker TJ, Koelemay MJW, Gouma DJ, Simons MP. Systematic review and meta-analysis of the effectiveness of antibiotic prophylaxis in prevention of wound infection after mesh repair of abdominal wall hernia. Br J Surg. 2006;93(1):5–10.
23. Erdas E, Medas F, Pisano G, Nicolosi A, Calò PG. Antibiotic prophylaxis for open mesh repair of groin hernia: systematic review and meta-analysis. Hernia. 2016;20(6):765–76.
24. Cevasco M, Itani KMF. Ventral hernia repair with synthetic, composite, and biologic mesh: characteristics, indications, and infection profile. Surg Infect. 2012;13(4):209–15.
25. Heniford BT, Park A, Ramshaw BJ, Voeller G. Laparoscopic ventral and incisional hernia repair in 407 patients. J Am Coll Surg. 2000;190(6):645–50.
26. Grant AM, EU Hernia Trialists Collaboration. Laparoscopic versus open groin hernia repair: meta-analysis of randomised trials based on individual patient data. Hernia. 2002;6(1):2–10.
27. Heniford BT, Park A, Ramshaw BJ, Voeller G. Laparoscopic repair of ventral hernias: nine years' experience with 850 consecutive hernias. Ann Surg. 2003;238(3):391–9; discussion 399-400
28. Sanchez-Manuel FJ, Lozano-García J, Seco-Gil JL. Antibiotic prophylaxis for hernia repair. Cochrane Database Syst Rev. 2012;2:CD003769.
29. Stremitzer S, Bachleitner-Hofmann T, Gradl B, Gruenbeck M, Bachleitner-Hofmann B, Mittlboeck M, et al. Mesh graft infection following abdominal hernia repair: risk factor evaluation and strategies of mesh graft preservation. A retrospective analysis of 476 operations. World J Surg. 2010;34(7):1702–9.
30. Simchen E, Rozin R, Wax Y. The Israeli Study of Surgical Infection of drains and the risk of wound infection in operations for hernia. Surg Gynecol Obstet. 1990;170(4):331–7.
31. Samel S, Keese M, Kleczka M, Lanig S, Gretz N, Hafner M, et al. Microscopy of bacterial translocation during small bowel obstruction and ischemia in vivo—a new animal model. BMC Surg. 2002;2:6.
32. Edwards JR, Peterson KD, Mu Y, Banerjee S, Allen-Bridson K, Morrell G, et al. National Healthcare Safety Network (NHSN) report: data summary for 2006 through 2008, issued December 2009. Am J Infect Control. 2009;37(10):783–805.
33. Malone DL, Genuit T, Tracy JK, Gannon C, Napolitano LM. Surgical site infections: reanalysis of risk factors. J Surg Res. 2002;103(1):89–95.
34. Meagher H, Clarke Moloney M, Grace PA. Conservative management of mesh-site infection in hernia repair surgery: a case series. Hernia. 2015;19(2):231–7.
35. Cobb WS, Carbonell AM, Kalbaugh CL, Jones Y, Lokey JS. Infection risk of open placement of intraperitoneal composite mesh. Am Surg. 2009;75(9):762–7; discussion 767-768
36. Eriksen JR, Gögenur I, Rosenberg J. Choice of mesh for laparoscopic ventral hernia repair. Hernia. 2007;11(6):481–92.
37. Engelsman AF, van Dam GM, van der Mei HC, Busscher HJ, Ploeg RJ. In vivo evaluation of bacterial infection involving morphologically different surgical meshes. Ann Surg. 2010;251(1):133–7.
38. Baucom RB, Ousley J, Oyefule OO, Stewart MK, Phillips SE, Browman KK, et al. Evaluation of long-term surgical site occurrences in ventral hernia repair: implications of preoperative site independent MRSA infection. Hernia. 2016;20(5):701–10.

39. Hawn MT, Gray SH, Snyder CW, Graham LA, Finan KR, Vick CC. Predictors of mesh explantation after incisional hernia repair. Am J Surg. 2011;202(1):28–33.
40. Jezupovs A, Jezupors A, Mihelsons M. The analysis of infection after polypropylene mesh repair of abdominal wall hernia. World J Surg. 2006;30(12):2270–8; discussion 2279-2280
41. Falagas ME, Kasiakou SK. Mesh-related infections after hernia repair surgery. Clin Microbiol Infect. 2005;11(1):3–8.
42. Sanchez VM, Abi-Haidar YE, Itani KMF. Mesh infection in ventral incisional hernia repair: incidence, contributing factors, and treatment. Surg Infect. 2011;12(3):205–10.
43. Taylor SG, O'Dwyer PJ. Chronic groin sepsis following tension-free inguinal hernioplasty. Br J Surg. 1999;86(4):562–5.
44. Yerdel MA, Akin EB, Dolalan S, Turkcapar AG, Pehlivan M, Gecim IE, et al. Effect of single-dose prophylactic ampicillin and sulbactam on wound infection after tension-free inguinal hernia repair with polypropylene mesh: the randomized, double-blind, prospective trial. Ann Surg. 2001;233(1):26–33.
45. Paton BL, Novitsky YW, Zerey M, Sing RF, Kercher KW, Heniford BT. Management of infections of polytetrafluoroethylene-based mesh. Surg Infect. 2007;8(3):337–41.
46. Trunzo JA, Ponsky JL, Jin J, Williams CP, Rosen MJ. A novel approach for salvaging infected prosthetic mesh after ventral hernia repair. Hernia. 2009;13(5):545–9.
47. Slomka JM, Laker S, Chandrasekar P, Paull DE. Failure to obtain microbiological culture and its consequence in a mesh-related infection. BMJ Case Rep. 2013;2013 https://doi.org/10.1136/bcr-2013-009123.
48. Szczerba SR, Dumanian GA. Definitive surgical treatment of infected or exposed ventral hernia mesh. Ann Surg. 2003;237(3):437–41.
49. Langer C, Schaper A, Liersch T, Kulle B, Flosman M, Füzesi L, et al. Prognosis factors in incisional hernia surgery: 25 years of experience. Hernia. 2005;9(1):16–21.
50. Nobaek S, Rogmark P, Petersson U. Negative pressure wound therapy for treatment of mesh infection after abdominal surgery: long-term results and patient-reported outcome. Scand J Surg. 2017;106(4):285–93.
51. Tamhankar AP, Ravi K, Everitt NJ. Vacuum assisted closure therapy in the treatment of mesh infection after hernia repair. Surgeon. 2009;7(5):316–8.
52. Berrevoet F, Vanlander A, Sainz-Barriga M, Rogiers X, Troisi R. Infected large pore meshes may be salvaged by topical negative pressure therapy. Hernia. 2013;17(1):67–73.
53. Kathju S, Nistico L, Melton-Kreft R, Lasko L-A, Stoodley P. Direct demonstration of bacterial biofilms on prosthetic mesh after ventral herniorrhaphy. Surg Infect. 2015;16(1):45–53.
54. Liang MK, Li LT, Nguyen MT, Berger RL, Hicks SC, Kao LS. Abdominal reoperation and mesh explantation following open ventral hernia repair with mesh. Am J Surg. 2014;208(4):670–6.
55. Nguyen MT, Li LT, Hicks SC, Davila JA, Suliburk JW, Leong M, et al. Readmission following open ventral hernia repair: incidence, indications, and predictors. Am J Surg. 2013;206(6):942–8; discussion 948-949
56. Perencevich EN, Sands KE, Cosgrove SE, Guadagnoli E, Meara E, Platt R. Health and economic impact of surgical site infections diagnosed after hospital discharge. Emerg Infect Dis. 2003;9(2):196–203.
57. Plymale MA, Ragulojan R, Davenport DL, Roth JS. Ventral and incisional hernia: the cost of comorbidities and complications. Surg Endosc. 2017;31(1):341–51.
58. Wade A, Plymale MA, Davenport DL, Johnson SE, Madabhushi VV, Mastoroudis E, et al. Predictors of outpatient resource utilization following ventral and incisional hernia repair. Surg Endosc. 2018;32(4):1695–700.
59. Deysine M. Infection control in a hernia clinic: 24 year results of aseptic and antiseptic measure implementation in 4,620 "clean cases.". Hernia. 2006;10(1):25–9.
60. HerniaSurge Group. International guidelines for groin hernia management. Hernia. 2018;22(1):1–165.
61. Simons MP, Aufenacker T, Bay-Nielsen M, Bouillot JL, Campanelli G, Conze J, et al. European Hernia Society guidelines on the treatment of inguinal hernia in adult patients. Hernia. 2009;13(4):343–403.

62. Köckerling F, Bittner R, Jacob D, Schug-Pass C, Laurenz C, Adolf D, et al. Do we need antibiotic prophylaxis in endoscopic inguinal hernia repair? Results of the Herniamed Registry. Surg Endosc. 2015;29(12):3741–9.
63. Birindelli A, Sartelli M, Di Saverio S, Coccolini F, Ansaloni L, van Ramshorst GH, et al. 2017 update of the WSES guidelines for emergency repair of complicated abdominal wall hernias. World J Emerg Surg. 2017;12:37.
64. Wiegering A, Sinha B, Spor L, Klinge U, Steger U, Germer CT, et al. Gentamicin for prevention of intraoperative mesh contamination: demonstration of high bactericide effect (in vitro) and low systemic bioavailability (in vivo). Hernia. 2014;18(5):691–700.
65. Reinbold J, Hierlemann T, Urich L, Uhde A-K, Müller I, Weindl T, et al. Biodegradable rifampicin-releasing coating of surgical meshes for the prevention of bacterial infections. Drug Des Devel Ther. 2017;11:2753–62.
66. Gurusamy KS, Allen VB. Wound drains after incisional hernia repair. Cochrane Database Syst Rev. 2013;12:CD005570.
67. Ehrlich G, Hu F, Lin Q. Intelligent implants to battle biofilms. ASM News. 2004;70(3):127–33.
68. Williamson ED, Savage VL, Lingard B, Russell P, Scott EA. A biocompatible microdevice for core body temperature monitoring in the early diagnosis of infectious disease. Biomed Microdevices. 2007;9(1):51–60.
69. Schmidt DJ, Moskowitz JS, Hammond PT. Electrically triggered release of a small molecule drug from a polyelectrolyte multilayer coating. Chem Mater. 2010;22(23):6416–25.

13 Basic Principles of Health Technology Assessment, Economic Evaluation, and Costing of Healthcare Programs

Rosanna Tarricone and Aleksandra Torbica

13.1 Introduction

Continuously increasing healthcare expenditure that has been verified in last decades in almost all the countries in the world has undoubtedly established grounds for spread of evidence-based approach in healthcare policy. Choices imposed by unavoidable scarcity of resources (people, time, facilities, equipment, knowledge, etc.) from one side, and increasing healthcare demand in quantitative and qualitative terms on the other, have made it necessary to introduce economic criteria in decision-making processes at different government levels [1].

Health technology assessment paradigm originated from growing concern about the expansive diffusion of costly medical equipment in the 1970s and third payers' ability to fund their use. Since then, HTA has grown remarkably to inform policy and decision-making in health care, especially on how best to allocate limited funds to health interventions and technologies [2]. The assessment is conducted by interdisciplinary groups using explicit analytical frameworks, drawing on clinical, epidemiological, health economic, and other information and methodologies.

R. Tarricone (✉) · A. Torbica
Department of Social and Political Science, Bocconi University, Milan, Italy

Division of Government, Health and Non Profit, SDA Bocconi School of Management, Milan, Italy

CERGAS-SDA, Bocconi University, Milan, Italy
e-mail: rosanna.tarricone@unibocconi.it; aleksandra.torbica@unibocconi.it

D. P. Greco, E. Borgonovi (eds.), *Abdominal Wall Surgery*,
https://doi.org/10.1007/978-3-030-02426-0_13

Health technology assessment is intended to provide a bridge between the world of research and the world of decision-making. HTA is an active field internationally and has seen increasing growth fostered by the need to support management, clinical, and policy decisions. It has also been advanced by the evolution of evaluative methods in the social and applied sciences, including clinical epidemiology and health economics.

Within the HTA framework, economic evaluation analysis (cost-effectiveness, cost-utility, and cost-benefit analysis)—together with the assessment of clinical effectiveness—has the role of supporting decision-making process in public domain, by providing necessary information concerning the economic aspects of resource absorption by different healthcare technologies, pharmacological treatments, or other interventions.

The aim of this chapter is to introduce the basic principles of health technology assessment (HTA), economic evaluation, and costing of healthcare programs and services.

The chapter is divided into several sections in order to provide the reader with the basics about the HTA objectives and what are the methods and stages of this activity. More specifically, the focus is on the economic evaluation analysis, i.e., one of the major pillars of HTA paradigm. Furthermore, greater attention is made on costing of healthcare programs and services to illustrate the most common methodological approaches.

Given the rich literature on the topic, the chapter has no ambition to be exhaustive on the issue but it is intended to provide a basic but comprehensive overview on a discipline that in recent years has aroused great interest among national and international policy makers.

13.2 What Is Health Technology Assessment

HTA is "a multi-disciplinary field of policy analysis studying the clinical, economic, social and ethical implications of the development, diffusion and use of health technologies." It is a structured, multi-dimensional process of analysis and decision: it requires a structured collection and systematic analysis of data to support the evaluation of technologies; it is multi-dimensional since the impact of technology should be evaluated on several dimensions [3]. The main objective of HTA is to support the health-related decision-making process as to the introduction of health technologies in clinical practice.

The evaluation of scientific and technological innovations in the healthcare sector has recent history. Until the introduction of experimental clinical studies such as randomized clinical trials in the mid-thirties, health technologies were evaluated on anecdotal basis [2]. Despite early technologies in healthcare have appeared at the beginning of the nineteenth century, the concept of HTA was established only in 1976 [4]. Health technology means "all the tools, equipment, drugs and procedures used to provide health services, as well as the organizational units for the provision of such services" [5]. It follows that a drug is a technology, instrumentation for monitoring the heart beat is a technology, an intensive care unit is a technology, and a mobile APP is a technology. From that moment onwards, HTA has had a rapid development.

13.3 Overview of the HTA Process

The full process of HTA includes the following phases (Fig. 13.1):

1. Identifying topics for assessment and specifying the decision problem.
2. Assessment:
    a. Systematic review of the clinical evidence.
    b. Economic evaluation.
    c. Assessing social, legal, ethical, and organizational implications.
3. Synthesis, dissemination, and implementation of policies.

13.3.1 Identifying Topics for Assessment

At this stage, it is necessary to clearly identify the object of evaluation that can be a new technology or an existing technology for which one can foresee new application areas. The criteria used for topic identification include: disease burden, existence of treatment alternatives, clinical impact, economic or budgetary impact, level of controversy, existence of evidence, variation in practice, timeliness of the assessment, ethical, legal, or social implications, and general level of interest.

In this phase it is also important to distinguish between diagnostic technologies and technologies for therapeutic purposes. The diagnostic procedures have in fact

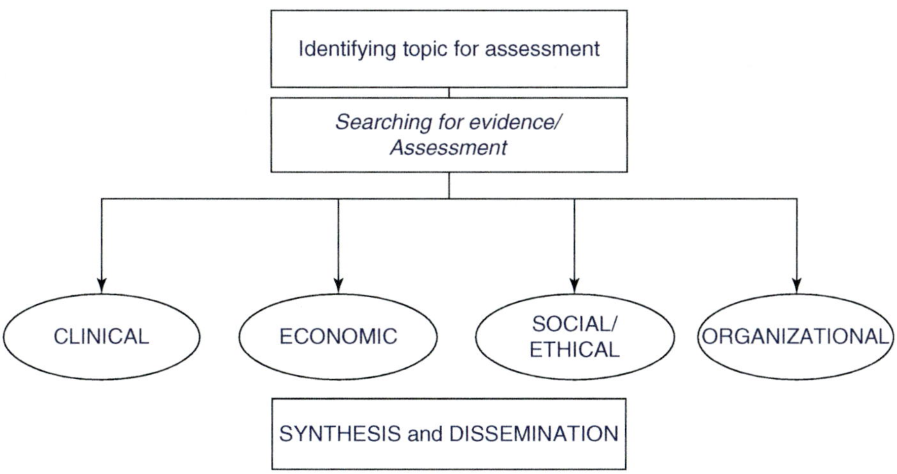

Fig. 13.1 Overview of HTA process

peculiar characteristics that distinguish them from therapeutic ones and are the cause of considerable difficulties in the evaluation phase. This refers in particular to the fact that diagnostic technologies can have an extremely wide field of use. This is, for example, the case of computed tomography or magnetic resonance imaging. Which efficacy parameters and disease indications should be considered for the evaluation of these technologies? What is the alternative to be considered? Generally, when a diagnostic technology is evaluated, the field must necessarily shrink to specific indications. An example is the evaluation conducted on neonatal ECG screening for the long QT syndrome in Italy which can prevent cardiac deaths in infancy and childhood [6]. Finally, it is important to clearly identify at which stage of the technology's life cycle the evaluation process is performed. In the early stage, technologies may have a relatively limited use but they could have enormous potential for use as they grow and intrude in areas that often were not even envisaged in the initial phase. This obviously has a huge impact on the following stages, and it requires an effort by the researchers who must estimate the future conditions of use on the basis of insufficient data to provide a complete assessment.

Specifying the decision problem requires to be clear on the purpose of the HTA (e.g., what possible decisions could result from this HTA?) and to convert a general idea for study to a study design that can be executed (e.g., what is the relevant treatment population? which treatment alternatives should be studied? what are the settings in which care could be delivered? what outcomes are relevant? what would be acceptable study designs?).

In general, identifying programs/technologies and specifying the decision problem should strike a balance between the relevance of the assessment and the feasibility of conducting the study.

13.3.2 Assessment

This phase consists of several aspects. In operational terms, it is the systematic collection of data and information needed to perform the evaluation across several dimensions: clinical, economic, social, ethical, legal, and organizational. The methods used to undertake an evaluation of the different dimensions belong to different disciplines.

13.3.2.1 Systematic Review of the Clinical Evidence

The clinical dimension refers to the concept of effectiveness. In healthcare, the effectiveness of an intervention or program is defined as the ability to achieve positive results in terms of health for the community of patients. Basically, a program is effective if it contributes to a positive change of the state of health of the patients. Evaluating the effectiveness of a healthcare technology is not a simple process. The best indicator for the assessment of the effectiveness of technologies and health programs shall be represented by survival, measured through "life years gained," i.e., the indicator must be connected to a final outcome. It may happen that effectiveness cannot be measured in terms of survival and that other physical units are contemplated instead. This is the case, for example, of a screening program. The outcome of the program can be identified in terms of "ability of early detection of positive cases" and the comparison with another program (in the case where the technology aims to replace an existing one) may thus be performed in terms of "number of positive cases diagnosed." This is an example of an intermediate outcome. The general principle is to use intermediate outcome measures when there is a proven positive relationship between the intermediate outcomes and the final outcome or when the intermediate outcome has a finite value itself. It has been scientifically proven, for example, that early detection of breast cancer is a predictor of survival. In this case the measurement of effectiveness based on an intermediate outcome (e.g., the number of diagnosed cases) is adequate because a certain relationship with the final outcome does exist, linked to the survival of patients. It may happen, however, that early detection of the screening program does not lead to a longer life expectancy. However, the program's ability to reveal the negative cases has such a value itself as it reassures the patient and avoids the healthcare system to undertake unnecessary diagnostic and therapeutic procedures. If, however, there is no proven positive relationship between the outcome of a healthcare program and the survival of patients, the comparison of the two technologies or healthcare programs should not be based on a cost-effectiveness analysis—as we will see—and an alternative technique should be chosen. The antiemetic treatment for cancer patients does not lengthen the survival of patients—for example—but it is effective in the prevention of acute events. In this case, the comparison between different antiemetic treatments cannot be conducted through a cost-effectiveness analysis but a different technique is preferred, for example, the analysis of rising and avoided costs.

13.3.2.2 Economic Evaluation

The economic dimension is properly related to economic evaluations. Economic evaluation analysis aims at identifying the alternatives that maximize health benefits per unit of cost. Economic evaluation can be defined as: "the comparative analysis of alternative courses of action in terms of both their costs and consequences" [7]. In short, economic evaluations provide decision makers with information on the trade-offs in resource costs and health benefits involved in choosing one intervention over another.

Economic techniques such as cost-benefit analysis (CBA), cost-effectiveness analysis (CEA), and cost-utility analysis (CUA) [7, 8] are full economic evaluations, and they all have the objective to identify, measure, value, and compare the costs and consequences of alternatives being considered.

The three techniques are very similar in terms of cost estimation: they tend, in fact, to provide a value of the cost elements expressed in monetary units. Differences emerge in the evaluation of the effects (Table 13.1).

In a nutshell, in the CBA health effects are measured in monetary terms, with a unit of measure that is consistent with the one used for the quantification of costs. In the CEA health outcomes are measured in physical units (e.g., life years gained). In the CUA the outcomes to be evaluated can be more than one, also not similar for the different alternatives and not achieved at the same level of effectiveness. The most widely used measure is the QALY (quality adjusted life years), which adjusts the life years gained for the quality of life associated with them.

Table 13.1 Types of full economic evaluations

Type of analysis	Measurement/ evaluation of costs	Effects identification	Measurement/ assessment of the effects
CEA	Monetary units	Singles result-goal common to all the alternatives, reached at different levels of effectiveness	Physical units (life years gained, diagnosed cases, etc.)
CBA	Monetary units	One or more outcomes not necessarily common to the alternatives and achieved at different levels of effectiveness	Monetary units
CUA	Monetary units	One or more outcomes not necessarily common to the alternatives and achieved at different levels of effectiveness	QALYs

13.3.2.3 Costs Identification and Measurement

As economic resources are limited, any decision to undertake a health care program will redirect resources from alternative uses. The economic cost recognizes the cost of using resources that could have been productively used elsewhere. This is the concept of opportunity cost. This means that the benefits from the expenses in question should be compared with the benefits that would have been obtained if the money had been used elsewhere.

In practice, what we have to measure when we are dealing with the costs of a healthcare program is the opportunity cost of using a resource in the program, instead in its best alternative. This is valued by its "shadow" price. Shadow prices are identical to market prices in the case of perfect competition where market prices are equal to marginal costs. However, most markets deviate from the ideal competitive model. There are also goods and services that are not sold on the market (for example, health and education). In all these cases, the market prices do not correspond to the value of the resources or simply do not exist. This does not mean, however, that these resources do not have a price. If there is no observable price, or the observable price is misleading, there is a shadow price, as each unit must have an opportunity cost in terms of a lost alternative. Shadow prices can be assigned using different strategies. Firstly, a survey can be used to obtain the willingness to pay of consumers. Secondly, there may be markets for similar products outside the public sector (for example, the private sector). Thirdly, the cost of providing a service could be used to indicate its social value. The assumption is that revenue costs with the addition of capital costs and overheads can be used as a reasonable proxy for long-term marginal costs [9]. The first approach can be complicated to implement and the second is not always feasible when health services are the object of the analysis, so the assessment of production costs to provide healthcare services is the preferred option and the objective of this chapter.

In all economic evaluations the costs can be classified into direct costs and productivity losses. Direct costs are divided into direct healthcare and non-healthcare costs. The direct healthcare costs include all costs incurred by the healthcare service, by patients and their families to implement the new technology or to organize and implement the new program. Typical examples are the medical staff, medical supplies and devices, drugs, and hospital stay. The monetary estimation of direct healthcare costs follows accounting principles as better described below.

Direct Healthcare Costs

Costing healthcare programs requires identifying all components that generate costs and assigning them a monetary value. Two approaches can be used: micro-costing and gross-costing. With the first method, the cost of a program is evaluated by summing up each individual cost component (input) that has contributed to the provision of the service/program. If, for example, the service to be evaluated is "hospital admission," resources such as personnel, drugs, tests, and meals used to produce the service must be identified, measured, and evaluated. This means that the micro-costing is a "bottom-up" approach, i.e., the calculation of production (full) costs consists in transferring the inputs to the outputs. Conversely, with the gross-costing approach, the cost of a service (e.g., hospitalization) is assessed in a "top-down" manner, i.e., by dividing the total cost of the service unit (e.g., hospital ward) for the total number of services (e.g., hospital admissions) produced over a period of time. Both methods aim to evaluate unit cost of services; however, the level of accuracy achieved by them is quite different. The result of the micro-costing approach is the "actual" cost of the service, while the "average" cost is the product of the gross-costing approach [10].

The micro-costing approach is very accurate and can somehow be considered the "gold standard" for cost assessment. However, it is expensive and time consuming and its widespread use must be offset by the benefits derived from such a detailed analysis. As a general rule, micro-costing is preferred because it explicitly indicates the production and cost functions related to the service in question. Micro-costing is recommended when the objective is to highlight the cost differences related to the service under consideration. Special attention must, however, be paid to the representativeness and comparability of these costs since it is very likely that they differ across healthcare providers. Since this approach is time consuming, it is important to evaluate when it is worthwhile to adopt it. There are healthcare services whose main components are less sensitive to how budgets are formed and spread in healthcare centers. This means that micro- and gross-costing approaches would tend to comparable results, thus making the micro-costing approach not applicable. On the other hand, for services with a significant component of personnel and overhead costs and significant sharing of personnel or facilities among patient groups, a micro-cost approach is the best approach since, by specifying cost components, it improves comparability.

Direct Non-healthcare Costs

The non-healthcare direct costs are those incurred by the patient and his/her family members or others outside the healthcare cycle, such as the costs of transportation to access the technology.

Whenever possible, these costs should be measured in monetary terms through market prices (i.e., the best proxy of opportunity cost) as it happens for cost categories such as transportation or home adaptations. If there are no market prices, it is important to use other approaches. Informal care is care provided by lay people. Specifically, informal caregivers can be defined as family, friends, acquaintances, or neighbors of a patient who provide care for which they do not have to be financially compensated. Informal care is a component of direct costs but its assessment follows the methods used for productivity costs. The valuation of informal care is rather difficult as caregivers do not lose just part of their time, but they also experience intangible effects like fatigue, leisure time forgone, and fewer social contacts. The first problem is assessing the exact quantity of time spent on informal caregiving. During the time providing informal care, many normal activities often can continue as usual; thus joint production occurs, as in the case of surveillance. It may be very difficult to separate normal activities from caregiving activities. Preparing and serving meals may be defined a normal activity, but helping someone to eat is not. This problem may be solved by using a structured interview or questionnaire in which caregivers are asked about the type of care provided and loss of time from paid work, unpaid work, and leisure time. If informal care is provided at the expense of paid labor, the worker's labor costs may be used to estimate informal care. The method follows that used for estimating productivity costs. If, however, informal care is provided at the expense of unpaid work and/or leisure time the cost measurement is not straightforward. As for patients, the valuation of unpaid working time by caregivers can be valued by the market wage, that is by using the wage a person would have received for a similar work in the market. If caregivers' time allocated to the provision of caring and nursing of patients involves a displacement of non-working time, the cost can be given by the value (to the individual) of leisure activities forgone, that is by using the net hourly income caregivers would earn had they provided that activity in the market. There is not, however, much agreement on the valuation of leisure time. The costs of informal care can be assessed through the replacement approach, by assuming that a professional worker would have been hired had the lay person (i.e., caregiver) not been available. The last is thought to be the most consistent method with those used to estimate the other cost components since what is important is the type of activity provided to patients more than the nature of time (i.e., leisure or work) displaced [11].

Productivity Losses

Productivity costs measure production lost because of morbidity and mortality. The theoretical grounds on which productivity cost estimation can be traced to is the human capital approach (HCA). Expected future earnings are used on the assumption that they reflect the individual's potential contribution to the economy, or more precisely, that a worker's wage equals the value of his marginal product. Although its basic principles have been used at least since the seventeenth century, the substantial development of the HCA occurred in the early 1960s, at the time when interest among economists was turning to human resources as a neglected component of the US economy. The main work using the HCA in the health care field to evaluate the potential for growth was Mushkin's article "health as an investment."

The approach suggested by Mushkin is that of using earnings as a measure of labor product added. The rationale is that wages and salaries are paid in direct return for productive services and correspond to the individual's contribution to production. Adjustments were also made for those who were out from the labor market. The category that received more attention was that of housewives' services. Housewives' services were estimated on the basis of their corresponding value in the market, that is by using the replacement value approach. Another approach was that of the opportunity cost. It assumes the economic value of unpaid work to be at least as much as the wage rate that the same person would command in the market place. Basically, if a woman chooses housework over employment, the housework must be equal to or greater than the value of the employment. However, it was argued that this approach was inconsistent with that used to value the employed population where what one does is valued rather than what one could be doing [11].

13.3.2.4 Outcome Identification and Measurement

While the cost assessment is a common part of all three types of full economic evaluations, the differences rise in outcome identification and measurement [7]. In the following paragraphs we illustrate the main approaches to outcome measurement within each economic evaluation technique. For more comprehensive discussion on different techniques consult the reference textbook by Drummond et al. Methods for Economic Evaluation of Healthcare Programs, 2015.

Cost-Benefit Analysis (CBA)

The CBA is a full economic evaluation technique in which the measurement of costs and benefits takes place in monetary terms. If the benefits outweigh the costs—that is, if the net benefits are greater than zero—the health program is considered eligible for funding.

The particularly sensitive issue in the CBA relates to the identification and measurement of the benefits. There are two approaches. The first one identifies and measures the benefits based on the willingness to pay of consumers. The second identifies and measures the benefits of a technology or program in terms of resources freed up. In the latter case, technology costs (rising costs) are compared to savings (avoided costs). In this case, however, it is not strictly correct to refer to a cost-benefit analysis but to the analysis of rising and avoided costs.

The identification of the benefits according to the approach of the willingness to pay is based on the assumption that what matters are the preferences expressed by consumers and what they are willing to pay to receive the benefits of the good or service technology. The maximum amount of money that the consumer is willing to pay reveals the monetary utility value of the benefits obtained from consuming a certain good or service. With the approach of the willingness to pay, it is possible to measure the benefits of the technology also not strictly medical, such the ones—for example—related to the value of information, to the reduction of the state of anxiety and to the healthcare program delivery process (non-health benefits), and to the external benefits that relate substantially from knowing that it is possible to access to the technology when it is needed.

The willingness to pay is measured by estimating what would be the behavior of consumers in a hypothetical market: the contingent evaluation method. This is the case when a question is asked directly to individuals to estimate their willingness to pay to receive the benefits of a specific technology (e.g., assisted insemination) described in terms of a hypothetical scenario.

Once measured the benefits in monetary terms, these are compared with the costs of the technology and its introduction and implementation in the healthcare system. If the benefits outweigh the costs, the technology can eventually be funded because the community estimates its value greater than its costs, in other words the return on investment is greater than one. Conversely, if the monetary benefits are lower than cost, the technology should not be considered among those eligible for funding because it means that the community does not judge its benefits greater than its costs.

The CBA is an extremely attractive technique because it measures the value of benefits through individual preferences, but it is a technique also extremely complex and often poorly adapted to the healthcare context [8]. These are some of the reasons that make CBA less used in a HTA process.

Cost-Effectiveness Analysis (CEA)

As the CBA, the CEA also aims to identify, measure, and compare the costs and the results of health technologies. Unlike CBA, in the CEA the evaluation of the benefits is conducted on the basis of physical units (non-monetary), and the results are expressed in terms of "cost per unit of effectiveness." The rationale of the CEA is to maximize the benefits considering a budget constraint.

The aim of a CEA is to make a comparison between two or more technologies or programs using the same measure of effectiveness (e.g., number of life years gained). After choosing the unit for the measurement of effectiveness, it is possible that the level of effectiveness achieved by the various programs is identical (e.g., same number of life years gained). In this case, the CEA is called "cost-minimization analysis," and it is sufficient to assess and compare the costs of different programs by choosing the one—equally effective—having the lowest cost. The effectiveness of the programs should represent the survival of patients, measured, for example, in terms of life years gained. It should therefore be connected to a final outcome.

Once having estimated the cost and the effectiveness of technologies or health programs, the next step is to calculate the cost-effectiveness of the different programs and comparing them.

Let's suppose to compare costs and effectiveness of two programs: A and B, where A is the innovative program. Let's refer to C_A for costs related to program A and to C_B for costs related to program B. Analogously, the effectiveness of A is E_A and the effectiveness of B is E_B. From the comparison between programs it may emerge that:

1. The costs for A are greater than the costs for B and the effectiveness of A is less than B ($C_A > C_B$; $E_A < E_B$). In this case the program A is dominated by program B and the new program A will have to be discarded;

2. The costs for A are less than the costs for B and the effectiveness of A is greater than B ($C_A < C_B$; $E_A > E_B$). In this case the program A is defined as "cost-saving," i.e., program A frees resources, making them available for alternative purposes and program B must be abandoned;
3. Program A costs are greater than the costs of program B and the efficacy of program A is greater than B ($C_A > C_B$; $E_A > E_B$). In this case the calculation of the incremental cost-effectiveness ratio is requested.

The incremental cost-effectiveness ratio is obtained by calculating the difference in costs divided by the difference in effectiveness. Once calculated the cost-effectiveness, the next question is whether the program is eligible for funding. To answer to this question it is necessary to distinguish between mutually exclusive and non-mutually exclusive programs. The first group includes programs intended to replace the comparison program (e.g., two alternative drugs for the treatment of hypertension); the second group includes independent programs, i.e., they can be activated within the limits of financial budget. In the first case, the incremental cost-effectiveness ratio can be used as a decision rule on the admissibility of the program funding, evaluating it in relation with an acceptability threshold value. The threshold value can be identified, for example, by analyzing past investment decisions. Programs with an incremental cost-effectiveness ratio lower than the threshold value would be defined as eligible for funding. In the second case, the programs—non-mutually exclusive—are ordered according to the incremental cost-effectiveness ratio, starting from the one with the lower value up to the program with the highest ratio. In this case, the choice of programs to be funded will be dictated by resources availability, so programs whose total costs exhaust the available budget will be chosen.

Cost-Utility Analysis (CUA)

Cost-utility analysis (CUA) attempts to incorporate the dimension of quality of life into the measurement of benefits. Benefits are measured as "quality adjusted life years," or QALYs, in which the gain in expected lifespan resulting from an intervention is weighted by the quality of that life, as assessed through some type of systematic surveying of the affected (or general) population. Thus, an intervention that leads to a 10-year gain in life expectancy, but implies considerable pain during those years might be estimated to have a lower QALY than an intervention that results in only an 8-year gain in years, but with less pain during that period.

The outcomes of a program for a CUA are measured in QALYs, quality adjusted life years, a unit of measure that combines the quantitative and qualitative dimensions of life years gained by the patient. Since the quality of life is a function of the preferences of different individuals for different temporary or permanent health states, its value is calculated through "utilities" that represent individuals' preferences about their health states.

The QALY is a measure of the value of health outcomes which assigns to each period of time a weight (from 0 to 1) corresponding to the QoL during that period, where a weight of 1 corresponds to perfect health and a weight of 0 to death. It assumes that health is a function of length of life and quality of life, and combines these values into a single index number. To determine QALYs, one multiplies the utility value associated with a given state of health by the years lived in that state. A year of life lived in perfect health is worth 1 QALY (1 year of life × 1 utility value). A year of life lived in a state of less than perfect health is worth less than 1 QALY, for example, 1 year of life lived in a situation with utility 0.5 (e.g., bedridden, 1 year × 0.5 Utility) is assigned 0.5 QALYs. Similarly, half a year lived in perfect health is equivalent to 0.5 QALYs (0.5 years × 1 utility). Death is assigned a value of 0 QALYs, and in some circumstances it is possible to accrue negative QALYs to reflect health states deemed worse than dead.

The utility values between 0 and 1 are usually determined by the following methods:

a. Rating scale or visual analogue scale (VAS): Respondents are asked to rate a state of ill health on a scale from 0 to 100, with 0 representing being dead and 100 representing perfect health. This method has the advantage of being the easiest to ask, but is the most subjective.
b. Time-trade-off (TTO): Respondents are asked to choose between remaining in a state of ill health for a period of time, or being restored to perfect health but having a shorter life expectancy.
c. Standard gamble (SG): Respondents are asked to choose between remaining in a state of ill health for a period of time, or choosing a medical intervention which has a chance of either restoring them to perfect health or killing them.

Another way of determining the utility associated with a particular health state is to use standard descriptive systems such as the EuroQol Group's EQ-5D questionnaire, which categorizes health states according to five dimensions: mobility, self-care, usual activities (e.g., work, study, homework, or leisure activities), pain/discomfort, and anxiety/depression.

The CUA result is given by the incremental cost-utility ratio. Similarly, to the incremental cost-effectiveness ratio, also in this case for the interpretation of the incremental cost-utility it is necessary to use an acceptability threshold value as a comparison value. The basic hypothesis is that the incremental cost-utility ratio of the last program—including those currently used in clinical practice—is the threshold value, that is the economic value of a QALY beyond which the system is not prepared to allocate additional resources. The CEA and the CUA are the chosen techniques by policy makers because they measure the effects of new technologies on patients' health, considering whether survival or quality of life. However, the CUA is a technique that—for the methodological complexity that characterizes it—must be used only when the quality of life is really the discriminating element, and therefore decisive, for the technological innovation under investigation (i.e., cancer drugs).

The main advantages of QALYs can be summarized in:

- Provide a framework for valuing the health gains associated with interventions.
- Can be used to help guide priority settings.
- Combine estimates of both the extra length of life gained and the quality of extra life gained.
- Allow comparison of the effectiveness of one intervention for a problem with the effectiveness of another intervention for the same problem.
- Allow comparisons across disease areas to help show which programs provide the greatest allocative efficiency.

The main criticisms of QALYs include:

- Values assigned to the quality of life component of the QALY may not reflect the values of patients receiving the intervention.
- Controversial—whose quality values should be used?
- May lack sensitivity within disease area.
- Can over-simplify complex healthcare issues and suggest "quick and easy" resource allocation decisions.

Although there is considerable debate about the optimal ways to assess the subjective "quality" dimension, analysts generally agree that QALYs are closer to the fundamental concept of health benefits than are the standard physical measures used in cost-effectiveness analysis.

13.3.2.5 Assessing Social, Legal, Ethical, and Organizational Implications

The ethical dimension is likewise important although often overlooked in the assessments of technologies. The introduction of new technologies can entail changes in the individuals' survival curve (e.g., maintaining in a vegetative health state) or faces individuals (e.g., therapeutic abortion in cases of congenital malformations detected through prenatal diagnosis) and society as a whole (e.g., artificial insemination programs) with choices that are ethical in nature and whose assessment should therefore also reconcile this dimension. The social dimension concerns the fact that a technology can be a good investment for the hospital or for the entire healthcare system, but gives rise to costs for others outside the system. A home care program, a process of de-institutionalization of psychiatric patients may induce costs for the family and the society that must be considered before providing a conclusive judgment about the introduction of the program.

Finally, the organizational dimension refers to the impact that technology has on the organization of the hospital or structure and the healthcare system as a whole. An effective technology may require space, procedures, and expertise that are not ready and not yet developed within healthcare structures, or alternatively may require a different balance between spaces and existing skills (e.g., technologies that can replace surgical interventions with no invasive interventions) which, however, cannot be achieved in the short and medium terms [12].

13.3.3 Synthesis, Dissemination, and Implementation of Policies

The evaluation process is not complete unless it is followed by the dissemination of the information generated. This phase aims to provide an overall framework to be used in the time of the decision on the adoption of a technology. It should include all the dimensions discussed above although it must be emphasized that the social and ethical dimensions are rarely considered.

It is important to distinguish between the assessment and the appraisal. The assessment is driven by scientific principles and conducted by rigorous methods and paves the way to the appraisal phase, i.e., the decision-makers' recommendations that is driven by political and social values. This implies that policy decisions in terms of coverage and reimbursement of technologies are evidence-based, which is a benefit per se. Examples of appraisals include issuing guidance, developing treatment protocols, and changing payment and/or procurement systems for hospitals or health professionals. In some countries, appraisals are also used to determine positive or negative lists of health technologies such as drugs and devices thus regulating patients' access to technological innovation based upon scientific considerations. Policy decisions based upon the HTA framework belong to the broader paradigm of value-based healthcare, i.e., the capacity (or necessity) in times of resource constraints, of healthcare systems and, more in general, governments to select and priorities only those technologies whose value offsets the costs [13].

13.4 Conclusions

In all major countries, health technology assessment has definitely become the predominant framework to be used to assess, select, and prioritize technologies in the healthcare sector [14]. If this originated from the increasing awareness of scarcity of resources by governments who had been struggling between financial constraints and populations' limitless, health needs, the HTA has now become even more relevant, and it is here to stay, because it is consistent with the more recent value-based healthcare paradigm. Regardless of budget availability, it is important to ascertain whether the benefits outweigh the costs of any technology, be it a device, a pharmaceutical, a mobile APP, or a procedure so to make it sure that any intervention does create and bring value to patients and to the healthcare system as a whole.

HTA has become so attractive and irrevocable that, besides singles countries, the European Commission has decided to make an important step ahead and has proposed a new Regulation on HTA to the European Parliament and the European Council aimed at centralizing the clinical assessment of innovative health technologies. If the Regulation will be passed and come to force, "Joint Clinical Assessments" will be carried out by a pool of experts drawn from different Member States whose recommendations will be binding for all Member States who, however, will still be in charge for deciding the economic implications in terms of coverage and reimbursement.

In view of this irreversible trend, it is, however, relevant to remember that HTA is made of two important parts: assessment and appraisal. In both cases, it is important that the players (i.e., researchers and policy makers) are sufficiently trained and skilled to carry out their own part so to make it sure that the results are soundly grounded in rigorous methods and actually aim at maximizing patients' health given available budgets. At this regard, specific training becomes of paramount importance and capacity building is advisable before HTA is spread in jurisdictions that are quite new in this field.

It must also be noted that not all technologies will and can be assessed through a formal HTA process. As we have seen, HTA requires resources (e.g., skilled researchers) whose cost must be worth allocating. The great majority of HTA Agencies across the world has defined a set of criteria to select the technologies that actually deserve to be assessed through a HTA process. For example, in the new Regulation on HTA, the European Commission has proposed to consider all new active substances and new therapeutic indications of those pharmaceuticals that are centrally authorized; the medical devices classified as class IIb and III (i.e., article 51 of Regulation (EU) 2017/745); in vitro diagnostic medical devices classified as class D (i.e., article 47 of Regulation (EU) 2017/746) and any additional device that responds to the following criteria: unmet medical needs, potential impact on patients, public health, and healthcare systems, significant cross-border dimension, and major union-wide added value.

HTA not only makes the resource allocation process more rational and transparent but also requires a collaborative approach among all relevant stakeholders. This means that the decision-making process has now become more pluralistic and takes into considerations the perspectives of previously neglected actors such as patients, the academia, and in some cases the industry. Although the final decisions will still be with policy makers, all other stakeholders have now the opportunity but also the responsibility of constructively participating to the process and to shaping the future of our healthcare systems.

References

1. Mossialos E, Le Grand J, editors. Health care and cost containment in the European Union. London: Ashgate; 1999.
2. Banta D. The development of health technology assessment. Health Policy. 2003;63:121–32.
3. Velasco-Garrido M, Busse R. Health technology assessment. An introduction to objectives, role of evidence, and structure in Europe. European Observatory on Healthcare Systems and Policies; 2005.
4. Office of Health Technology Assessment. Development of medical technology: opportunities for assessment. Washington: U.S. Government Printing Office; 1976.
5. Office of Health Technology Assessment. Development of medical technology: opportunities for assessment. Washington: U.S. Government Printing Office; 1978.
6. Quaglini S, Rognoni C, Spazzolini C, Priori SG, Mannarino S, Schwartz PJ. Cost-effectiveness of neonatal ECG screening for the long QT syndrome. Eur Heart J. 2006;27(15):1824–32.
7. Drummond MF, Scuplher M, Claxton K, Stoddart GL, Torrance GW. Methods for economic evaluation in health care. Oxford: Oxford University Press; 2015.

8. Tarricone R. Valutazioni economiche e management in sanità. Milano: McGraw-Hill; 2004.
9. Allen C, Beecham J. Costing services: ideals and reality. In Netten A, Beecham J. (eds) Costing community care. Ashgate, 1993.
10. Tarricone R, Torbica A. Costing and performance in healthcare management. In: Faltin FW, Kenett RS, Ruggeri F, editors. Statistical methods in healthcare. Hoboken: Wiley; 2012. p. 386–404.
11. Tarricone R. Cost-of-illness analysis—what room in health economics? Health Policy. 2006;77(1):51–63.
12. Drummond MF, Tarricone R, Torbica A. Economic evaluation of medical devices. Oxford research encyclopedia: economics and finance; 2018.
13. Drummond M, Tarricone R, Torbica A. Assessing the added value of health technologies: reconciling different perspectives. Value Health. 2013;16(1):S7–S13.
14. Ciani O, Torbica A, Tarricone R. Diffusion and use of health technology assessment in policy making: what lessons for decentralised healthcare systems? Health Policy. 2012;108(2–3):194–202.

14 Economic Modeling and Budget Impact Analysis in Abdominal Surgery: The Case of Mesh

Carla Rognoni

14.1 The Budget Impact Analysis (BIA)

The budget impact analysis (BIA) is increasingly demanded by regulators as an essential part of a comprehensive economic evaluation of a new healthcare intervention [1]. The purpose of a BIA is to estimate the consequences, in financial terms, of the adoption and diffusion of a new technology or treatment for a specific medical context. In particular, a BIA assesses whether a therapeutic choice, rather than another one, used for a given disease, can affect the healthcare expenditure related to this condition.

Given the intention of a BIA, the suggested perspective is that of the budget holder, who may be a single payer, responsible for the entire healthcare system, or a specific provider (e.g. hospital) or single patients or families. A BIA should be flexible to produce estimates that may include different combinations of healthcare or social services and costs, depending on the perspective considered. In this way, the BIA becomes a tool to show decision-makers the broader economic implications of the intervention and the impact on other budget holders.

Importantly, the BIA should be seen as complementary to the cost-effective analysis (CEA) and not as a substitute. The CEA estimates incremental costs and effectiveness of a new therapy, compared to the standard of care used in the clinical practice or to different alternatives; the BIA, however, estimates the impact of the use of resources and direct healthcare costs of the introduction of a new therapy.

The description of the health condition, its treatment and the eligible population are essential components of the analysis.

C. Rognoni (✉)
Centre for Research on Health and Social Care Management (CERGAS), SDA Bocconi School of Management, Bocconi University, Milan, Italy
e-mail: carla.rognoni@unibocconi.it

D. P. Greco, E. Borgonovi (eds.), *Abdominal Wall Surgery*,
https://doi.org/10.1007/978-3-030-02426-0_14

In a BIA, the considered population should be all patients eligible for the new intervention during the time horizon of interest. The estimation of the eligible population starts from the number of individuals covered by the approved treatment indication. The population is then considered "open" since it enters and remains in the analysis according to predefined inclusion criteria (e.g. presence of symptoms). The analysis may also be performed for population subgroups, defined for example according to age, gender, disease severity or comorbidities.

The purpose of a BIA is to realize a model of analysis that can help to understand the relationship between the characteristics of its own context and the possible consequences on the budget relating to the introduction of a new therapy or to the replacement of a therapy in use. In particular, a BIA compares a current scenario, which represents the current intervention mix for the eligible population, with a future scenario, which considers the introduction of a new intervention. The uptake of the new intervention is generally not known at the time of analysis and the same holds for the impact on the current intervention mix. Three types of changes can be envisaged: (1) substitution: the new intervention may replace one or more current interventions, (2) combination: the new intervention is added to current interventions mix and (3) expansion: the new intervention is added in situations where there is no active intervention.

Once the current and future scenarios are defined, their cost should be calculated. The costs are estimated by multiplying the yearly cost of each option by the proportion of the eligible population using that option and by the number of patients in the eligible population, taking into account subsequent yearly incident cohorts.

The impact of the new intervention on other cost components outside the healthcare system (e.g. patients' productivity losses) should not be generally included in a BIA, because these aspects are not usually important for the budget holder.

As regards the time perspective, the BIA considers a limited time horizon (1–5 years) since this is of interest for decision-makers, in relation to their programming activities; in general, in order to provide more complete information, the impact is assessed for the first year and then for the first years following the introduction. In cost-effectiveness analyses, the time horizon can also be extended to the whole life of the subjects when a chronic disease is under investigation.

Similar to the CEA, the budget impact assessments should then make explicit the assumptions underlying the models used, the information sources of the data and any rules for estimating the same; the evaluation must also include a sensitivity analysis and should highlight in a clear and distinct way the components of the expenditure, such as healthcare resource consumption and unit prices.

In general, the BIA models should present a sufficiently simple structure so that who use them can verify any changes related to modifications in assumptions and estimates.

Finally, the budget impact analyses should reflect as much as possible the characteristics of local areas not only epidemiologically but also of clinical practice and, most importantly, the unit costs of healthcare services, where these present a high variability. It is also important to try to populate the model with local data, although this is not always possible.

14.2 The Case of Mesh

In the last 20 years, abdominal wall surgery has undergone changes in the treatment of hernias. Many changes have been reported, but innovations have definitely improved with the introduction of prostheses, the so-called meshes. On the market, there are different types of prosthesis and the choice of the most suitable one can be performed among the following:

- Synthetic non-absorbable or partially absorbable meshes: are considered permanent implants and are used to provide everlasting reinforcement to the repaired hernia;
- Biosynthetic meshes: constitute a new class of materials which can be absorbed completely from the surrounding tissue over time;
- Biologic meshes: are able to "transform" themselves in the tissue with which they come in contact. This regards layers obtained from animal tissues that after implantation are progressively replaced and "colonized" by the patient's cells, so as to disappear completely after having exercised their containment effect.

The synthetic non-absorbable materials or partially absorbable, when are implanted in the tissues, being extremely compatible with them, act as foreign bodies creating a scar reaction around the prosthesis itself. These materials are successfully used in the treatment of abdominal wall hernias, leading to a low risk of recurrence.

Biological and biosynthetic tissues are the result of the most recent studies in the field and are called re-shareable, because after their implantation they are replaced, through a process of incorporation, by a new tissue formed in the site where the prosthesis is inserted and has the anatomical and functional characteristics of the original one: in the patient, there is no trace of the prosthesis, but a "new" tissue is regenerated. Biological and biosynthetic meshes are now broadly used in cases of abdominal wall hernias associated with infections, but their use in clinical practice is still limited since there are no scientific evidence that demonstrate their effectiveness after many years from surgery.

The considerable variety of materials and surgical techniques gives the surgeon the opportunity to choose the most appropriate technology for the individual patient, according to a "tailored surgery" approach.

The materials used to close the abdominal wall incisions and the surgical technique applied are of utmost importance to avoid a high frequency of incisional hernias.

With the development of newer prosthetics and approaches for hernia repair, it is nevertheless difficult to understand the total cost involved in the use of these advanced medical devices. Recently, Gillion and colleagues [2] performed a systematic literature review and highlighted that there is lack of studies evaluating the cost of incisional hernia repair: significant heterogeneity in time periods, surgical approaches and cost items considered by few published studies make it challenging to perform a quantitative evaluation. The same authors performed a cost analysis in

France considering both direct and indirect costs; direct costs included all consumption of resources resulting from the treatment, while indirect costs were those related to the outpatient care during the sick leave, but mainly related to the inability to work, such as the costs of a replacement, the productivity loss and the costs of the daily allowance. Direct costs were estimated from a cost analysis performed in 2011 among public hospitals, while the sick leave and the inability to work (including the hospital stay) were estimated using data extracted from a prospective registry on abdominal wall hernias. The weighted average direct cost of a "mean" incisional hernia repair resulted 4731€ (range 3497€–16,367€ according to the severity level). The mean total cost for an incisional hernia repair in France, taking into account both direct and indirect costs, was estimated to be 6451€, ranging from 4731€ for unemployed patients to 10,107€ for employed patients whose indirect costs were slightly higher than the direct costs. This study gives estimates of the total cost of incisional hernia repair in a European country but the analysis is limited to the surgical intervention and no information is reported on costs sustained in the follow-up for the management of complications.

The aim of the present analysis is to develop knowledge about the clinical and economic implications that can support the "stakeholders" in an Italian hospital in the overall evaluation of the choices related to the prostheses offered to patients with abdominal incisional hernia. The evaluation takes into account different aspects of the management of patients undergoing incisional hernia repair, including the approaches for the management of different complications.

14.3 Methods

The research main objective is to perform a BIA to estimate the current economic impact of the management of patients with incisional abdominal hernia through biosynthetic mesh implants, synthetic or biologic meshes, from the hospital perspective in Italy [3]. As regards biosynthetic meshes, we referred to poly-4-hydroxybutyrate (P4HB) resorbable meshes. The BIA is also performed to evaluate changes in the hospital budget considering a future scenario with increased utilization rates of biosynthetic meshes in the next 5 years.

The clinical efficacy for the three types of devices was derived from the published literature. In particular, a literature review has been performed in December 2016 to retrieve clinical studies reporting complications related to the use of biologic, biosynthetic and synthetic meshes in complex abdominal wall repair.

The Ventral Hernia Working Group (VHWG) developed a 4-level grading system to classify patients according to the risk of developing a surgical site occurrence based on patient and wound characteristics (grade 1 = low risk, grade 2 = comorbid, grade 3 = potentially contaminated and grade 4 = infected) [4]. Another classification, according to Centers for Disease Control and Prevention (CDC), considers a different risk classification: class I (clean), class II (clean-contaminated), class III (contaminated) or class IV (dirty-infected) [5]. For our analysis, we considered studies on patients reporting grade 1–2–3 of both VHWG and CDC classifications since this is the context in which clinicians generally perform the choice among the different types of prostheses. Only studies with at least 18 months of follow-up (mean or median) were considered.

For the three types of meshes, weighted frequencies have been calculated for the different complications, taking into account the number of patients involved [6–17] (Table 14.1).

Cost data were estimated based on the use of specific healthcare resources for main repair and for the management of the main complications. As the analysis was performed from the hospital perspective, all costs related to the consumption of hospital direct healthcare resources were estimated and expressed in Euro (2017 value).

Clinical pathways and healthcare resource consumption for the management of complications were estimated by a study-specific questionnaire administered to key opinion leaders in the field, with great experience on mesh implants, belonging to 12 Italian hospitals. All the clinicians received an electronic version of the questionnaire between January and February 2017. The questionnaire included different sections: (1) relevant exams, lab tests, visits, drugs and surgical materials related to hernia repair intervention, with personnel time for the different figures involved in the healthcare services and in the surgical activity; (2) costs for drugs and surgical materials, including meshes; (3) exams, lab tests, visits, drugs, negative-pressure wound therapy and hospitalizations for the management of main complications (recurrence, infected mesh removal, infection—superficial, deep, organ space—and seroma) and (4) a forecast of possible future scenarios (1, 3 and 5 years) of utilization of the different types of meshes in Italy.

The results from the questionnaires were summarized to estimate healthcare resource utilization. For each healthcare item (exam, visit, hospitalization, etc.) reported, a weighted mean was calculated on the basis of the number of responders. Hospital costs were associated to the different healthcare resources. During the hospital stays for the management of complications, the DRG reimbursement has been considered a proxy of the hospital cost.

The model was integrated with epidemiological data (40,000 incisional hernia per year) [18] to perform a BIA comparing the current scenario with 60%, 10% and 30% utilization rates for synthetic, biosynthetic and biologic meshes, respectively, with future hypothetical scenarios considering increasing utilization rates of biosynthetic meshes, in place of the other types of mesh, in the next 5 years, as reported by the key opinion leaders.

Table 14.1 Summary of the different complication rates for the three kinds of meshes

	Synthetic mesh (%)	Biologic mesh (%)	Biosynthetic mesh (%)
Recurrence	15.2	8.0	5.4
Infected mesh removal	12.5	4.6	–
Superficial infection	8.0	15.1	12.0
Deep infection	4.4	6.1	8.0
Organ space infection	3.4	2.4	–
Seroma	3.5	12.9	4.0

The cost of the current and new scenarios was determined by multiplying the cost for each strategy by the proportion of the eligible population using it, taking into account subsequent yearly incident cohorts. Financial streams were presented as undiscounted costs, since the focus of the analysis was expected budget at each point [1].

14.4 Results

Eight of 12 clinical centres, completed the questionnaire, representing institutions with the highest volumes of treated patients in Italy.

Costs related to the healthcare resource consumption are summarized in Fig. 14.1, while Fig. 14.2 reports the mean cost per patient for the surgical intervention, for the mesh and for the management of complications (weighted according with complication frequencies reported in Table 14.1). The mean overall cost per patient resulted 3838€, 7531€ and 3949€ for synthetic mesh, biologic mesh and biosynthetic mesh, respectively.

The BIA was performed comparing the current scenario with future hypothetical scenarios considering increasing utilization rates of biosynthetic meshes of 25%, 38% and 44% in the next 1, 3 and 5 years, as estimated by the clinicians.

Considering 40,000 incisional hernia repairs per year, an increasing use of biosynthetic meshes, and P4HB resorbable meshes in particular, may result in a decrease of the total hospital budget of about 140 million Euros in the next 5 years (Fig. 14.3), showing a saving per patient of about 700€ in the same time horizon.

14.5 Conclusions

Surgical repair with prosthesis implants is considered the choice method for the management of patients with incisional hernia. Patients undergoing incisional hernia repair impose a significant financial burden on the healthcare system, since complications such as recurrence or infections may develop and result in further hospitalizations and morbidity. Although several prostheses with different characteristics are available, there is currently no solid consensus on the type of mesh that is best. In the literature, studies report contrasting results. For example, if from one side the Ventral Hernia Working Group clinical recommendations endorse biological meshes for clean-contaminated fields [4], on the other side, the study by Fischer and colleagues [9] showed that a synthetic mesh may be more cost-effective than an acellular dermal matrix in the same clinical setting.

The present study showed that an increasing use of biosynthetic prostheses can result in a saving per patient of approximately € 700 over the next 5 years. This result should be considered with caution because the study has few limitations. First, we considered P4HB resorbable meshes as a proxy for all biosynthetic meshes and this could be a limitation because different biosynthetic meshes have different characteristics and may have different outcomes in terms of complication rates.

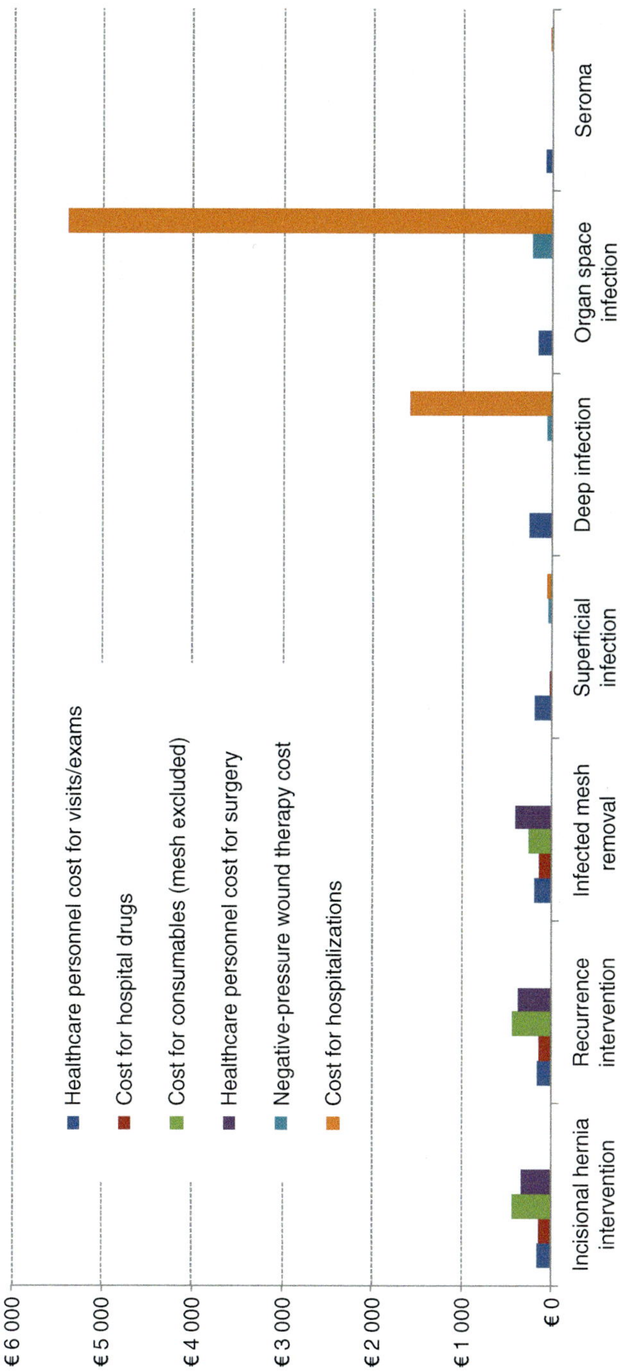

Fig. 14.1 Summary for the main cost items (costs are intended as mean cost per patient)

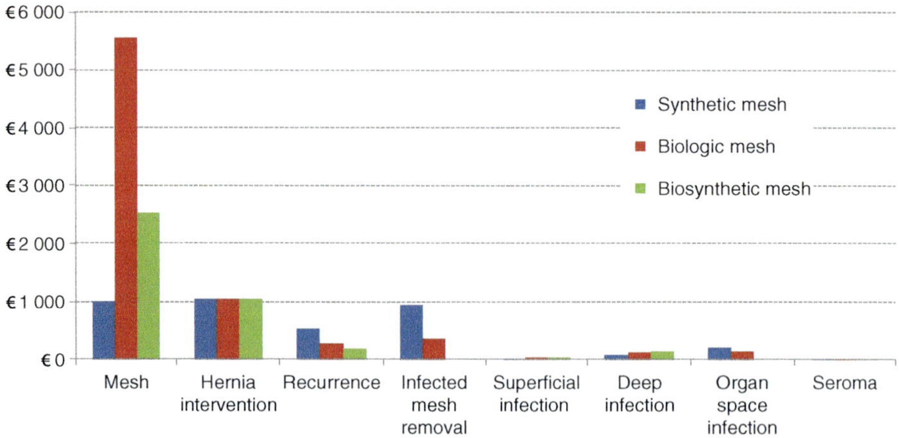

Fig. 14.2 Summary of mean costs for patient management for the different types of mesh

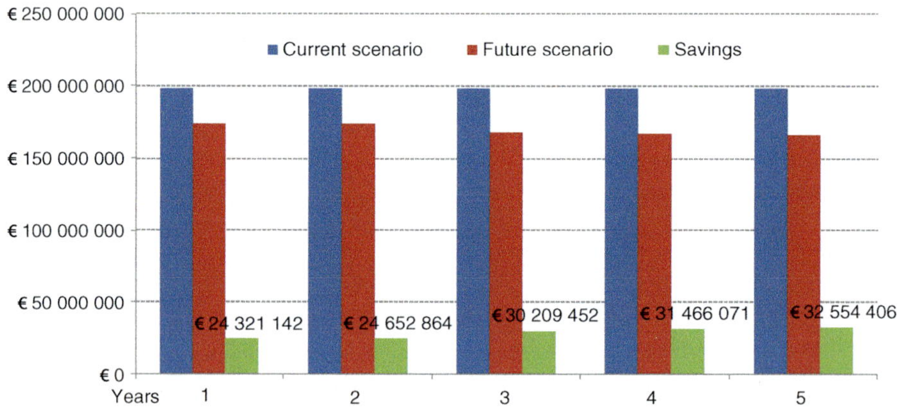

Fig. 14.3 BIA results: savings in comparison to current scenario at different years

Moreover, complication rates were obtained from a limited number of studies (only two that included biosynthetic meshes) with different lengths of follow-up (18–61 months), number of patients (25–428) and combination of levels of severity of the patients. In addition, the event rates varied between the studies, and the calculated weighted means may not completely represent the Italian setting.

As regards the estimation of the healthcare resources, it must be noted that data derived from self-reported questionnaires may be limited by varying recollection and poor generalizability. Moreover, the BIA model results are conditioned by the high future utilization rates of biosynthetic meshes over the other types of prostheses, as estimated by the clinicians. Lower future utilization frequencies may lead to more limited savings for the national healthcare service. Data derived from prospective observational multicentre studies would increase the validity of the current model. Moreover, observational studies in addition to RCTs would also provide a confirmation of the clinical evidence of the comparative effectiveness of the different meshes.

The analysis focused only on the hospital perspective. The study by Gillion and colleagues, already described above [2], showed that indirect costs represent more than 50% of the total cost for some patient categories. This suggests that a broader analysis considering the societal perspective would give supplementary information on the sustainability of these medical devices.

Considering the paucity of cost (and cost-effectiveness) data for Italy, the present budget impact analysis provides evidence about the clinical and economic advantages of the use of biosynthetic meshes but, at the same time, highlights the need for further data collection through studies or registries involving different types of meshes.

In the future, prospective randomized trials of different mesh materials, or registries, may offer a stronger level of recommendation. Ongoing and future cost-effectiveness and budget impact analyses taking into account the expense for materials, surgical procedures, potential complications and indirect costs would be greatly valuable to clinicians and policy makers.

Acknowledgements The author would like to thank Dr. Dalila Patrizia Greco for the support in the questionnaire development and the clinical expert group who provided clinical advice and data for the development of the model: Luigi Boccia and Francesco Di Lecce (ASST Mantova), Feliciano Crovella and Andrea Bassi (C.T.O.—Azienda Ospedaliera dei Colli, Napoli), Diego Cuccurullo (Ospedale Monaldi—Azienda Ospedaliera dei Colli, Napoli), Vincenzo Maria Greco (Policlinico S. Orsola Malpighi, Week Surgery, Sede di Budrio), Mauro Longoni and Giuseppe Faillace (Ospedale Cinisello Balsamo, Azienda ASST Nord Milano), Gennaro Nasti and Beatrice Di Venere (Presidio Ospedaliero Madonna delle Grazie, Matera), Micaela Piccoli and Vincenzo Trapani (Ospedale NOCSAE, Baggiovara, Modena) and Giorgio Soliani (Azienda Ospedaliero Universitaria di Ferrara).

References

1. Sullivan SD, Mauskopf JA, Augustovski F, Jaime Caro J, Lee KM, Minchin M, et al. Budget impact analysis-principles of good practice: report of the ISPOR 2012 budget impact analysis good practice II task force. Value Health. 2014;17(1):5–14.
2. Gillion JF, Sanders D, Miserez M, Muysoms F. The economic burden of incisional ventral hernia repair: a multicentric cost analysis. Hernia. 2016;20(6):819–30.
3. Rognoni C, Tarricone R. Budget impact analysis of incisional hernia repairs considering Poly-4-hydroxybutyrate resorbable meshes. Value Health. 2017;20(9):A596.
4. Ventral Hernia Working Group, Breuing K, Butler CE, et al. Incisional ventral hernias: review of the literature and recommendations regarding the grading and technique of repair. Surgery. 2010;148(3):544–58.
5. Horan TC, Gaynes RP, Martone WJ, et al. CDC definitions of nosocomial surgical site infections, 1992: a modification of CDC definitions of surgical wound infections. Infect Control Hosp Epidemiol. 1992;13:606e608.
6. Buell JF, Sigmon D, Ducoin C, et al. Initial experience with biologic polymer scaffold (Poly-4-hydroxybuturate) in complex abdominal wall reconstruction. Ann Surg. 2017;266(1):185–8.
7. Chand B, Indeck M, Needleman B, et al. A retrospective study evaluating the use of Permacol™ surgical implant in incisional and ventral hernia repair. Int J Surg. 2014;12(4):296–303.

8. De Noto G, Reaven N, Funk S. Ventral hernia: retrospective cost analysis of primary repair, repair with synthetic mesh, and repair with acellular xenograft implant. Open Access Surg. 2013;6:23–32.
9. Fischer JP, Basta MN, Wink JD, et al. Cost-utility analysis of the use of prophylactic mesh augmentation compared with primary fascial suture repair in patients at high risk for incisional hernia. Surgery. 2015;158(3):700–11.
10. Köhler G, Weitzendorfer M, Kalcher V, et al. Synthetic mesh repair for incisional hernia treatment in high-risk patients for surgical site occurrences. Am Surg. 2015;81(4):387–94.
11. Krpata DM, Blatnik JA, Novitsky YW, Rosen MJ. Evaluation of high-risk, comorbid patients undergoing open ventral hernia repair with synthetic mesh. Surgery. 2013;153(1):120–5.
12. Liang MK, Berger RL, Nguyen MT, et al. Outcomes with porcine acellular dermal matrix versus synthetic mesh and suture in complicated open ventral hernia repair. Surg Infect. 2014;15(5):506–12.
13. Majumder A, Winder JS Wen Y, et al. Comparative analysis of biologic versus synthetic mesh outcomes in contaminated hernia repairs. Surgery. 2016;160(4):828–38.
14. Novitsky YW, Fayezizadeh M, Majumder A, et al. Outcomes of posterior component separation with transversus abdominis muscle release and synthetic mesh sublay reinforcement. Ann Surg. 2016;264(2):226–32.
15. Novitsky YW, Towfigh S, Prabhu AS, et al. Prospective multicenter evaluation of ventral/incisional hernia repair with poly-4-hydroxybutyrate mesh (Phasix™). In: Abstract presented at AWR Conference. Washington; 2016.
16. Sbitany H, Kwon E, Chern H, et al. Outcomes analysis of biologic mesh use for Abdominal Wall reconstruction in clean-contaminated and contaminated ventral hernia repair. Ann Plast Surg. 2015;75(2):201–4.
17. Souza JM, Dumanian GA. Routine use of bioprosthetic mesh is not necessary: a retrospective review of 100 consecutive cases of intra-abdominal midweight polypropylene mesh for ventral hernia repair. Surgery. 2013;153(3):393–9.
18. Ipponi L, Gossetti F. Presentations at "impact of reimbursement system: case study on abdominal wall surgery" congress. Milan: Bocconi University; 2017.

Part III

Outcomes

How to Measure Outcomes in Surgery 15

Graziano Pernazza and Enrico Pernazza

15.1 Background

Historically, the concept of the value of a surgical procedure has been identified within a rather simple scheme. In the relationship between the surgeon, the patient, and the disease, the patient was the intermediate object. Patients were often identified by the disease and they were often the ground to measure the technical value of a surgeon.

The perceived value was about the procedure, the act itself, regardless of the result [1, 2].

Since the 1980s the scenario has progressively changed, not because of a change in the sequence of events, but owing to overlapping phenomena [3–5]. Every element of the relationship has undergone drastic modifications. In universalistic healthcare systems, the surgeon has abandoned the role of a "solitary hero" to become an element of an organic model. The disease has become a more complex entity: the "surgical disease" is increasingly being treated by a multidisciplinary approach, based on diagnostic-therapeutic protocols and assistential pathways), guidelines, and appropriateness criteria [6–12].

Moreover, the concept of the patient has changed, from being an object, to becoming the main actor of the care process, in an "empowerment" pathway that involves a conscious acceptance of the proposed treatment, the evaluation of alternative options, and the final outcome evaluation [13, 14].

In this environment we have moved from the strict value of the surgical act to a more extensive value of surgical "performance". The qualifying elements include

G. Pernazza
Department of Surgery, General and Robotic Surgery Unit, AO San Giovanni-Addolorata, Rome, Italy

E. Pernazza (✉)
TIISO Interprofessional Interdisciplinary Table for Operating Room Safety, Rome, Italy

D. P. Greco, E. Borgonovi (eds.), *Abdominal Wall Surgery*,
https://doi.org/10.1007/978-3-030-02426-0_15

admission and discharge criteria, information and consent, safety and hygiene, clinical organization, and technological innovation.

The introduction of the Diagnosis-Related Groups (DRG) system [15] has codified the value of healthcare provision in financial terms.

Probably, the relevance of the financial aspect itself has generated opportunistic behavior. In private hospitals the procedure coding was occasionally aimed at generating more profitable DRG, while selecting, in public hospitals, the most rewarding DRG, with the result being, in times of serious economic crisis, on the one hand, to foreclose access to treatment for patients with diseases with a weaker DRG, and, on the other, to favor high-cost procedures which often do not find financial equilibrium in the related DRG fare.

We are therefore facing the expressed objective value of the performance, affected by all the distortions we have mentioned above, and the *perceived value*, each with different perspectives: the patient's perspective, which is greatly enhanced by "taking care" (the ability of the facility to assist the patient in all phases of the illness, including correct procedures in the scheduling and counseling process); the healthcare system's perspective (based on appropriateness, efficiency, and resource rationalization); and the professional's perspective (looking for the availability of innovative technologies), even including efforts to provide an internal "benchmarking" system [16–21].

15.2 Assessing the Value of Surgical Treatment

Given that all human activities are aimed at creating value, *how can we correctly measure the value of surgical treatment*?

Highly professional services, which are essentially based on interpersonal relationships such as those between surgeon and patient, are affected by a paradox. On the one hand, they are entrusted to professionals whose qualification is considered high and who act, through the patient, directly on society. On the other hand, in the past, no effective measuring instruments were provided, nor was there any obligation for the professionals to provide transparency and accountability, perhaps with the implication being that society must be able to trust those who can claim the requisite qualifications at this level.

Ethical, fairness, and competence issues and issues related to the need to understand and be understood, to be accountable, and to clearly assume all the responsibilities in the professional field, as well as issues related to the substantial litigation in the medical and, specifically, surgical field, risk throwing a dark shadow on the professional skills and the social relevance of the surgical profession.

The recent introduction of outcome measurement tools (Programma Nazionale Esiti [PNE] by Agenas [The National Agency for Regional Health Services]) in Italy has certainly been a dramatic change to defeat the prevailing self-referentiality and to reveal the reality and make performance evaluation homogeneous. The endpoint is certainly not to create competition within the healthcare system, but to establish a standard level of assistance to guarantee the best clinical results, considering the available resources.

Quality costs, but quality is not a cost. The social value of a treatment process is measured by the ability of the process to guarantee health to citizens, in a rigorous and uniform way.

15.3 How to Measure the Value of Surgical Treatment?

The set of relationships among managers and doctors, decision makers and managers, and structures and citizens must be outlined in the health organization to enable everyone involved to be able to report about their activity, to realize the concept of "accountability". This is the proper and inalienable element of these relationships.

The consequent measurement/evaluation process, carried out with the appropriate technical tools (such as indicators and standards) provides the foundation for actions to improve the organization.

The fundamental tools for properly measuring and evaluating a system/organization are, essentially, indicators and standards.

15.3.1 Tools

15.3.1.1 Indicators

Indicators are synthetic measures that aim to best describe a system/organization with the least possible number of elements. They help us to "understand" systems or organizations, to compare them with others (benchmark) and to improve them (The Good Indicators Guide 2008) [19, 22–25].

Basically, there are three levels of use for the proposed indicators:

1. Quality improvement
2. Accountability
3. Research.

The explored dimensions are:

1. The "facility-process-outcome" relationship
2. The "technical-organizational-perceived quality" relationship.

In the first relationship, "facility" means all the available resources; "process" means the set of interventions carried out, with their ideal characteristics; and "outcome" means the effect of activities on the wellbeing of the users [12, 26].

In the second relationship, "technical quality" is the set of *appropriateness*, *effectiveness* (experimental "efficacy" and practice "effectiveness"), *patient safety*, and *adherence to guidelines*; "organizational quality" is *efficiency and integration between business processes*; "perceived quality" is communication, the patient's right to be informed, humanization, respect for and attention to the patient, simplification, environmental comfort, and accommodation services.

15.3.1.2 Standard

The term "standard" comes from the Old French "estendart" (meaning "banner"). The term "standard" may have different meanings:

1. Threshold level or acceptable threshold;
2. Value, model, reference to which a comparative judgment can be expressed;
3. Requirement or acceptable level of an organization or an individual.

The "standard" is a widely accepted reference model, because it conforms to experimental observations, although it is not necessarily complete or coherent, so new experimental results can lead to corrections or extensions of the model.

"Gold standard" is a technical term to indicate a material, a drug, a specific examination, or a medical or surgical treatment that is the most reliable at the time of definition.

15.3.1.3 How to Measure and Why?

Once the instruments have been examined, we must answer the inevitable question: What do we measure?

We certainly know that:

1. Indicators do not measure quality
2. Quality is a value-based concept
3. To switch from measurement to quality, an evaluation model is needed.

We therefore think it is fair to believe that, if a performance measure is generic and potentially universal, then performance assessment, not only in the Italian system, should be local or regional.

We have plenty of data ... but who looks at the data?

We know that 45.4% of doctors do not receive patient safety data, while 34.4% of doctors do not talk about data with other doctors [27].

"Data become information when they are capable to modify the probability of decisions"; that is, when the data lead to changes in decisions, or at least to the possibility of making changes in decisions [28, 29].

Authors who have dealt with the issue of how to maintain and improve performance quality have emphasized that the possibility to dynamically "measure", to monitor the activity in progress, and to direct the changes, is an essential tool.

"Measuring without change is a waste. To change without measuring is foolhardy" [30].

And again, according to Berwick [31], to measure is essential, because, in the act of defining the measures, the objectives are clarified and because the measures are essential for deciding on whether to continue doing what you do or whether you have to change. Measures are also essential to assess whether it is worthwhile to introduce an innovation.

The first issue, therefore, is not to "explain" measures to the public or to the "buyers", but to the managers!

The second issue, even more relevant, is to train all healthcare professionals, especially surgeons, to question themselves, because "Everyone wants measures, but nobody wants to be measured" (Deming).

The aim should be to stimulate professionals by enhancing their role and the knowledge that their skills are essential for the development of a health organization, since a positive relationship between the level of professionals' involvement and the quality of observed clinical performance is now evident.

15.4 International Environment

15.4.1 International Quality Indicator Project (IQIP)

In the United States, the attention to "clinical performance" issues dates back to the early 1980s. In 1985, in the state of Maryland, a pilot project called the "Quality Indicator Project" took place, on the initiative of some hospitals that wanted to integrate their economic and clinical performance data [32].

Subsequently, the project involved many institutions throughout the United States and after 1992 other institutions joined from abroad, with the total reaching about 600 hospitals. About 250 of them were outside the United States (Great Britain, Taiwan, Portugal, Austria, Germany, Italy, Switzerland, Japan, Singapore, Ireland, Luxembourg), and the project evolved into the International Quality Indicator Project (IQIP).

The IQIP is the largest international project and database related to clinical outcome and performance indicators. Compared with other systems of indicators used in the Italian healthcare field, the IQIP project allows each hospital, by virtue of the high number of participants worldwide, to evaluate, for each chosen indicator, its positioning compared with the national average, the European average, and the international average, both with respect to groups of structures, selected on the basis of having characteristics similar to their own ("peer groups"). https://www.ihciqip.com/.

15.4.2 Agency for Healthcare Research and Quality (AHRQ)

Recently, the United States Government set up a new data bank through the Agency for Healthcare Research and Quality (AHRQ); this data bank includes indicators that pass a rigorous filter selecting the best ones based on their methodological quality and detectability. Another organization, the National Quality Measures Clearinghouse, contains many quality indicators of clinical and screening services, derived from those proposed by seven different American agencies.

The classification categories adopted are the following:

1. Accessibility
2. Assistential pathway
3. Outcome
4. Perceived quality.

They are mainly outcome (and volume) indicators that are linked to the SAS (statistical analysis system) query: a flexible system that allows organizations to achieve business objectives and to obtain the higher profit from the corporate information assets [33].

15.4.3 Joint Commission (JC)

The Joint Commission (JC) collects indicators for accreditation. These indicators do not allow the dynamic evaluation of current practice and are all about process flows; they are limited to 12 pathologies and their related areas of care [34].

15.4.4 Indicators in Various Countries

Under the acronym of AQUA (Institute for Applied Quality Improvement and Research in Health Care) there is a collection of mandatory indicators from many German hospitals. The indicators refer to 30 clinical-care areas with very high scientific and methodological levels. The values expressed throughout 2013 can be used as a standard.

In most countries, each health organization has developed its own set of indicators.

Australian indicators for hospital care and day hospital care are found in: Hospital Wide Medical Indicators—Australian Council on Healthcare Standards (ACHS) Care Evaluation Program (https://www.safetyandquality.gov.au/our-work/indicators/) [35].

The Joint Commission of Accreditation of Healthcare Organizations (JCAHO) has published the Core measures ORYX® project [36] when began including outcomes and other performance data into the accreditation process. Information gained allowed the Joint Commission to develop National Patient Safety Goals to promote specific improvements in patient safety.

Danish indicators are found at the Health Maintenance Organizations (HMO) [37] and NCQA (National Committee for Quality Assurance) website.

Performance indicators in the British National Health Service (NHS) can be found in details on their website [38].

15.5 Italian Scenario

The Italian Ministry of Health has published a "Training manual for clinical governance: performance monitoring" [39].

This is the fundamental document in which the new concepts for monitoring and evaluating performance are well indicated and defined; they do not exclusively concern professionals, but have assumed a systemic character, becoming fundamental elements of the system.

The following items, respectively, are included:

1. General principles and characteristics of performance evaluation
2. Evaluation criteria
3. Definition and selection of indicators
4. Purpose of the evaluation intended as a benchmark and as part of the clinical government models.

Finally, mention is made about the positive and negative effects that could follow the publication of the obtained results.

On the one hand, as documented by the literature, it is known that following the adoption of these initiatives in individual hospitals, greater attention has been paid to the quality of care, while on the other hand, the publication of results may lead to some negative effects, such as the adoption, by the professionals and services under evaluation, of opportunistic behaviors, e.g., the selection of favorable cases or a reduced motivation in individual professionals and teams.

15.5.1 National Outcome Evaluation Program (Programma Nazionale Esiti; PNE)

The PNE is an institutional activity of the Italian National Healthcare System (SSN-Sistema Sanitario Nazionale) and provides comparative assessments on the efficacy, safety, efficiency and quality of care produced within the country. PNE is developed by Agenas on behalf of the Ministry of Health. The first publication of data was made in March 2012 by Carlo Perucci, and the study has been subsequently conducted by Marina Davoli [40].

The goal of the project was clearly stated: "…PNE measures are assessment tools to support clinical and organizational auditing programs aimed at improving effectiveness and equity in the NHS. PNE does not produce rankings, judgments…". Nevertheless, PNE data have had a dramatic impact; unfortunately, the data have been used in a distorted way by the media, provoking a certain diffidence in healthcare professionals.

15.5.2 The Performance Evaluation System of Regional Health Systems

The Performance Evaluation System of the Regional Health Systems, developed by Sant'Anna School of Advanced Studies of Pisa, responds to the aim of providing each Italian Region with a method to measure, compare, and represent the level of its health supply. The Regional Health Systems Performance Evaluation System was activated in 2008, through the collaboration of four Regions: Tuscany, Liguria, Piedmont, and Umbria. In 2010 the following Regions were added: Valle d'Aosta, Marche, Autonomous Province of Trento and Bolzano and Marche. In 2011 the

Basilicata Region, in 2012 the Veneto Region, and in 2014 the Regions of Emilia Romagna and Friuli-Venezia Giulia were added. Since 2015, the Calabria Region, Lombardy, and Puglia have also joined.

An inter-regional sharing process has led to the selection of about 300 indicators, of which 150 are regarding evaluation and 150 are regarding observation, aimed at describing and comparing, through a benchmarking process, the different dimensions of the health system performance: the status of population health, ability to pursue regional strategies, health assessment, evaluation of user and employee experience, and, finally, the assessment of economic-financial dynamics and operational efficiency.

The results are represented by a target scheme, which offers an intuitive overview of the performance obtained by the region, immediately illustrating its strengths and weaknesses.

The indicators are elaborated at the regional and organization level; some regions also choose to process the data of their own hospital establishments and their districts. Since 2008, a report has been drawn up annually, with the results of the regions and organizations. Since 2010, the report has been made public and is accessible by all stakeholders. The regions participating in the network consider the transparency and accountability of their actions as value and make their results public.

15.5.3 Patient-Reported Outcome Measures (PROMs)

PROMs allow the integration of the outcome indicators, based on clinical evaluations, produced by health professionals with the assessments that the patients themselves express directly in regard to their own states of health. In this sense, the PROMs allow us to understand whether a specific treatment or intervention has made a difference for the patient, both in terms of specific and general health conditions, and in terms of quality of life.

The PROMs, in fact, are questionnaires that are able to collect different kinds of information. The multidimensionality of the PROMs allows us to grasp a wide range of aspects that includes symptoms, functionality, mental health/psychological distress, perception of one's own health, and health-related quality of life.

In order to produce a score, each parameter is measured using metrics that associate a value with the patient's responses.

In more detail, the questionnaires used for the collection of PROMs include standardized disease/condition-specific tools, which are designed to investigate the outcomes of a specific intervention or pathology, and generic tools, which are able to measure the quality of life and the state of health perceived by the patient. In recent years, the number of specific measures has grown exponentially, allowing the use of PROMs for the evaluation of outcomes produced in different care paths and numerous treatments, be they surgical, pharmacological, psychotherapeutic, rehabilitative, etc.

PROMs are usually accompanied by general questionnaires, such as the EuroQol five-dimensions questionnaire (EQ-5D) [41] and the short-form health survey

(SF-36) [42]. These are PROMs that measure well-being, quality of life, and perceived health status from the patients' point of view, regardless of their specific condition, pathology, and individual characteristics.

These tools are particularly useful for making comparisons between groups or aggregated levels, as in the case of clinical trials.

The method for administering PROMs is now subject to guidelines; these guidelines are aimed at standardizing the data collection procedures and are used to maximize the comparability between different clinical trials or observational studies, as well as the comparability between different health organizations or health systems within continuous PROMs collection systems.

15.6 Conclusion

Great progress has been made both in the definition of professional quality indicators and in the awareness of identifying these indicators in a complete, reproducible, and accurate way.

There are many differences between the indicators proposed by Mediobanca in the early 1990s [23] and those selected in the PNE of The National Agency for Regional Health Services (Agenas). A great contribution came from the adoption of evidence-based medicine, which oriented the definition of professional process indicators linked to health outcomes.

It is, however, always advisable to consider the difficulties in interpreting the values of the indicators, and, in particular, to note that differences in outcomes may be due not to differences in professional quality, but to errors in detection and/or coding, to random fluctuations, and to confounding factors, among which the most significant seems to be differences in the complexity of the cases. The importance of "verifying the quality and completeness of the database used, specifying the method of calculating the indicator, having more indicators and not basing decisions on a single value" [43] should always be kept in mind.

It should be stressed, however, that if these difficulties often make the comparison between different organizations problematic, they do not undermine their internal use in the worthy evaluation process for the continuous improvement of quality; if there are unfavorable values or those that worsen over time compared with values in similar organizations, actions of correction and improvement must be imposed.

The potential offered by the theoretical developments in the field of professional indicators and the more favorable orientation of the most "advanced" population of health professionals should lead to the use of information systems in the detection of data that allows the monitoring of not only productivity but also of other important aspects of professional quality.

However, we should think carefully about the opportunity to publicize data. Following the Australian example [35], it could be appropriate, in our country, to work toward getting approval for a law that protects "confidentiality" on adverse events and "near misses". The recent law n.24 08.03.2017 (so-called Gelli law) in Italy still seems to be an insufficient political answer from this point of view.

Regarding the often repeated analogy between the cockpit of a plane and an operating room, it should not be forgotten that one of the reasons for the rapid decrease in air accidents was the establishment of the Aviation Safety Reporting System. This is a system to which pilots and flight controllers can voluntarily communicate accidents and near accidents, with the absolute certainty of the absence of negative consequences for the professionals involved. If ministerial "incident reporting" in Italy is struggling dramatically to take off, perhaps, even in the pathway of prevention, quality, and safety, something has yet to change.

References

1. Ballard DJ. Indicatori per il miglioramento della qualità dell'assistenza clinica in un sistema sanitario integrato. QA. 2004;15(4):231–44.
2. Baraghini G, Trevisani B, Roli L. Le ISO 9000 in Sanità/la Vision. In: Per governare bisogni e richieste. Milano: Franco Angeli; 2001.
3. Reeve BB, Wyrwich KW, Wu AW, et al. ISOQOL recommends minimum standards for patient-reported outcome measures used in patient-centered outcomes and comparative effectiveness research. Qual Life Res. 2013;22:1889.
4. Curtis LH, Phelps CE, McDermott MP, et al. The value of patient-reported health status in predicting short-term outcomes after coronary artery bypass graft surgery. Med Care. 2002;40(11):1090–100.
5. Greenhalgh J. The applications of PROs in clinical practice: what are they, do they work, and why? Qual Life Res. 2009;18:115. https://doi.org/10.1007/s11136-008-9430-6.
6. Black N. Patient reported outcome measures could help transform healthcare. BMJ. 2013;346:f167.
7. Agency for Health Care Policy and Research. Using clinical practice guidelines to evaluate quality of care. 1. Issues. Rockville, MD: US Department of Health and Human Services, Public Health Services; 1995. (AHCPR publication No 95-0045.)
8. Arcà M, Fusco D, Barone AP, Perucci CA. Introduzione ai metodi di risk adjustment nella valutazione comparativa degli esiti. Epidemiol. Prev. 2006;30(4 Suppl):1–48.
9. Freeman T. Using performance indicators to improve health care quality in the public sector: a review of the literature. Health Serv Manag Res. 2002;15:126–37.
10. Grilli R, Ballini L. L'implementazione delle linee-guida: valore e limiti della ricerca sull'efficacia delle diverse strategie per orientare i comportamenti professionali. In: Liberati A, editor. La medicina basata sulle prove di efficacia. Roma: Il Pensiero Scientifico; 2004.
11. Gubb J. Have targets done more harm than good in the English NHS? Yes. BMJ. 2009;338:a3130.
12. Canadian Council on Health Services Accreditation. A guide to the development and use of performance indicators. Ottawa: CCHSA; 1996.
13. Marshall MN. Accountability and quality improvement: the role of report cards. Qual Health Care. 2001;10:67–8.
14. Oliver A, Brown LD. Incentivizing professionals and patients: a consideration in the context of the United Kingdom and the United States. J Health Polit Policy Law. 2011;36:59–87.
15. Piano Sanitario Nazionale 1994-1996 (D.P.R.1/3/94), par. 8.
16. Raleigh VS, Foot C. Getting the measure of quality. Opportunities and challenges. London: The King's Fund; 2010.
17. ACHS Care Evaluation Program. Internal medicine indicators. Sydney: The Royal Australian College of Physicians, ACHS; 1997.
18. Kazandjiian VA, Matthes N, Thomas T. Errors: can indicators measures the magnitude? J Eval Clin Prat. 2001;7:252–60.
19. Liva C. Le iniziative dell'Agenzia per i Servizi sanitari Regionali sugli indicatori di performance. Relazione tenuta al Convegno Internazionale "Introdurre gli indicatori di performance clinica nel sistema sanitario nazionale", Ferrara 20–22 novembre 2003. http://www.assr.it.

20. Morosini P, Palumbo G. Indicatori per l'accreditamento professionale e il benchmarking. In: Liva C, Di Stanislao F, editors. Accreditamento dei servizi sanitari in Italia. Torino: Centro Scientifico Editore; 1998.
21. Murray CJL, Salomon JA, Mathers CD, Lopez AD, editors. Summary Measures of Population Health: concepts, ethics, measurements and applications. Geneva: World Health Organization; 2002. http://www.who.int/health-systems-performance/docs.
22. The good indicators guide: Understanding how to use and choose indicators. Copyright © 2008 NHS Institute of Innovation and Improvement. http://www.apho.org.uk/resource/item.aspx?RID=44584.
23. Mediobanca. Indicatori per il controllo dell'efficienza e dell'economicità della spesa nel S.S.N. Milano: Mediobanca; 1993.
24. Solberg LI, Mosser G, McDonald S. The three faces of performance measurement: improvement, accountability and research. Jt Comm J Qual Improv. 1997;23:135–47.
25. Tommassini C, Turco L, Faraoni T, Mannacci A, Cecchi A, Nerattini M, Filomena A, Veneri F. IL progetto indicatori del presidio ospedaliero del Mugello – ASL 10 di Firenze. Relazione tenuta al Convegno Introduzione agli indicatori di performance clinica nel sistema sanitario, Ferrara 21–22 novembre 2003.
26. Donabedian A. The quality of healthcare assistance, vol. 1. Florence: NIS; 1990.
27. Scagliarini M, Apreda M, Wienand U, Valpiani G. Monitoring operating room turnaround time: a retrospective analysis. Int J Health Care Qual Assur. 2016;29(3):351–9.
28. Morosini P, Perraro F. Enciclopedia del Miglioramento Continuo di Qualità in Sanità. 2nd ed. Torino: Centro Scientifico Editore; 2001.
29. Morosini P, Palumbo G, editors. Variabilità nei servizi sanitari in Italia. Centro Scientifico Editore: Torino; 2004.
30. Berwick DM. Continuous improvement as an ideal in health care. N Engl J Med. 1989;320:53.
31. Berwick DM. A primer on leading the improvement of systems. BMJ. 1996;312:619–22.
32. Scheiderer KJ. The Maryland Quality Indicator Project: searching for opportunities for improvement. Top Health Inf Manage. 1995;15(4):26–30.
33. Inpatient Quality Indicators Technical Specifications - Version 5.0, March 2015. https://www.qualityindicators.ahrq.gov/Modules/IQI_TechSpec.aspx.
34. The Joint Commission Performance Measurement. https://www.jointcommission.org/performance_measurement.aspx.
35. Hospital Wide Medical Indicators—Australian Council on Healthcare Standards (ACHS) Care Evaluation Program. https://www.achs.org.au/programs-services/clinical-indicator-program/.
36. JCAHO. Managing performance measurement data in health care. Oakbrook Terrace, IL: Joint Commission; 2000.
37. Health Maintenance Organizations (HMO). http://www.pni.dk.
38. NHS Clinical Performance Indicators. https://www.gov.uk/government/publications/performance-management-of-nhs-a-e-services-using-theclinical-quality-indicators.
39. Ministero della Salute - DIPARTIMENTO DELLA PROGRAMMAZIONE E DELL'ORDINAMENTODEL SERVIZIO SANITARIO NAZIONALE DIREZIONE GENERALE DELLA PROGRAMMAZIONE SANITARIA Ufficio III ex DG.PROG. Manuale di formazione per il governo clinico: monitoraggio delle performance cliniche (2012). http://www.salute.gov.it/imgs/C_17_pubblicazioni_1984_allegato.pdf.
40. Fusco D, Barone AP, Sorge C, D'Ovidio M, Stafoggia M, Lallo A, Davoli M, Perucci CA. P. Re.Val.E.: outcome research program for the evaluation of health care quality in Lazio, Italy. BMC Health Serv Res. 12:25.
41. EuroQol Office Marten Meesweg 107 3068 AV Rotterdam, The Netherlands. https://euroqol.org.
42. RAND 1776 Main Street Santa Monica, CA 90401-3208. https://www.rand.org/healthcare/surveys_tools/mos/36-item-short-form.html.
43. Lattuada L, Burba I. Quali cautele sono consigliabili nell'interpretazione delle informazioni prodotte dagli indicatori? QA. 2004;15(4):277–85.

Suggested Readings

ACHS Care Evaluation Program. Hospital-wide medical indicators, version 6. Sydney: Australian Council on Healthcare Standards (ACHS); 1998.

AHRQ (Agency for Healthcare Research and Quality). CONQUEST overview: a computerised needs-oriented quality measurement evaluation system. Rockville, MD: CONQUEST; 1999. http://www.ahcpr.gov/qual/conquest.htm.

Altman DG, Machin D, Bryant TN, Gardner MJ. Statistics with confidence. 2nd ed. London: BMJ Publishing Group; 2000.

Atherton PJ, Sloan JA. Rising importance of patient-reported outcomes. Lancet Oncol. 2006;7:883–4.

Baker R, Fraser RC. Development of review criteria: linking guidelines and assessment of quality. BMJ. 1995;311:370–3.

Barbieri P, La Pietra L, Liva C. La qualità delle attività ospedaliere. Salute e Territorio. 2004a;144:186–92.

Barbieri P, Duca G, Liva C, La Pietra L. Gli indicatori di qualità per la valutazione dell'attività ospedaliera. Alcuni problemi metodologici. QA. 2004b;15(4):245–59.

Barletta C, Trotta MC, Gregori M, Barletta P, De Simone M. Efficacia degli indicatori in medicina di urgenza: strumento per migliorare la qualità della cure, indurre il cambiamento ed acquisire consapevolezza. Relazione al Convegno Internazionale "Introdurre gli indicatori di performance clinica nel sistema sanitario nazionale". Ferrara 20–22 novembre 2003.

Bellini P, Braga M, Rebba V, Rodella S, Vendrami E, editors. Indicatori per il monitoraggio e la valutazione dell'attività sanitaria. Atti del seminario organizzato dalla Commissione per la garanzia dell'informazione statistica, Roma, giugno 2002 (scaricabile dal sito https://www.palazzochigi.it/Presidenza/statistica/attitiva/rapporti).

Berti E, Grilli R. Practice guidelines and clinical governance: do the means match with the end? A quality appraisal of local practice guidelines. Clin Govern Int J. 2003;8(4):312–7.

Birnbaum D. Mandatory public reporting. Clin Govern Int J. 2008;13(2):142–6.

Browne J, Jamieson L, Lewsey J, van der Meulen J, Black N, Caims J, Lamping D, Smith, CL, Horrocks J. Patient reported outcome measures (PROMs) in elective surgery. Report to the Department of Health. 2007.

Campbell SM, Reeves D, Kontopantelis E, Sibbald B, Roland M. Effects of pay for performance on the quality of primary care in England. N Engl J Med. 2009;361:368–78.

Canadian Council on Health Services Accreditation. AIM achieving improved measurement accreditation. Ottawa: CCHSA; 2002.

Checkland K, Marshall M, Harrison S. Re-thinking accountability: trust versus confidence in medical practice. Qual Saf Health Care. 2004;13:130–5.

Cook DJ, Manning DM, Holland DE, et al. Patient engagement and reported outcomes in surgical recovery: effectiveness of an e-health platform. J Am Coll Surg. 2013;217(4):648–55.

Department of Health. NHS Performance Indicators: national figures 2002. London; 2003. vari documenti visibili nel sito in http://www.doh.gov.uk/nhsperformanceindicators

DH, Department of Health. Guidance on the routine collection of Patient Reported Outcome Measures (PROMs). 2008/9; NHS Operating Framework and 2009/10 Guidance on the Standard NHS Contract for Acute Services.

Feldman-Stewart D, Brundage MD. A conceptual framework for patient–provider communication: a tool in the PRO research tool box. Qual Life Res. 2009;18:109.

Frazzica RG, Giambelluca SE, Perraro F, Morosini P, Arnone R, Centineo G, Pinco M, Testaquadra S, Vancheri O. Miglioramento Continuo della Qualità negli ospedali in Sicilia. QA. 2002;13(3):142–53.

Goddard M, Jacobs DC. Using composite indicators to measure performance in health care. In: Smith PC, Mossialos E, Papanicolas I, Leatherman S, editors. Performance measurement for health system improvement. Experiences, challenges and prospects. Cambridge: Cambridge University Press; 2009. p. 339–68.

Gray M, Jani A. Promoting triple value healthcare in countries with universal healthcare. Healthc Pap. 2016;15(3):42–8.
Health Services Research Group University of Newcastle. Trends in quality of care. Clinical indicators. Sydney: ACHS (Australian Council on Healthcare Standards); 2002. p. 1998–2000.
Institute of Medicine. To err is human: building a safer health system. Washington, DC: National Academic Press; 1999.
Institute of Medicine. The quality chasm: a new health system for the 21st century. Washington, DC: National Academic Press; 2001.
Institute of Medicine. Priority areas for national action: transforming health care quality. Washington, DC: Institute of Medicine; 2003.
Jackson S. Il modello EFQM in sanità: guida ad una applicazione di successo. Torino: Centro Scientifico Editore; 2003.
James S, Daubert JC, Werf FV. Commentary: use of registries to investigate the past and develop the future. BMJ. 2011;342:d2826.
JCAHO. The measurement mandate. Oakbrook Terrace, IL: Joint Commission; 1993.
JCAHO. A guide to establishing programs for assessing outcomes in clinical settings. Oakbrook Terrace, IL: Joint Commission; 1994.
JCAHO. National library of healthcare indicators. Oakbrook Terrace, IL: Joint Commission; 1997.
Kazandjiian VA, Matthes N, Wicker KG. Are performance indicators generic? The international experience of the Quality Indicators Project. J Eval Clin Prat. 2003;9:265–76.
Le Grand J. The other invisible hand. Delivering public services through choice and competition. Princeton, NJ: Princeton University Press; 2007.
Macleod D, Clarke N. Engaging for success: enhancing performance through employee engagement. London: Department for Business, Innovation and Skills; 2009.
Mannion R, Davies HTO. Payment for performance in health care. BMJ. 2008;336:306–8.
Mathers CD, Sadana R, Salomon JA, Murray CJ, Lopez AD. Healthy life expectancy in 191 countries, 1999. Lancet. 2001;357:1685–91.
Mays N. Use of targets to improve health system performance: English NHS experience and implications for New Zealand. Working Paper 06/06. In: New Zealand Treasury; 2006.
McGlynn EA, Ash SM, Adams J, Keesey J, Hicks J, DeCristofaro A. The quality of health care delivered to adults in the United States. N Engl J Med. 2003;348:2635–45.
Montaguti U. Per raggiungere l' appropriatezza degli interventi serve una metodologia di gestione dei quadri clinici. Quaderni de Il Sole 35 Ore Sanità. 2003;3(5):7–12.
Morosini P. Nuove tendenze dell'accreditamento alla luce del sistema dell'accreditamento australiano. QA. 1992;2:13–22.
Morosini P. Griglie di valutazione in sanità. Torino: Centro Scientifico Editore; 2000.
NCQA (National Committee for Quality Assurance). 2001. HEDIS 2001. Vol. 2: Technical specifications; Vol. 3: Specifications for Survey Measures; Vol. 5: HEDIS compliance audit; Washington 2000L Street NW, NCQA. http://www.ncqa.org.
NQMC (National Quality Measures Clearinghouse). 2003. http://www.qualitymeasures.ahrq.gov/resources.
Ovretveit J. What are the best strategies for ensuring quality in hospitals? Copenhagen: WHO Regional Office for Europe; 2003.
Piergentili P, Focarile F. Indicatori sanitari per la qualità dell'assistenza sul territorio. Una guida pratica. QA. 2004;15(4):2676.
Rabin R, de Charro F. EQ-5D: a measure of health status from the EuroQol Group. Ann Med. 2001;33(5):337–43.
Rodella S, editor. Numero monografico: Indicatori di qualità dei servizi socio-sanitari. Salute e Territorio. 2004;144:138–200.
Rodella S, Maistrello M. Rassegna di esperienze internazionali. Salute e Territorio. 2004;144:140–56.
Shekelle PG, Lim YW, Mattke S, Damberg C. Does public release of performance results improve quality of care? London: The Health Foundation; 2008.

Shore DA. The trust crisis in health care. Causes, consequences, and cures. Oxford: Oxford University Press; 2007.

Smith PC. Performance measurement in health care: history, challenges and prospects. Public Money Manag. 2005;2005:213–20.

Snyder CF, Aaronson NK. Use of patient-reported outcomes in clinical practice. Lancet. 2009;374(9687):369–70.

Spurgeon P, Mazelan PM, Barwell F. Medical engagement: a crucial underpinning to organizational performance. Health Serv Manag Res. 2011;24:114–20.

Sussex J. Paying for better outcomes - the English way. J Health Serv Res Policy. 2009;14:131–2.

The Health Foundation. Are clinicians engaged in quality improvement? A review of the literature on healthcare professionals' views on quality improvement initiatives. London, The Health Foundation. 2011.

UNI (ente nazionale italiano di unificazione). Norma UNI EN ISO 9004:2001: sistemi di gestione per la qualità e linee guida per il miglioramento delle prestazioni. UNI, Via Battistotti Sassi 11b, 20133 Milano; 2000.

Veillard J, Champagne F, Klazinga N, Kazandijan V, Arah OA, Guisset A-L. A performance assessment framework for hospital: the WHO regional office for Europe PATH project. Int J Qual Health Care. 2005;17(6):487–96.

Wachter RM, Pronovost PJ. Balancing "no blame" with accountability in patient safety. N Engl J Med. 2009;361:1401–6.

WHO Regional Office for Europe. Measuring hospital performance to improve quality of care in Europe: a need for clarifying concepts and defining the main dimensions. 2003. http://www.euro.who.int/Document.

Present and Future of EBM in Inguinal Hernia Repair and Abdominal Wall Reconstruction

16

Umberto Bracale, Giovanni Merola, Cesare Stabilini, Maurizio Sodo, and Giuseppe Cavallaro

16.1 Introduction

Evidence-based medicine (EBM) means the adequate use of current, best scientific evidences in the process of decision-making about treatment of patients. Randomized controlled study (RCT) is conducted on patients that can prove the effectiveness of many procedures, as well as the loss and the effectiveness of others comparing with the best existing intervention [1]. However, RCTs have some limits because they represent complex studies with possible ethical issues and restrictions about its generalization. In 1979, a system of rating evidence (Table 16.1) was developed when determining the efficacy of a particular procedure [2]. RCT's and the meta-analysis of them represent the highest levels of evidence, and case series or expert opinions the lowest level. RCTs are given the highest level because they are designed to be unbiased and have less risk of systematic errors [2].

Subsequently, the recommendation levels to be disseminated in the scientific community were established, which are closely connected to the level of scientific evidence present in the literature (Table 16.2).

U. Bracale (✉) · G. Merola · M. Sodo
Department of Public Health, University "Federico II" of Naples, Naples, Italy
e-mail: sodo@unina.it

C. Stabilini
Department of Surgical Sciences and Integrated Diagnostics (DISC), University of Genoa, Genoa, Italy

G. Cavallaro
Department of Surgery "P. Valdoni", Sapienza University, Rome, Italy
e-mail: giuseppe.cavallaro@uniroma1.it

D. P. Greco, E. Borgonovi (eds.), *Abdominal Wall Surgery*,
https://doi.org/10.1007/978-3-030-02426-0_16

Table 16.1 Levels of evidence of papers

Level	Type of evidence
1A	Systematic review of RCTs
1B	Individual RCT (with narrow confidence intervals)
1C	All or none study
2A	Systematic review of cohort studies (with homogeneity of papers)
2B	Individual cohort study (also with low-quality RCT, e.g. high loss of pts at follow-up)
2C	"Outcomes" research; ecological studies
3A	Systematic review of case-control studies
3B	Individual case-control study
4	Case series (and poor quality cohort and case-control study)
5	Expert opinion without explicit critical appraisal or based on physiology bench research or "first principles"

Table 16.2 Grade practice recommendations

Grade	Descriptor	Qualifying evidence	Implications for practice
A	Strong recommendation	Level I evidence or consistent findings from multiple studies of levels II, III, or IV	Clinicians should follow a strong recommendation unless a clear and compelling rationale for an alternative approach is present
B	Recommendation	Levels II, III, or IV evidence and findings are generally consistent	Generally, clinicians should follow a recommendation but should remain alert to new information and sensitive to patient preferences
C	Option	Levels II, III, or IV evidence, but findings are inconsistent	Clinicians should be flexible in their decision-making regarding appropriate practice, although they may set bounds on alternatives; patient preference should have a substantial influencing role
D	Option	Level V evidence: little or no systematic empirical evidence	Clinicians should consider all options in their decision-making and be alert to new published evidence that clarifies the balance of benefit versus harm; patient preference should have a substantial influencing role

Inguinal hernia repair and abdominal wall reconstructions represent one of the most commonly performed surgical procedures worldwide. More than 348,000 ventral hernia repairs are performed in the USA each year [3]. In the same way, nearly 800,000 patients undergo surgery for inguinal hernia repair (IHR) in the USA each year [4]. However, both for IHR and for abdominal wall reconstruction (AWR), many different approaches and treatment indications were reported in the literature. Consequently, there is considerable heterogeneity in the levels of evidence of the various issues concerning this type of surgery.

In the following paragraphs, we intend to report both the issues with the high or moderate level of evidence and those that have not yet reached an adequate level. These last issues will represent the efforts of future scientific researches.

16.2 EBM in Inguinal Hernia Repair

Since 2009, the European Hernia Society (EHS), the International Endo Hernia Society (IEHS) and the European Association for Endoscopic Surgery (EAES) published guidelines covering all aspects of IHR in adult patients. More recently, these three societies decided to develop a universal set of guidelines for groin hernia treatment, reporting the international guidelines for groin hernia management by the HerniaSurge Group [5–7].

During this period, the level of evidences of many aspects regarding IHR have upgraded with consequent higher grade of recommendations. For other aspects, however, the level of evidence remained unchanged with the consequent impossibility of giving an adequate level of recommendation.

Among the issues that are achieving a high level of evidence, there is certainly that of the treatment for symptomatic and asymptomatic patients. It seems to be established with a moderate level of evidence that there is a low complication risk of incarceration and strangulation in asymptomatic or minimally symptomatic men with inguinal hernias [7]. With higher evidence, although most of these patients will develop symptoms and consequently need to be operated, watchful and waiting strategy could be safe. Nevertheless, there is not a clear consensus on recommending this strategy because of the lower morbidity of elective IHR against the higher one during an emergency setting [7].

Regarding the most suitable inguinal hernia repair technique, many efforts have been made without reaching a consensus. It seems to be moderately recommended the use of Shouldice technique in non-mesh inguinal hernia repair [7]. However, this recommendation does not seem to be fully sharable since today there are no studies that have directly compared the Shouldice technique with the Desarda technique, which is one of the most used ones in Asian countries in case of non-mesh repair.

Similarly, the EHS guidelines recommend the use of Lichtenstein technique as the best mesh treatment option in case of symptomatic unilateral hernia in an adult man [5]. The more recent international guidelines for groin hernia seem to overpass this recommendation. They didn't recommend three-dimensional implants (like plug-and-patch) because of the excessive use of foreign materials [7]. Moreover, they suggested a laparo-endoscopic technique for male patient with a primary unilateral hernia. They justified this because of the lower post-operative and chronic pain incidence for mini-invasive approach [7]. This recommendation seems to be influenced by the largest number of studies carried out by institutions, which have high experience in the mini-invasive treatment. The use of laparoscopic approach is strongly recommended also in case of inguinal or femoral hernia repair in women as well as in case of recurrent hernia after a prior anterior approach.

In our opinion, the wide use of a laparo-endoscopic approach cannot be so easily generalized, considering that the spread of laparoscopic surgery in many countries is still limited. Probably for this reason, the HerniaSurge Group sets this recommendation provided that a surgeon with a specific expertise and sufficient resource are available. Moreover, they reported that there are patients and hernia characteristic that warrant a Lichtenstein as first choice treatment [7]. In this way, it has been enshrined the concept of "tailored" treatment which is affected by many factors such as surgeon expertise, local and national resource, patient comorbidity, contra-indication to general anaesthesia, primary or recurrent hernia, unilateral or bilateral hernia, reducibility and emergency situation.

Moreover, the debate about the best technique between TAPP and Tep techniques would seem to be solved, thanks to the publication of some high evidence level paper on this issue. The spread of these techniques seems to be connected to a different historical diffusion in different country more than a real advantage of one over the other. This is the case of a wide adoption of Tep repair in the UK as well as the wide spread of TAPP in France, Germany or Italy.

However, both techniques have gained similar results when performed by skilled surgeons [8].

Another debating issue concerns about the existence of an ideal mesh. Today, it seems widely accepted that an ideal mesh does not exist. It is recommended that hernia surgeons would be aware about the characteristics of the mesh that they used. In future, it would be useful to investigate not only characteristics such as lightweight (LWM) and heavyweight (HWM) as classification criteria but also to specify the grade of porosity and the type of polymer of which the prosthesis is made.

Another key point of the future research concerns the type of fixation in different techniques. The recommendation to use an atraumatic mesh fixation system in an open anterior repair seems to be weak. In the same way, the IHES recommends during a TAPP to not use tacks as methods of fixation except in cases of large direct defects. They suggest to not use any type of fixation during a Tep procedure and to use a fibrin sealant in case of TAPP [6].

About perioperative procedural steps, subject that would seem to be enshrined is the role of antibiotic prophylaxis during an open repair. In high-risk patient, it is strongly recommended. In contrast, with a lower grade it is not recommended to any patients in any risk environment during a laparoscopic repair [7].

In the same way, local anaesthesia is recommended for open repair of reducible inguinal hernias, provided that surgeons or anaesthesiologists are confident with local anaesthesia use. It seems to be associated with early hospital discharge and lower incidence of urinary retention as well as a higher hernia recurrence rate when inexperienced surgeons administer it. The International Hernia Guidelines suggested the use of local or general anaesthesia in patients aged over 65 years because of the higher risk of general complications related to regional anaesthesia [7].

Another important issue that was highly debating during last years is the chronic pain and its prevention and management. The International Association for the Study of Pain defines it as pain lasting more than 3 months [9]. Some authors extend the period from 3 to 6 months.

The incidence of clinically significant chronic pain is around 10–12%, decreasing over time [10, 11]. Debilitating chronic pain affecting normal daily activities ranges from 0.5 to 6% [11].

Many risk factors for chronic pain post-inguinal hernia repair were recognized: young age, female gender and post-operative pain intensity [6].

However, other factors could be inexperience of surgeon as well as inadequate knowledge of inguinal anatomy rather than the wrong use of mesh fixation tools.

Nerve anatomy recognition and awareness is recommended during inguinal hernia surgery, and the planned neurectomy seems to not reduce chronic pain incidence but rather increases the incidence of post-operative sensitivity loss. Only in case of iatrogenic injury, the nerve resections have to be recommended [7].

The handling of hernia sac has been another issue that was investigated. The HerniaSurge Group reported that sac invagination without ligation is associated with lower incidence of acute post-operative pain but with an increase of recurrence rate. In the same way, they recommend to minimize the surgical trauma of the spermatic cord in order to reduce the incidence of orchialgia [7].

For the management of post-operative chronic pain, there is a wide consensus for a multidisciplinary approach. However, there are weak evidence about the medical treatment strategy as well as about the mesh removal without neurectomy. The decision about the selective or triple neurectomy is left to the surgeon discretion [7].

Other two issues that have been addressed were the management of incarcerated or strangulated inguinal hernia as well as the learning curve of inguinal hernia repair.

About the incarcerated or strangulated inguinal hernia management, there is a lack of evidence. A tailored approach is recommended to a patient given the lack of adequate evidence [7].

About the learning curve, from a recent but yet unofficial literature review conducted by the Italian Society of Hernia and abdominal wall surgery, some interesting considerations have emerged. There is a lack of evidence about the learning curve of the anterior open approach. Only one paper fixes at 60 cases the minimum number of procedures needed to achieve a learning curve. Similarly, but with a slightly higher evidence, the value of 60 cases was indicated as the minimum number of procedures needed to achieve a learning curve during TAPP or Tep [6].

16.3 EBM in Ventral/Incisional Hernia Repair

Differently from the treatment of groin hernias, repair of ventral and incisional hernias presents several questions that still need to be properly answered. There is a multitude of studies regarding most aspects of abdominal hernia surgery in the literature, even with high level of quality and large series, but their results can often create confusion to the surgeon choice.

There is a great difference between primary ventral hernias and secondary (incisional) hernias; in fact, while the first kind of hernia can be easily categorized (umbilical, epigastric or rare hernias), incisional hernias may be extremely variable (site, size, previous surgery, number of defects and presence of contaminated field), and the currently used EHS classification [12] does not include parameters that are really important to establish the optimal treatment, such as the correlation between hernia width and the abdominal wall area that typically depends on sex, BMI, height and other factors.

The diffusion of a large number of different techniques to repair ventral and incisional hernias can give an important variety of choices but can even create confusion and not univocal interpretation of data. During the last two decades, laparoscopic approach with defect bridging by an intraperitoneal mesh has gained more and more popularity since this procedure can be easily performed. It is quick and does not require extensive dissection of the wall, often resulting in a quicker recovery and good short-term results [13]. Furthermore, the development of new products (both meshes and devices to fix them) created to be used on the peritoneal surface contributed to the diffusion of this approach. So, several guidelines from IEHS and SICE have been introduced in order to guide the decisional process and to give the correct indications to laparoscopic treatment on ventral and incisional hernias [14–16]. Nevertheless, in recent years the concept of abdominal wall hernia repair has gradually moved to the more proper concept of abdominal wall reconstruction. In fact, the restoration of the midline has to be considered as the crucial point in this kind of surgery. So, while maintaining the principles of tension-free repair remains mandatory, new techniques of dissection and reconstruction have been more recently introduced: the anterior component separation, with detachment of the external oblique muscles from the internal oblique muscle on its anterior aspect [17] and the posterior component separation with transversus abdominis release (TAR) [18], starting from the classical rives technique. Both these approaches permit to gain several centimetres from each side of the anterior abdominal wall and achieve a good and tension-free closure of the midline in most cases, so they become very useful mainly in complex abdominal wall reconstruction, as in case of larger defects or complex situations (previous repairs, contaminated fields and loss of domain) [19]. Furthermore, the large use of intraperitoneal meshes, mostly by laparoscopic approach, has created a large number of mesh-related complications, such as bowel adhesions and injuries, and consequently the number of legal controversies has increased. Even for these reasons, the use of intraperitoneal meshes should nowadays be limited to very selected cases. The tendency to place the mesh outside the peritoneal surface and the concept of abdominal wall functionality restoration has permitted the development of new mini-invasive approaches to the extraperitoneal space to aid the component separation techniques, such as the endoscopic anterior component separation [20] and the laparoscopic component separation [21]. The robotic approach has developed during the last years and permits to achieve a better and easier dissection of the intermuscular space [13].

Another crucial issue in abdominal wall reconstruction is clearly the choice of the mesh to be implanted. Even for this matter, there is no clear evidence, as clinical scenarios may be extremely variable. Obesity, recurrent hernias, complex hernias (such as in case of the presence of ostomies, and contaminated fields) and emergency surgery are challenging situations for the surgeon, and the choice of the best repair with the best mesh for that specific situation requires skill and experience in this kind of surgery [22]. Permanent synthetic meshes having a macroporous structure are considered the gold standard in most situations in clean surgical fields. However, partially or even totally long-term resorbable synthetic meshes have recently been developed following the evidence that less is more, i.e. less foreign body reaction if not needed can be more physiological and lead to a better long-term outcome [23]. These new meshes seem to be an effective and cheaper alternative to biological meshes (that are used and preferred in contaminated fields), utilization of which in abdominal wall surgery still lacks clear evidence [24]

16.4 Future Perspectives

Abdominal wall surgery is probably most frequently performed in general surgery settings. Despite this, there is still no general agreement on indications to repair, choice of approach and materials, mainly for ventral and incisional hernias than for inguinal (and crural) hernias; in fact, there are many consensus and guidelines for the treatment of groin hernias, regarding both open and mini-invasive repairs, and this reflects the high level of agreement and evidence on this specific item. Conversely, as yet debated, abdominal wall reconstruction surgery is a "larger space" with a lot of serious and interesting studies but still no general consensus. So, the real need is the creation of evidence-based guidelines regarding all aspects of this kind of surgery, both for the laparoscopic and for the open approach. These guidelines should have the purpose to serve as a real guide to everyday clinical activity.

References

1. Sackett DL, Rosenberg W, Mc Gray JA, haynes RB, Richardson WS. Evidence-based medicine: what it is and what it isn't. BMJ. 1996;312:71–2.
2. The periodic health examination. Canadian Task Force on the Periodic Health Examination. Can Med Assoc J. 1979;121:1193–254.
3. Bower C, Scott Roth J. Economics of abdominal wall reconstruction. Surg Clin N Am. 2013;93:1241–53.
4. Bracale U, Rovani M, Picardo A, Merola G, Pignata G, Sodo M, Di Salvo E, Ratto EL, Noceti A, Melillo P, Pecchia L. Beneficial effects of fibrin glue (Quixil) versus Lichtenstein conventional technique in inguinal hernia repair: a randomized clinical trial. Hernia. 2014;18(2):185–92. https://doi.org/10.1007/s10029-012-1020-4.
5. Miserez M, Peeters E, Aufenacker T, Bouillot JL, Campanelli G, Conze J, Fortelny R, Heikkinen T, Jorgensen LN, Kukleta J, Morales-Conde S, Nordin P, Schumpelick V, Smedberg S, Smietanski M, Weber G, Simons MP. Update with level 1 studies of the European Hernia Society guidelines on the treatment of inguinal hernia in adult patients. Hernia. 2014;18(2):151–63. https://doi.org/10.1007/s10029-014-1236-6.
6. Bittner R, Montgomery MA, Arregui E, Bansal V, Bingener J, Bisgaard T, Buhck H, Dudai M, Ferzli GS, Fitzgibbons RJ, Fortelny RH, Grimes KL, Klinge U, Köckerling F, Kumar S, Kukleta J, Lomanto D, Misra MC, Morales-Conde S, Reinpold W, Rosenberg J, Singh K, Timoney M, Weyhe D, Chowbey P. International Endohernia Society. Update of guidelines on laparoscopic (TAPP) and endoscopic (TEP) treatment of inguinal hernia (International Endohernia Society). Surg Endosc. 2015;29(2):289–321. https://doi.org/10.1007/s00464-014-3917-8.
7. HerniaSurge Group. International guidelines for groin hernia management. Hernia. 2018;22(1):1–165. https://doi.org/10.1007/s10029-017-1668-x.
8. Bracale U, Melillo P, Pignata G, Di Salvo E, Rovani M, Merola G, Pecchia L. Which is the best laparoscopic approach for inguinal hernia repair: TEP or TAPP? A systematic review of

the literature with a network meta-analysis. Surg Endosc. 2012;26(12):3355–66. https://doi.org/10.1007/s00464-012-2382-5.
9. Merskey H, Bogduk N. Classification of chronic pain. Description of pain terms. Prepared by the International Association for the Study of pain, Subcommittee on Taxonomy. Pain Suppl. 1986;3:1–226.
10. Alfieri S, Amid PK, Campanelli G, et al. International guidelines for prevention and management of post-operative chronic pain following inguinal hernia surgery. Hernia. 2011;15(3):239–49. https://doi.org/10.1007/s10029-011-0798-9.
11. Nienhuijs SW, Rosman C, Strobbe LJA, Wolff A, Bleichrodt RP. An overview of the features influencing pain after inguinal hernia repair. Int. J. Surg. 2008;6(4):351–6. https://doi.org/10.1016/j.ijsu.2008.02.005Hernia. 2014 Apr;18(2):151-63. https://doi.org/10.1007/s10029-014-1236-6. Epub 2014 Mar 20.
12. Muysoms FE, Miserez M, Berrevoet F, Campanelli G, Champault GG, Chelala E, Dietz UA, Eker HH, El Nakadi I, Hauters P, Hidalgo Pascual M, Hoeferlin A, Klinge U, Montgomery A, Simmermacher RK, Simons MP, Smietański M, Sommeling C, Tollens T, Vierendeels T, Kingsnorth A. Classification of primary and incisional abdominal wall hernias. Hernia. 2009;13:407–14.
13. Vorst AL, Kaoutzanis C, Carbonell AM, Franz MG. Evolution and advances in laparoscopic ventral and incisional hernia repair. World J Gastrointest Surg. 2015;7:293–305.
14. Cuccurullo D, Piccoli M, Agresta F, Magnone S, Corcione F, Stancanelli V, Melotti G. Laparoscopic ventral incisional hernia repair: evidence-based guidelines of the first Italian consensus conference. Hernia. 2013;17:557–66.
15. Bittner R, Bingener-Casey J, Dietz U, Fabian M, Ferzli GS, Fortelny RH, Köckerling F, Kukleta J, Leblanc K, Lomanto D, Misra MC, Bansal VK, Morales-Conde S, Ramshaw B, Reinpold W, Rim S, Rohr M, Schrittwieser R, Simon T, Smietanski M, Stechemesser B, Timoney M, Chowbey P, International Endohernia Society (IEHS). Guidelines for laparoscopic treatment of ventral and incisional abdominal wall hernias (International Endohernia Society (IEHS)-part 1). Surg Endosc. 2014;28(1):2–29.
16. Silecchia G, Campanile FC, Sanchez L, Ceccarelli G, Antinori A, Ansaloni L, Olmi S, Ferrari GC, Cuccurullo D, Baccari P, Agresta F, Vettoretto N, Piccoli M. Laparoscopic ventral/incisional hernia repair: updated Consensus Development Conference based guidelines. Surg Endosc. 2015;29:2463–84.
17. Ramirez OM, Ruas E, Dellon AL. Component separation method for closure of abdominal wall defects: an anatomic and clinical study. Plast Reconstr Surg. 1990;86:519–26.
18. Novitsky YW, Elliott HL, Orenstein SB, Rosen MJ. Transversus abdominis muscle release: a novel approach to posterior component separation during complex abdominal wall reconstruction. Am J Surg. 2012;204:709–16.
19. Hodgkinson JD, Leo CA, Maeda Y, Bassett P, Oke SM, Vaizey CJ, Warusavitarne J. A meta-analysis comparing open anterior component separation with posterior component separation and transversus abdominis release in the repair of midline ventral hernias. Hernia. 2018;22(4):617–26. https://doi.org/10.1007/s10029-018-1757-5.
20. Dauser B, Ghaffari S, Ng C, Schmid T, Köhler G, Herbst F. Endoscopic anterior component separation: a novel technical approach. Hernia. 2017;21:951–5.
21. Malik K, Bowers SP, Smith CD, Asbun H, Preissler S. A case series of laparoscopic components separation and rectus medialization with laparoscopicventral hernia repair. J Laparoendosc Adv Surg Tech. 2009;19:607–10.
22. Deerenberg EB, Timmermans L, Hogerzeil DP, slieker JC, Eilers PHC, Jeekel J, Lange JF. A systematic review of the surgical treatment of large incisional hernia. Hernia. 2015;19:89–101.
23. Koscielny A, Widenmayer S, May T, Kalff J, Lingohr P. Comparison of biological and alloplastic meshes in ventral incisional hernia repair. Lancgenbecks Arch Surg. 2017;403(2):255–63. https://doi.org/10.1007/s00423-017-1639-9.
24. Trippoli S, Caccese E, Tulli G, Ipponi P, Marinai C, Messori A. Biological meshes for abdominal hernia: lack of evidence-based recommendations for clinical use. Int. J. Surg. 2018;52:278–84.

Health Technology Assessment in Abdominal Wall Surgery

17

Valentina Beretta, Michele Tringali, and Antonio Marioni

17.1 Introduction to the Technologies used in Abdominal Wall Surgery

Abdominal wall surgery can be performed using different technologies.

First, *open surgery* refers to the cases in which the surgeon made an incision to expose the entire operative area. This technology allows the repair of the defect by placing, in the majority of the cases, a mesh over the abdominal opening. While usually synthetic or plastic mesh is adopted, in the case of severe circumstances bioprosthetic mesh are implemented and will become an integral part of the body over few weeks.

Second, *laparoscopic surgery* occurred when a slender tool with a tiny camera and light is inserted in the abdominal cavity. Patients can benefit from laparoscopic surgery in terms of early recovery, while medical institutions can benefit of the lower costs associated with a shorter length of stay [1]. But, on the other side, among the disadvantages, higher attention to avoid damages to the internal structures is needed [2]. In addition, meticulous attention is needed for blood aspiration [2]. This implies that many procedures are more difficult for surgeon to perform [1]. In fact, even if the quality of image and video provided is excellent, it requires a longer and more specific training for professionals, with a learning curve longer than open surgery.

V. Beretta (✉)
Department of Economics and Management, University of Pavia, Pavia, Italy
e-mail: valentina.beretta02@universitadipavia.it

M. Tringali
Hospital Programming Unit, HTA Office, Regional Government Health Care Directorate, Lombardy Region, Italy
e-mail: michele_tringali@regione.lombardia.it

A. Marioni
Surgery Department, University Hospital of Pisa, Pisa, Italy
e-mail: a.marioni@ao-pisa.toscana.it

D. P. Greco, E. Borgonovi (eds.), *Abdominal Wall Surgery*,
https://doi.org/10.1007/978-3-030-02426-0_17

Third, *robotic surgery* is used when miniaturized surgical instruments are used instead of previously described techniques. It has been introduced to potentially overcome some of the limitations connected to the laparoscopic surgery [1, 3]. Many advancements are associated with the use of robotic support in performing the operation: "The view is spectacular, the movements are intuitive, and, during a case with a long operative time, the chair is like a first-class seat on a transcontinental flight" ([3], p. 19S). While the major advantage of the robot surgery is that also professionals without laparoscopic competences can approach and adopt this technology, it is somewhat surprising that the dominant trend of diffusion of robot surgery is not from open surgery but from conventional laparoscopic surgery, as registered in the USA [4] and in Italy [5]. On the contrary, the main disadvantage of the robotic surgery is undoubtedly the costs associated with the technology [6, 7].

17.2 How to compare different Technologies?

Previous studies in the literature analyzed the main differences across different techniques that can be adopted to perform abdominal wall surgery.

17.2.1 Open Surgery and Laparoscopic Surgery

According to Jain and Jain, similar results between open and laparoscopic surgery have been found [8]. However, small differences have been detected in the literature:

- Groin pain is higher in open surgery with respect to laparoscopic repair. This causes patients to be restricted from daily physical and sporting activities [8];
- Higher operating time in laparoscopic surgery [1, 8–10];
- Higher complications in laparoscopic surgery than open one, caused by long learning curve [8, 11];
- Even if the assessment of the costs associated with different procedure is difficult, since they mainly depend on institutional policies and procedures [12], laparoscopic surgery is associated with higher reimbursement [13, 14].

Despite these small differences, the choice between the two approaches is dictated by the preferences of surgeons and circumstances, since there is no evidence in the literature for a clear superior procedure [8].

17.2.2 Open Surgery and Robotic Surgery

Very little is known about the comparison between open surgery and robotic surgery, since the latter is meant to compete with or replace laparoscopic surgery [1].

The study conducted by Menon et al. in 2002 found that, while similar results have been found for the features before the surgery, its duration, and the pathological stages, the outcomes differ significantly, favoring robotic surgery [15].

17.2.3 Laparoscopic Surgery and Robotic Surgery

This is the area of major interest since robotic surgery is intended to replace laparoscopic one [1]. According to D'Annibale et al., robotic and laparoscopic techniques can obtain similar results in terms of operativity and postoperative outcomes [7]. However, since the operating times related to the robotic surgery are longer, advantages that are able to justify the choice of conducting robotic surgery are needed [1]. In this regard, results of previous studies are controversial.

Some authors found that only little advantages are provided by robotic surgery with respect to laparoscopic surgery [1]. Others found that in certain stages of the surgical procedure, the dexterity and the flexibility of robotic surgery may be advantageous for the surgeon [7]. Finally, the greatest advantage is related to the possibility for the surgeon to stay at the console, which is connected to more comfortable workplace, less fatigue, and enhanced ability to perform fine tasks [1].

In summary, robot-assisted mininvasive surgery can provide some benefits to surgeons, scarce benefits to health care organizations (but at higher costs), and questionable, if any, benefits to patients, with some exceptions, e.g., reduced blood loss and transfusion requirements at least in some indications [5, 16, 17].

17.3 Health Technology Assessment for Abdominal Wall Surgery evaluation

Despite previous studies for the comparison of different technologies used in performing abdominal wall surgery exist in the literature, there is a lack of systematic comparison between them. As identified in previous studies, cost is considered the most important barrier for performing robotic surgery [6, 7], but additional studies are need in order to evaluate the efficacy, the effectiveness, and the cost-effectiveness of using this technique [7]. In fact, as highlighted by Gutt et al., trials are needed in order to evaluate the benefits of robotic surgery since the literature available does not produce valuable support to the modern evidence-based medicine [1, 3]. In fact, even if technological advancements are changing the abdominal surgery practice [3], clear advantages for transiting from one practice to robotic surgery are needed [1].

In this sense, Health Technology Assessment (HTA) would provide a useful tool for the systematic assessment of different technologies. HTA aims at systematically evaluating the properties, effects, and impacts of health technologies, in order to support policy-makers in taking decisions [18]. Over the years, many definitions of HTA have been provided in the literature, underlying different aspects of the topic. In particular, the World Health Organization defined HTA as a multidisciplinary process aimed at evaluating the different implications (from clinical to economic) of a health technology for supporting decision-making processes (World Health Organization). Also, EUnetHTA provided a definition of HTA, considered as the process that evaluates health technologies in a systematic, transparent, unbiased, and robust manner (EUnetHTA).

The importance of technology assessment (TA) raised in the 1960s, because of the critical role of the technology in the society [18]. Subsequently, in 1965, the role of TA has been clarified by the congressman Emilio Daddario, during the deliberations of the Committee on Science and Astronautics of the US House of Representatives, who affirmed that the purpose of TA was to serve policy-makers in taking decisions, considering social, economic, and legal implications of any course of action [18]. In 1969, TA was defined as a support tool aimed at aiding the Congress in fully considering both the private and the public interests when assessing a new technology, in order to maximize the society's welfare [19].

During the 1970s, there has been a growing interest in the topic by many scholars. In particular, there was the necessity to find a common and shared meaning for the term "technology" and to define the role of technology assessment. At this purpose, Galbraith, in 1977, defined technology as "the systematic application of scientific or other organized knowledge to practical tasks" [20], while Brooks and Bowers, in 1970, stated that TA was aimed at identifying both the intended effects of technologies and the unintended social, economic, and environmental effects [21].

Subsequently, the TA started being applied to other fields of research. In particular, after the Congress in 1967, the Office of Technology Assessment was authorized, founded in 1973, operationalized in 1974, and adopted in the health programs in 1975. Just in 1976, the first Office of Technology Assessment (OTA) Health Program report was issued, as a proof of the fact that, before the advent of HTA, health technologies were analyzed in terms of safety, effectiveness, and cost [18].

The spread of HTA in the rest of the world occurred starting from the 1980s [22]. In the late 1980s, the establishment of the Swedish Council on Technology Assessment in Health Care (SBU) represents an important step towards the diffusion of HTA in Europe [22]. The HTA showed a rapid dissemination outside the boundaries of the USA, and, in particular, in Europe, where several countries have established agencies to perform HTA in order to set priorities [23].

After the first application of the term, many steps have been undertaken to reinforce the knowledge of HTA. It was especially in the 1980s and 1990s when, the emerging concern about the real effectiveness of health technologies and the sharp increase in health expenditures gave assistance to the development of HTA in Europe [24, 25].

In 1992, the Cochrane Collaboration (CC) has been established as a worldwide network of centers and people aiming at critically reviewing the literature related to health care effects of healthcare interventions. The objective of the collaboration is to provide a database in which extensive and accurate information are provided to physicians in order to make decisions [26].

In the following years, a number of forces have driven the development of HTA [27]:

- Robust science upon which to base the choice of interventions was needed. In fact, as the Department of Health stated in 1991, there were many categories of health technologies [28]:
  - Ineffective widely used technologies;
  - Valuable technologies introduced in delay;
  - New technologies falsely promoted over existing ones;
  - Technologies with a variation in their value.

  Because of the existence of nonvaluable technologies, decision-makers had to provide evidence of the value of the new health technologies, in order to reduce waste in monetary and nonmonetary terms;
- Costs containment was required since the unit cost of new technologies was usually higher with respect to the technologies they replaced;
- The rise in consumers' expectations increased both the use and the demand for better information.

Despite many advancements have been done in HTA in the last years, many collaborations are now in place, and many health technologies are now subject to assessment, there is a scarcity of literature focusing on the application of HTA processes to robotic abdominal wall surgery.

The most widespread technology used in abdominal wall robotic surgery is the Da Vinci robot. Even if no HTA reports have been identified, different systematic reviews exist [1, 5, 16, 17, 29, 30].

Results of these studies found that robotic surgery with Da Vinci robot is secure and feasible, and that the associated mortality and morbidity rates are low. The duration of the operation is higher with respect to open surgery, while lower with laparoscopic surgery. In particular, a faster learning curve is associated with robotic surgery with respect to laparoscopic surgery. However, no specific advantages for the patients have been found using this technique [29].

In addition, the potential of HTA can be even enhanced with the support of the hernia registries. Different alternative classifications of hernias have been proposed and tested in the literature [31–36], with the aim of supporting future guidelines and therapeutic choices with most valuable and important risk factors [37]. Despite registries vary according to the classification factors that are considered, the main aim of any classification should be the improvement of extent to which different studies and related results can be compared [37]. At this purpose, the existence of registries allows the development of evidence-based guidelines [37] that, together with HTA reports, should be at the basis of investment choices for the introduction of new technologies in healthcare systems, and/or for public procurement procedures.

17.4 HTA in Abdominal Wall Surgery: the Tuscany Case

Abdominal wall reconstructive surgery in recent years has had a positive impulse.

Open anterior treatment remained the gold standard in the reconstruction of the midline for the treatment of primitive or incisional abdominal wall hernia.

Laparoscopic surgery determines a bridge treatment without reconstruction of the midline.

In the last few years, with the advent of robot-assisted surgery, the treatment of incisional or primitive abdominal wall hernias has been seen again with positioning of the extra-abdominal retromuscular prosthesis and reconstruction of the midline.

In Tuscany, thanks to the collaboration of University Hospital of Pisa and Grosseto Hospital, this technique plays an important role in the treatment of the abdominal wall hernia.

The decision algorithm we developed is as follows:

1. Incisional or primitive abdominal wall hernia with a <5-cm hole with the remaining wall functionally effective in an obese subject or with associated pathology: IPOM PLUS.
2. Incisional or primitive abdominal wall hernia with a 5–10-cm hole: repair with placement of a retromuscular prosthesis according to Rives–Stoppa with anterior open technique or in selected cases with a robot-assisted technique.
3. Incisional or primitive abdominal wall hernia with a hole between 10 and 15 cm: endoscopic components separation and subsequent repair according to Rives–Stoppa with retromuscular prosthesis with anterior open technique or in selected cases with robot-assisted technique.
4. Incisional or primitive abdominal wall hernia with >15-cm hole is performed: posterior component separation with transversus abdominis release with anterior open technique or in selected robot-assisted cases.
5. Abdominal wall hernia associated with muscular diastasis (hernia of abdominal wall associated with muscular diastasis): midline reconstruction with traditional open technique with placement retromuscular prosthesis and dermolipectomy or abdominoplasty, and in selected cases with muscular diastasis <5 cm and abdominal hernia reconstruction of the median line with robot-assisted Costa technique.

The Tuscany group experience (Antonio Marioni MD, General Surgery, University Hospital of Pisa and Luca Felicioni MD, Grosseto Misericordia Hospital) in collaboration with Carlo De Nisco PhD (Santa Lucia Hospital of Nuoro—Sardinia) started the robot-assisted experience about 1 year ago (2017) and the interventions performed so far with robot-assisted technique have shown a shorter hospital clinical course, with less acute postoperative pain, even if the results in terms of postoperative recurrence given the short post-surgical follow-up cannot be assessed yet.

17.5 Conclusions

HTA has shown to be a good decision-making tool, which can allow to achieve the best results in investments for high cost technologies, as surgical robot. However, for the evaluation of everyday devices, as sutures or meshes, the use of registries, combined with HTA, could be more suitable. The Tuscany case shows that an important change is ongoing: surgeons and institution (NHS) have joined forces to find the best solution both from the side of science and of economy. This opens a window to the future, in order to pass from opposing fields to a system of cooperation with the same aim: a safe surgery.

References

1. Gutt CN, Oniu T, Mehrabi A, Kashfi A, Schemmer P, Büchler MW. Robot-assisted abdominal surgery. Br J Surg. 2004;91(11):1390–7.
2. Monson JR. Advanced techniques in abdominal surgery. BMJ. 1993;307(November):1346–50.
3. Hanly EJ, Talamini MA. Robotic abdominal surgery. Am J Surg. 2004;188(4 Suppl. 1):19–26.
4. Armijo PR, Pagkratis S, Boilesen E, Tanner T, Oleynikov D. Growth in robotic-assisted procedures is from conversion of laparoscopic procedures and not from open surgeons' conversion: a study of trends and costs. Surg Endosc. 2018;32(4):2106–13.
5. Jefferson T, Abraha I, Chiarolla E, Corio M, Paone S, Piccoli M, et al. HTA report robotic surgery. Vol. Agenas, Ro. 2017.
6. Hanly EJ, Zand J, Bachman SL, Marohn MR, Talamini MA. Value of the SAGES Learning Center in introducing new technology. Surg Endosc Other Interv Tech. 2005;19(4):477–83.
7. D'Annibale A, Morpurgo E, Fiscon V, Trevisan P, Sovernigo G, Orsini C, et al. Robotic and laparoscopic surgery for treatment of colorectal diseases. Dis Colon Rectum. 2004;47(12):2162–8.
8. Jain S, Jain M. Comparison between laparoscopic and open hernia repair: a clinical trial. Int J Adv Multidiscip Res. 2018;5(4):1–5.
9. Kuhry E, Van Veen RN, Langeveld HR, Steyerberg EW, Jeekel J, Bonjer HJ. Open or endoscopic total extraperitoneal inguinal hernia repair? A systematic review. Surg Endosc. 2007;21(2):161–6.
10. Smink DS, Paquette IM, Finlayson SRG. Utilization of laparoscopic and open inguinal hernia repair: a population-based analysis. J Laparoendosc Adv Surg Tech. 2009;19(6):745–8.
11. McCormack K, Scott N, Go PM, Ross SJ, Grant A. Laparoscopic techniques versus open techniques for inguinal hernia repair. Cochrane Database Syst Rev. 2003;1:CD001785.
12. Khajanchee YS, Kenyon TAG, Hansen PD, Swanström LL. Economic evaluation of laparoscopic and open inguinal herniorrhaphies: the effect of cost-containment measures and internal hospital policy decisions on costs and charges. Hernia. 2004;8(3):196–202.
13. Jacobs VR, Morrison JE Jr. Comparison of institutional costs for laparoscopic preperitoneal inguinal hernia versus open repair and its reimbursement in an ambulatory surgery center. Surg Laparosc Endosc Percutaneous Tech. 2008;18(1):70–4.
14. Payne JH, Grininger LM, Izawa MT, Podoll EF, Lindahl PJ, Balfour J. Laparoscopic or open inguinal herniorrhaphy?: a randomized prospective trial. Arch Surg. 1994;129(9):973–81.
15. Menon M, Tewari A, Baize B, Guillonneau B, Vallancien G. Prospective comparison of radical retropubic prostatectomy and robot-assisted anatomic prostatectomy: the Vattikuti Urology Institute experience. Urology. 2002;60(5):864–8.
16. Tan A, Ashrafian H, Scott AJ, Mason SE, Harling L, Athanasiou T, et al. Robotic surgery: disruptive innovation or unfulfilled promise? A systematic review and meta-analysis of the first 30 years. Surg Endosc. 2016;30(10):4330–52. https://doi.org/10.1007/s00464-016-4752-x.
17. Roh HF, Nam SH, Kim JM. Robot-assisted laparoscopic surgery versus conventional laparoscopic surgery in randomized controlled trials: A systematic review and meta-analysis. PLoS One. 2018;13:1–12.
18. Goodman CS. Introduction to health technology assessment. 2014.
19. National Academy of Engineering C on PEP. A Study of Technology Assessment. 1969.
20. Galbraith JK. The New Industrial State. Princeton: Princeton University Press; 1977. 577p
21. Brooks H, Bowers R. The assessment of technology. Sci Am. 1970;222:13–21.

22. Banta D, Jonsson E. History of HTA: introduction. Int J Technol Assess Health Care. 2009;25(Suppl.S1):1–6.
23. Sorenson C, Chalkidou K. Reflections on the evolution of health technology assessment in Europe. Heal Econ Policy Law. 2012;7(1):25–45.
24. Oliver A, Mossialos E, Robinson R. Health technology assessment and its influence on health-care priority setting. Int J Technol Assess Health Care. 2004;20(1):1–10.
25. Banta D, Jonsson E. History of HTA: introduction. Int J Technol Assess Health Care [Internet]. 2009;25(S1):1–6. Available from: http://www.journals.cambridge.org/abstract_S0266462309090321.
26. Bero L, Rennie D. The cochrane collaboration: preparing, maintaining, and disseminating systematic reviews of the effects of health care. JAMA. 1995;274(24):1935–8.
27. Stevens A, Milne R, Burls A. Health technology assessment: history and demand. J Public Health. 2003;25(2):98–101.
28. Department of Health L. Assessing the effects of health technologies. London: Department of Health; 1991.
29. Ballantyne GH. Telerobotic gastrointestinal surgery: phase 2—safety and efficacy. Surg Endosc. 2007;21(7):1054–62.
30. Taylor GW, Jayne DG. Robotic applications in abdominal surgery: their limitations and future developments. Int J Med Robot Comput Assist Surg. 2007;3(1):3–9.
31. Schumpelick V. In: Schumpelick V, editor. Narbenhernie. Stuttgart: Hernien Thieme; 2000. p. 266–9.
32. Chevrel JP, Rath AM. Classification of incisional hernias of the abdominal wall. Hernia. 2000;4(1):7–11.
33. Korenkov M, Paul A, Sauerland S, Neugebauer E, Arndt M, Chevrel JP, et al. Classification and surgical treatment of incisional hernia. Langenbeck's Arch Surg. 2001;386(1):65–73.
34. Dietz UA, Hamelmann W, Winkler MS, Debus ES, Malafaia O, Czeczko NG, et al. An alternative classification of incisional hernias enlisting morphology, body type and risk factors in the assessment of prognosis and tailoring of surgical technique. J Plast Reconstr Aesthet Surg. 2007;60(4):383–8.
35. Ammaturo C, Bassi G. The ratio between anterior abdominal wall surface/wall defect surface: a new parameter to classify abdominal incisional hernias. Hernia. 2005;9(4):316–21.
36. Miserez M, Alexandre JH, Campanelli G, Corcione F, Cuccurullo D, Pascual MH, et al. The European hernia society groin hernia classication: simple and easy to remember. Hernia. 2007;11(2):113–6.
37. Muysoms F, Miserez M, Berrevoet F, Campanelli G, Champault GG, Chelala E, et al. Classification of primary and incisional abdominal wall hernias. Hernia. 2009;13(4):407–14.

Part IV

Future Perspectives

18 Stakeholders' Opinion

Diego Orlando Freri

The aim of this chapter is to analyze the theme of "wall surgery," from the point of view of stakeholders other than medical surgeons and health economists, focusing on decision-makers, patients, and advocates. Some issues emphasized by the various interlocutors and their solution proposals will be highlighted and analyzed.

Without a doubt, the problem that strongly emerges, especially from the world of patients and their associations, is that of the excessive length of the waiting list for an operation [1, 2]. According to Enrica Mattioli, Vice President of the Associazione Diastasi Italia ODV [3], an organization created by a group of young women affected by diastasis of the rectus muscles of the abdomen following pregnancy, and which today collects over 13,000 members throughout Italy: "waiting lists arrive up to 5 or 6 years in some structures." According to Ms. Mattioli, the reason is to be found in the lack of specialized center which concentrates exclusively on pathologies affecting the abdominal wall, "which force those who have diastasis to turn to hospitals that give priority to other diseases."

The same concept is expressed and substantiated in more detail by Rodolfo Vincenti, co-founder of the Fondazione Chirurgo e Cittadino Onlus [4], created by the will of the surgeons, but which concurrently addresses physicians and citizens, with the aim of creating relationship and dialogue between the two worlds. Professor Vincenti recalls how the cases to be treated with wall surgery are hundreds of thousands every year, in a country like Italy. While "playing a role of primary importance for the insightful implications both at the clinical and socioeconomic level," due to their large number, in most cases, they present with forms that can be largely operated in day surgery or even outpatient as ambulatory surgery, under local or regional anesthesia, and only rarely for a surgical emergency.

Therefore, they fall into the category of pathologies that have suffered "the drastic reduction in the hospital bed/inhabitant ratio in Italy over the last decade, exacerbating the problem of access to care, especially for diseases that do not have emergency features [1, 2, 5].

D. O. Freri (✉)
HealthCom Consulting, Milan, Italy
e-mail: diego.freri@hcc-milano.com

D. P. Greco, E. Borgonovi (eds.), *Abdominal Wall Surgery*,
https://doi.org/10.1007/978-3-030-02426-0_18

It is important to remember—as professor Vincenti points out—that the average number of hospital beds per 1000 inhabitants in the OECD (Organization for Economic Cooperation and Development) area is 4.8, and in Italy only 3.4, against 6.3 in France and 8.3 in Germany (2016 OECD data). The hospitalization rate is also among the lowest in Italy: 13 admissions per 1000 inhabitants, with an OECD average of 16 and a German rate of 25" [1, 6, 7].

Furthermore, professor Vincenti underlines the importance of the indicator that evaluates the consistency of health personnel compared to the resident population [7]. According to the Survey of the Consorzio per la Ricerca Economica Applicata in Sanità "C.R.E.A. Sanità 2017" [5], tells us the representative of the Fondazione Chirurgo e Cittadino Onlus, compared to an average of 11.8 staff units of the Sistema Sanitario Nazionale (SSN, the Italian National Health Service) per 1000 residents nationwide, ranging from a figure of 8.6 of the Campania to 16.6 in Valle d'Aosta, with the Lazio to 11.1, the Lombardia to 11.7, and the Veneto to 13.6, a figure, the latter, among the highest for the regions with ordinary statute.

Hence, the combined arrangement of the "bed slashing associated with the turnover block and the consequent reduction of staff numbers, with the progressive increased access in the emergency room of the elderly population, often with different pathologies and with complex health needs, has created what it is called a 'funnel effect.' This, in the face of a clear improvement in the index of appropriateness of hospitalization, has as its direct consequence an increasing number of partially self-sufficient citizens, who need access to the planned treatment. Therefore, a widespread numerical and temporal increase in the waiting time to obtain the therapy, especially for those pathologies, such as wall defects, which, in fact, appear to show light symptoms and do not present emergency features."

The phenomenon of waiting lists [6, 8], which, as we will see later, is not exclusively a national problem, is associated with another, adds Ms. Mattioli, probably more critical for patients with diastasis. In fact, explains the Vice President of Associazione Diastasi Italia ODV [3]: "access to the intervention is not guaranteed in all the Regions and when it is, this happens unevenly. In some regions it is necessary to comply to rather rigid parameters such as a minimum gap of, for example, 5 cm—when a diastasis becomes pathological, and therefore not recoverable with exercise or other, above 2.5–3 cm—or mandatory presence of hernia or incisional hernia. Not only that, hospitals in the same city often have different criteria among them—it also happens with the same surgeons—so it becomes very difficult to understand where and to whom to turn. It is not uncommon, in addition, that some patients are denied the waiting list, without knowing that in another hospital, a few kilometers away, with the same parameters, you could instead undergo the operation." In a nutshell, there is a lack of uniformity of views and probably of a thorough and widespread knowledge of the matter.

He is not at all surprised by the situation, he confides to us, Marco Trivelli, Director General of the Niguarda Hospital in Milan [9], one of the largest and most important Italian hospitals, a national and international reference center for various diseases. "The theme of knowledge is fundamental; often, in healthcare, the in-depth knowledge of the dynamics of the sectors is lacking. This is because healthcare has always moved in relation to its abilities: it was the offer that created the demand," he says. In other words, what was the need to know? "Today things have changed—he continues—all this is no longer good. Today we need to measure and evaluate, to know and then make decisions happen." Measuring clinical outcomes, for example, is fundamental, according to Trivelli, to decide which type of procedure to favor, and which device would be more appropriate to use in an intervention.

"Given that any problem, disorder or illness, that a citizen claims, must be considered serious, because it is still a serious problem for those who suffer—Trivelli points out—certainly there are underestimated conditions, not for their intrinsic characteristics, but because they are considered less serious than others and therefore disadvantaged." Wall surgery is one of these. If we were more aware, we would know better and more, underlines the Director General, we could find appropriate solutions. "For wall surgery—he says—probably the solution could be to develop centers of excellence: dedicated surgical rooms in selected centers. I believe it can work. "Generally, in the dedicated-to-a-single-specialty centers services are performed, no treatment is carried out. I think that in the case of wall surgery we can reason for performance. In addition, specialized centers, which operate on large volumes, have the advantage of producing greater efficiency, for everyone—hospital organization, doctors, patients," he says.

Sweet words like honey, these, for Enrica Mattioli and Associazione Diastasi Italia ODV, which has, indeed, included among its proposals the institution of "centers of excellence that deal with the diastasis, from A to Z, and that follow every patient from the beginning of his journey. Unfortunately—she explains—the non-knowledge of the disease, which we find precisely among those who should guide us and diagnose it, is disconcerting. General practitioners who refuse to prescribe control ultrasounds, specialists who … 'Madam, has given birth, and does not claim to have returned like it was before,' who invites us to eat less, who to do massages. Yet, the health problems that our members highlight are many: abdominal swelling, urinary incontinence, prolapse, instability of the pelvis, back pain, nausea, digestive and respiratory difficulties, peristalsis, hernia, posture from hyper-lordosis. If these conditions were better known by the doctors, it would be possible to avoid long checkups between different specialists, which waste our time and money."

As in many situations of illness, the symptoms and disorders that patients accuse are not only physical. In the specific case of the diastasis they are also esthetic, with a serious impact on the psychological and social sphere. "In many cases—says Mattioli—the globose or pendulous abdomen significantly affects the well-being of the person, who does not find herself in such a different body and in such a short time, as in post-pregnancy cases. Often it is precisely the lack of knowledge of the pathology, even on the part of the doctors, which leads to close, to limit one's intimate and affective sphere, to generate misunderstandings with one's partner, family or friends, who may judge it only a superficial problem facing the joys of motherhood. All this leads to a state of intolerance that can also have serious psychological repercussions."

One of the solutions desired by the association, to overcome these problems, could be the establishment of a "network" of health professionals that represents a system at the forefront of prevention, diagnosis, and treatment, with all the benefits for both patients and the healthcare professionals who are part of it, in terms of training, learning, and competence. It could involve surgeons, gynecologists and midwives, sonographers, but also other professionals. Physiotherapists, for example, who could provide pregnant women with useful advice on which types of exercise are most suitable and which, on the other hand, are counterproductive, such as hypo-pensive gymnastics or for strengthening the pelvic floor, during and immediately after pregnancy. Or the psychotherapists, to support the patient in the path of reappropriation of their physical and mental health, when the problem arises, or to also help in the post-intervention phase, which sometimes is loaded with too many expectations. An operation, however, not easy to achieve, as we have seen and, in this regard, still asks the Association: "clinical studies would be useful to help determine how the surgery in some cases is decisive, and other studies would be important for investigate what causes the onset of the pathology during pregnancy, the risk factors, such as twin births or weight gain, with the aim of preventing this condition, rather than being forced to treat it."

Returning to the problem mainly stressed, the waiting lists, are we facing an exquisitely Italian matter? The answer, of course, is no [1, 6, 10, 11]. First, professor Vincenti recalls: "wall surgery almost always regards performance delivered in election and it is intrinsically burdened by long waiting times and is a generator of malaise and anxiety for the patient." Then, he adds: "in all the countries where there is a public health service totally or partially universal, there are discomforts for long waits. With free or almost free care, citizens demand more services than those administrators can or want to provide. The result is rationing through waiting and/or the introduction of deterrents such as performance tickets. Long waiting times have become a symbol of the inefficiency of health services, particularly in hospitals [1].

Ireland, Denmark, Finland, Sweden, Germany, Spain, Belgium in the recent decade have undertaken a national program aimed at reducing waiting times, but with alternate results often related to the partial payment of the performance. In Sweden: *any prescribed treatment should be fixed within 90 days after the specialist's visit*; in Spain: *no patient should wait more than 6 months for surgery*; in Germany: *patients with private insurance have significantly shorter waiting times than patients with public health coverage*; in Belgium: *for each health procedure the patient has to pay 15% of the fee from his own pocket*. So, as we can see, in Italy we are not the only ones, but the problem is widespread and strongly affects the level of quality delivered and above all perceived."

What can be done then? The great complexity of the problem cannot fail to consider the three aspects on which we must act: the hospital structure, the organization of services, and the empowerment of the citizen [11–13]. "In few words and simplifying—Vincenti adds—we believe it is essential to revise upward the availability of hospital beds and jointly open differentiated access routes for diseases considered 'minor,' non-acute, such as those that require repair surgery of the abdominal wall that often, not to say always, are—this being the case—understandably postponed with respect to major pathologies. Therefore, increase of beds, in favor of an autonomous Day Surgery for short hospitalization and for operating block, and the increase of the dedicated staff in addition to active and available H12 operating blocks. It is quite clear that this will be possible only with adequate investments in structural and human resources as well as the organizational involvement of surgeons and healthcare professionals."

Another aspect to consider is how to act towards the citizen [14]. "Paradoxically, it is the most difficult aspect of the problem—continues Vincenti. The tools to curb the access to inappropriate medical tests, or tests which may be delayed without dangers, are few and I would say very vague, depending more on the different moods and anxiety levels of the patient. If on the one hand it is the right of the citizen to have the appropriate listening by the doctor, to receive understandable information, to share treatment paths, on the other hand he must not substitute word of mouth or the web surfing to the doctor's opinion, who will try not to comply with every request of the patient, prescribing only what he deems appropriate and appropriate for that suspicion or certainty of illness and fully explaining the reasons for any refusal. We at the Fondazione Chirurgo e Cittadino [4] have among our statutory purposes the process of improving the empowerment of the citizen on the care pathway. We both plan CME training courses for doctors and nurses on dialogue and correct communication with the patient and create information materials for patients. We strongly believe that the correct and empathetic way, in which the doctor can describe the diagnostic and treatment pathways compatible with the diagnosed or suspected disease, providing certainty about the necessary time needed for it, will lead, if not to reduce waiting times, as said solvable exclusively with a radical rethinking of the current organizational forms, at least to a significant increase in perceived quality and a marked reduction in the levels of anxiety that we all have when faced with the need for surgery or before a diagnosis that is not yet certain. All the involved stakeholders—decision-makers, doctors, nurses, citizens—will have to, for their own fields of competence, take action for the future sustainability of our NHS (SSN) which, whatever it is said, is among the best in the world."

References

1. Health Consumer Powerhouse. Euro Health Consumer Index 2017 [Internet]. Available from: https://healthpowerhouse.com/publications/. Cited 4 Jun 2018.
2. Cittadinanzattiva. XX Rapporto PiT Salute. Sanità pubblica: prima scelta, a caro prezzo [Internet]. Available from: https://www.cittadinanzattiva.it/files/primo_piano/salute/xx-rapporto-pit-salute-sintesi-principali-risultati.pdf. Cited 7 Jun 2018.
3. Diastasi Addominale - Il primo sito italiano dedicato alla patologia [Internet]. Diastasi Italia | Il primo sito completo di informazione sulla patologia della diastasi addominale. 2015. Available from: http://www.diastasiaddominale.com/. Cited 4 Jun 2018.
4. La Fondazione Chirurgo e Cittadino Onlus [Internet]. Available from: http://www.chirurgocittadino.it/. Cited 4 Jun 2018.

5. Spandonaro F, D'Angela D, Giordani C, Polistena B. 13th Health Report. The change of Italian healthcare system between Transition and Leeway [Internet]. Mediaticamente S.r.l.; 2017. (C.R.E.A. Sanità). Available from: http://www.creasanita.it/13volume_dwn/dwn_flild/Rapporto_Sanita_2017.pdf. Cited 7 Jun 2018.
6. OECD. Waiting time policies in the health sector [Internet]. OECD iLibrary; 2013. Available from: https://read.oecd-ilibrary.org/social-issues-migration-health/waiting-times-for-elective-surgery-what-works_9789264179080-en#page1. Cited 7 Jun 2018.
7. Siciliani L, Moran V, Borowitz M. Measuring and comparing health care waiting times in OECD countries. 2013; Available from: https://www.oecd-ilibrary.org/content/paper/5k3w9t84b2kf-en.
8. Ministero della Salute. Piano Nazionale di Governo delle Liste di Attesa (PNGLA) 2010–2012 [Internet]. 2010. Available from: http://www.salute.gov.it/imgs/C_17_pubblicazioni_1931_allegato.pdf. Cited 7 Jun 2018.
9. Home Page | ASST Grande Ospedale Metropolitano Niguarda [Internet]. Available from: http://www.ospedaleniguarda.it/. Cited 4 Jun 2018.
10. What? No waiting lists? Bull. World Health Organ. 2010;88(4):249–50.
11. CERGAS-SDA Bocconi. Rapporto OASI 2017. Osservatorio sulle Aziende e sul Sistema sanitario Italiano [Internet]. Egea; (CERGAS). Available from: http://www.cergas.unibocconi.eu/wps/wcm/connect/Cdr/Cergas/Home/Resources/Reserved+Area/. Cited 7 Jun 2018.
12. Ballini L, Negro A, Maltoni S, Vignatelli L, Flodgren G, Simera I, et al. Interventions to reduce waiting times for elective procedures. Cochrane Database Syst. Rev. 2015;2:CD005610.
13. Almomani I, AlSarheed A. Enhancing outpatient clinics management software by reducing patients' waiting time. J. Infect. Pub. Health. 2016;9(6):734–43.
14. Rifkin J. The Zero Marginal Cost Society: The Internet of Things, the Collaborative Commons, and the Eclipse of Capitalism. New York: St. Martin's Press; 2014. 368 p.

Internet Sources

Diastasi Addominale - Il primo sito italiano dedicato alla patologia [Internet]. Diastasi Italia | Il primo sito completo di informazione sulla patologia della diastasi addominale. 2015. Available from: http://www.diastasiaddominale.com/. Cited 4 Jun 2018.

Cittadinanzattiva una organizzazione, fondata nel 1978 [Internet]. Available from: https://www.cittadinanzattiva.it/. Cited 4 Jun 2018.

La Fondazione Chirurgo e Cittadino Onlus [Internet]. Available from: http://www.chirurgocittadino.it/. Cited 4 Jun 2018.

Home Page | ASST Grande Ospedale Metropolitano Niguarda [Internet]. Available from: http://www.ospedaleniguarda.it/. Cited 4 Jun 2018.

19 Evolution of Abdominal Wall Surgery in Non-developed Countries

Giampiero Campanelli, Piero Giovanni Bruni, Marta Cavalli, and Francesca Martina Lombardo

19.1 Background

Inguinal hernia is a common pathology in Western countries (5%), although it is slightly more common in African countries (7.7%). This prevalence is mainly due to the need to carry out extreme physical work, on which their survival depends [1].

Also, the tissues of the abdominal wall present high variability of thickness and resistance among individuals of different races and ethnic groups, probably also due to nutritional deficiencies during the embryogenetic phase and for genetic factors.

The natural history of the hernias of the abdominal wall is to progressively increase in size until it reaches, in some case, conditions such as to affect the performance of normal daily activity; over the years, even working becomes difficult, determining important socio-economic consequences especially in developing countries where it is often neither covered nor protected the worker's illness.

The extreme dependence on work, the absence of alternative subsistence and the cost for the cure mean that everything that does not require urgent treatment is postponed until there is a condition for which an emergency treatment is indispensable and it is not possible to defer later.

Strangulated hernia is the most common cause of intestinal obstruction and it often results in death or permanent disability [2].

G. Campanelli (✉) · P. G. Bruni · M. Cavalli · F. M. Lombardo
General and Day Surgery Unit, Center of Research and High Specialization for the Pathologies of Abdominal Wall and Surgical Treatment and Repair of Abdominal Hernia, Milano Hernia Center, Istituto Clinico Sant'Ambrogio, Milan, Italy
e-mail: Giampiero.Campanelli@grupposandonato.it

D. P. Greco, E. Borgonovi (eds.), *Abdominal Wall Surgery*,
https://doi.org/10.1007/978-3-030-02426-0_19

There is an estimated mortality rate of nearly 87% for those who do not reach hospital; for those reaching hospital, the majority have had strangulation lasting longer than 72 h and the overall mortality rate is 40% [3].

A recent review shows that on 100 uncomplicated adult groin hernias reported a 21% complication rate, including: bladder injury, urinary retention, intestinal occlusion, neuralgia, haematoma or immediate recidivation [4].

With the exception of urgent cases, most patients undergo repair surgery when the size of the hernia is so large, abnormal, that we call it *hernia permagna.*

While the working conditions make the development of hernias of the abdominal wall very frequent in the male, in the female the high rate of multiple caesarean sections makes the laparocele an extremely widespread disease.

While caesarean section is not clinically justified, there is no scientific evidence of the benefits for women or children. However in the developed countries, the non-eutocic delivery is encouraged by the same health structures, they believe that it is more logistically manageable, requires less time and is burdened by fewer maternal post-partum complications.

The high prevalence of abdominal wall defects, associated with socio-economic difficulties, has led to the development of different channels of collaboration with the rest of the world and the creation of specific centres also in rural areas for the treatment of abdominal wall hernias [2, 5].

To reduce as much as possible the gap between the different countries of the world in the surgical treatment and in the perioperative management of abdominal hernias, various world organizations have supported humanitarian missions and educational programs.

A possible educational program for local surgeons could be divided into three steps, at the base there is the historical surgical adage “see one, do one, teach one”.

19.2 Competency-Based Training Programme

The surgeon trainer first explains the surgical indications and the various therapeutic strategies. The trainer performs the initial operation assisted by the local surgeon in training. During this first phase, the teacher tries to emphasize the key times of the intervention, in the case of inguinal hernia the identification of the three nerves of the region and the anatomical structures, the positioning of the mesh (if available), the management of less simple cases such as inguinoscrotal hernias and, of course, intra- and post-operating complications.

In all subsequent cases, the trainee performed the operations assisted by the trainer. At the end of each operation, the trainer evaluated the trainee's performance emphasizing the critical issues and giving food for thought about the intervention carried out.

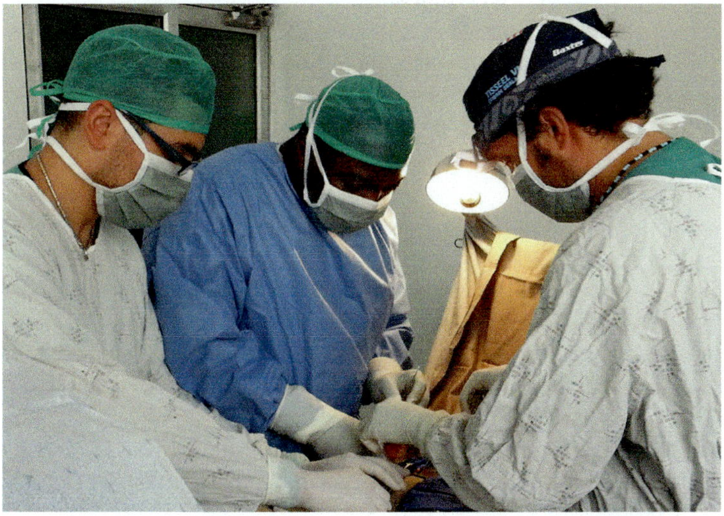

Different items can be evaluated including the surgical gesture, the choice of the incision, the dissection of the tissues, the respect for the anatomy, the fixation of the prosthesis, the dexterity, the choice of instruments, the time and the number of manoeuvres and the performance as a whole.

19.3 Independent Training Model

At the end of the mission, local instructor surgeons are appointed. These surgeons will select other local surgeons to teach and pass on what they have previously learned from surgeons on a humanitarian mission for second-rate training.

19.4 Maintenance of Proficiency

The surgeons in training are encouraged to send videos of their surgeries performed after the mission to the surgeons who trained them.

A study conducted with this educational program on the repair of inguinal hernia according to the Liechtenstein repair technique in 16 hospitals, Brazil, Ecuador, Haiti, Paraguay and the Dominican Republic [6] showed how all the surgeons who underwent this training program increased the score given to their performance over time with a rate of complications associated with intervention comparable to what happens in developed countries (USA and Europe) [7–9].

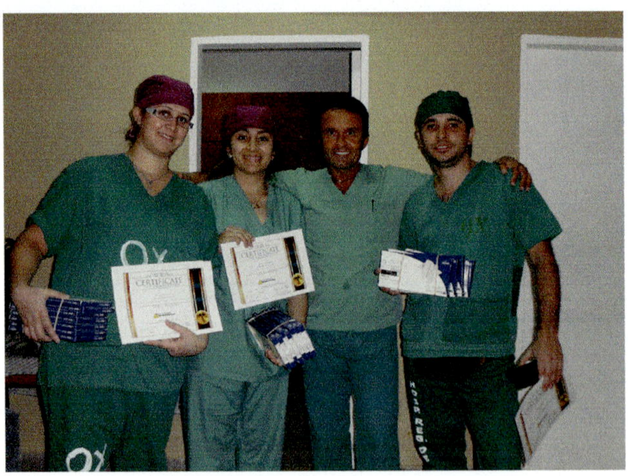

A program like this supports collaboration between international institutions and increases the capacity and level of surgical care directly in developing countries.

By forming regional experts, ethical infringements are avoided and the community becomes independent in providing adequate surgical care [10, 11].

Moreover, once the surgeons have become experts and familiar with the type of intervention, they will form, in turn, new local surgeons.

This will increase exponentially the number of local surgeons and the competence of the same in carrying out an abdominal wall surgery ensuring the patient a repair with standards equivalent to those of Western countries.

Each country has its own particular historical–cultural and political context that drastically influences the possibility for local doctors and for the general population to acknowledge the value of a specialized teaching that requires dedicated and regulated economic and structural means.

Prosthesis remains for many countries an unjustifiable or in any case with unaffordable cost.

In the case of abdominal hernia surgery, many areas of the world still tend to adopt open reparative techniques through direct sutures, and videolaparoscopy remains an unaffordable technology from the point of view of costs for over 95% of the population, a utopia reserved only for a few (and extremely rare) privileged centres, almost always located in large capitals.

Often, the absence of a University aggravates the lack of resident doctors and specialists who are able to update themselves on the international scientific reality and to cover the health needs of the territory.

The true relationship between costs and effectiveness of educational programs can only be assessed after some time by calculating how much the project has influenced the health finances of the countries involved in the study.

It remains that today it is very difficult to establish a true follow-up both for patients and for surgical training [12, 13].

An unresolved problem remains: reducing the cost of treatment to allow as many patient as possible the primary care and surgical treatment, hoping that the tendency to arrive at surgical observation only in an emergency should progressively go away in the face of an increase in patients who go to the hospital centres when there is still the possibility of benefit from the advantages of planning surgery.

References

1. Gil J, Rodríguez JM, Hernández Q, et al. Do hernia operations in African international cooperation programmes provide good quality? World J Surg. 2012;36(12):2795–801. https://doi.org/10.1007/s00268-012-1768-9.
2. Kingsnorth AN, Oppong C, Akoh J, Stephenson B, Simmermacher R. Operation hernia to Ghana. Hernia. 2006;10(5):376–9. https://doi.org/10.1007/s10029-006-0118-y.
3. Harouna Y, Yaya H, Abdou I, Bazira L. Prognosis of strangulated inguinal hernia in the adult: influence of intestinal necrosis. Apropos of 34 cases. Bull Soc Pathol Exot. 2000;93(5):317–20.

4. Fall B, Betel ME, Diarra O, Ba M, Dia A, Diop A. Complications of treatment of adult's groin hernia: a report of 100 cases comparative study between Bassini and Mac Vay's technics. Dakar Med. 2005;50(1):37–40.
5. Turaga KK, Garg N, Coeling M, et al. Inguinal hernia repair in a developing country. Hernia. 2006;10(4):294–8. https://doi.org/10.1007/s10029-006-0111-5.
6. Wagner JP, Schroeder AD, Espinoza JC, et al. Global outreach using a systematic, competency-based training paradigm for inguinal hernioplasty. JAMA Surg. 2017;152(1):66–73. https://doi.org/10.1001/jamasurg.2016.3323.
7. Amid PK. Lichtenstein tension-free hernioplasty: its inception, evolution, and principles. Hernia. 2004;8(1):1–7. https://doi.org/10.1007/s10029-003-0160-y.
8. Amid PK. Groin hernia repair: open techniques. World J Surg. 2005;29(8):1046–51. https://doi.org/10.1007/s00268-005-7967-x.
9. Vatansev C, Belviranli M, Aksoy F, Tuncer S, Sahin M, Karahan O. The effects of different hernia repair methods on postoperative pain medication and CRP levels. Surg Laparosc Endosc Percutan Tech. 2002;12(4):243–6.
10. Howe KL, Malomo AO, Bernstein MA. Ethical challenges in international surgical education, for visitors and hosts. World Neurosurg. 2013;80(6):751–8. https://doi.org/10.1016/j.wneu.2013.02.087.
11. Ramsey KM, Weijer C. Ethics of surgical training in developing countries. World J Surg. 2007;31(11):2061–7. https://doi.org/10.1007/s00268-007-9243-8.
12. Schroeder AD, Campanelli G, Cavalli M, et al. Humanitarianism in surgery. Hernia. 2017;21(6):963–71. https://doi.org/10.1007/s10029-017-1665-0.
13. Moore AM, Datta N, Wagner JP, et al. Centralized, capacity-building training of Lichtenstein hernioplasty in Brazil. Am J Surg. 2017;213(2):277–81. https://doi.org/10.1016/j.amjsurg.2016.10.011.

How Social Patterns Affect the Development of Science and Medicine

20

Ivan Cavicchi

20.1 What Is Medicine?

To the question "what is medicine", one answers the definition that recalls the complex of elements aimed at characterizing and circumscribing it on the conceptual level. Vocabulary medicine has been loosely defined as a science that has as its object in the study of diseases, their treatment and their prevention, and that studies the human body, in order to guarantee people's health, or as a discipline that considers various sciences and technologies to study human pathophysiology in order to maintain the state of health, in addition to studying the human person in normality and in diseases. Starting from the second half of the twentieth century throughout the Western World, there have been *super structural changes* in civil society and structural changes at the level of economics that have led to no longer recognizing the classic definition of medicine; in fact, we have the impression that this definition today has "cracked". A definition "cracks" when the complexity of the elements recalled to characterize it is no longer enough, or has become inadequate in spite of itself, or is no longer able to denote what it actually is, that is, when it does not correspond to reality. The changes that have occurred can be arranged into three groups:

- In the patient's: society, culture, ethics, demand for care and health,
- In the costs of medicine: the economic limitations that arise from the value of medicine that has become more and more subvenient,
- In science: not in the sense of the progress of knowledge, but in the sense of a paradigm that changes.

I. Cavicchi (✉)
"Tor Vergata" University, Rome, Italy
e-mail: info@ivancavicchi.it

D. P. Greco, E. Borgonovi (eds.), *Abdominal Wall Surgery*,
https://doi.org/10.1007/978-3-030-02426-0_20

All these things and others that we neglect for brevity have impacted the classical definition of medicine, creating numerous aporias and contradictions. Today, medicine:

- Is no longer just a biological science,
  - But it is also a science of organization, of management, a science of relationships, of communication, so it is clinical sociology, economics, ethics and all that concurrently,
- It does not cure only bodies or organisms or organs but cares for sick people,
  - Therefore, it does not cure diseases only but relates to the persons and the contexts that the diseases have, with their rights, their autonomies and therefore their opinions,
- It is not just a description of diseases,
  - But it is the interpretation of the sick of their singularities of their specificity,
- It is not just an empirical observation of symptoms,
  - But it is a relational knowledge with subjects and contexts,
- It is not just a prescription of the available scientific evidence,
  - It is negotiation between scientific evidence and personal opinions, so it is also proscribed validated not only by science but also by the existential choices of the citizen.

Each of these points represents a "lump'" of complexity that is a cluster of novelties, which to simplify we could represent with a simple "and", that is, with a simple conjunction:

- Science … and … ethics … and … economics,
- Observation … and … interpretation,
- Illness … and … the sick,
- Realization … and … knowledge,
- Symptoms … and words …

In grammar, the conjunction … *and* … serves to unite the parts of a discourse for which they could be considered the hyphen of complexity. For complexity in medicine, we mean the simultaneous coexistence in a patient of more things than more factors of more variables than more forms of reality, and of kinds of problems of different kinds; the conjunctions are the relationships between the many and different parts that make up the sick. In essence and in summary, the definition of medicine breaks out because of its increasing degree of complexity of its way of being of the multiplication of its fulfilments of its becoming more and more multiple knowledge. Until today, it was believed that medicine was only one that is described in medical books, because up to now we started from the belief that the disease was above all a scientific problem, therefore of clinical–biological knowledge. Medicine is this above all, but not only this, it is more and more related to concrete situations of care. Medicine is no longer predominantly scientific knowledge, but in spite of itself it becomes another matter when standardized diagnostic consumptions or when therapeutic consumption is limited for budgetary reasons, or when insurance companies fix their premiums to reimburse the benefits. Today, medicine implies a complexity that goes far beyond itself as science, and that calls into question people, subjects, behaviours, cultural qualities, organizations, professional knowledge, professional knowledge, relationships, communities and the resources available. Today to understand medicine only in one sense is to confess that there is a single thought. Conceiving medicine as a unique scientific thought means restricting its definition, simplifying its complexity, to exclude its important parts and anyhow other points of view, to define a low degree of pertinence and to pay the price of a low degree of realism. Faced with the risk of having medicine that is only scientific and not realistic, we must choose to adopt a definition of single-mindedness towards medicine and to implicitly exclude all variables outside that thought, or instead adopt a definition of complex medicine including more rationality and accepting the postulate that every rationality, therefore every logic, is not easily reducible to another rationality. Medicine of complexity thus becomes a medicine of equilibrium because its main effort is to find balanced solutions between the problems of resources and those of rights, between professional and organizational issues and between scientific evidence and the opinions of people. The logical ways of defining medicine are two—refer to:

- Its prevailing and essential meaning, such as the scientific one, or the ethical one,
  - Proposes a definition by essence, medicine is essentially a scientific question, so there is a "closed definition",
- A multiplicity of meanings of equivalent importance, comparable to each other,
  - Proposes an "open definition", medicine is a scientific question … and … economic … and … ethics … and … professional … and … social.

Scientific medicine was born in the second half of the nineteenth century, as a closed definition aimed at care of the human body and set with clinical logical and objectives, where today it has become an open definition in which the prevailing scientific rationality must make room for other types of rationality and oriented to different purposes from the clinic that affect the economy, the society and the relationships with the citizens. The right question is: how does one build an open definition consistent with complexity? That is, how do we get a realistic definition of medicine if by realism we mean the sharing of all the elements of reality to the definition of medicine? The reasoning to make is simple:

- The closed definition is always oriented to a prevailing or essential variable, (x), so that the term "medicine" will be used only as (x); if (x) are the diseases of the body, medicine will be mainly intended as the use of clinical knowledge; if instead it is ethics, it will be conceived essentially as respect for rights,
- The open definition is instead oriented to several variables (x, y, z …), in this case the term medicine will be used "as x y z …".

The two definitions of medicine, closed and open, are such because they come from two different assumptions.

What links the definition of medicine to its presuppositions, in logic, is defined as "function" f:

- The closed definition will be $f(x)$,
- The open definition will be $f(x, y, z \ldots)$.

Function f is the relationship between medicine and reality. Its realism will depend on the number of variables that it will be able to involve. The more the variables grow, the more its realism grows. What is medicine realistically? It is an "f" function related to its arguments. What is your degree of realism? Its ability through the arguments to represent reality in all its complexity. The closed or open definition of medicine is not to be seen with the logic of "true/false" (T/F). It would be wrong to consider one true and the other false, or more true or more false, for the simple reason that their unit of measurement is the practical effectiveness towards a chosen objective, given a non-random context of reference. If the chosen goal for medicine is for example "savings", the closed definition will be true in relation to its objective. So, it would be better to talk about convenience, meaning the latter as the ability of medicine to relate to reality. Repayment, for example in some regions, certainly reduces healthcare expenditure but discharges a large number of economic and social costs on citizens. In essence, the closed definition, faced with a high degree of complexity, will inevitably betray greater contradictions than the open one. If the problem is to save at all costs, it is clear that everything else is secondary. The actions decided to save while being priorities must not cause other kinds of costs; in this case, the closed definition will be open to other variables. In situations of high complexity, the open definition is always cheaper because it will have a greater degree of plausibility and convenience. For medicine, the distinction between closed and open definitions is not so distinct. The definition of how broad or narrow the definition is closely depends on the health policies, which decide "politically" the degree of complexity.

20.2 The Condition of Sustainability: Economics and Medicine

If the classic distinction between economic structure and social superstructure is tenable, it could be said that medicine, today, is part of the social superstructure, despite being particularly conditioned by the economy. This reference to the past is a historically unprecedented fact, and arises when medicine is public or private on the insurance form and inevitably posing the problem of its costs and its expenditure. With regard to the economy, it should be remembered that the objective, hitherto pursued by the various governments, is to reduce the incidence of health expenditure in relation to GDP, which implicitly states that medical spending is seen as an obstacle to economic growth. With respect to budgetary policies, it should be remembered that the objective of the various governments has so far been to definance over time the financial commitment to public health (progressive de-financing), which implies that medical spending is seen as a diseconomy. In this sense, today we can say that the economic structure greatly influences medicine and consequently the professional behaviour of the physician, considered the main effector of expenditure creating unprecedented ethical problems. The ethical issue that is created is the following: if medicine is in fact conditioned by the availability of resources and health expenditure has an incremental nature, it is to be expected that over time these conditions will increase, i.e. the limits imposed on this. To what extent, deontologically speaking, is this possible? Are there any inviolable thresholds or inviolable ethical values? On the contrary, are these values destined to become relative and flexible, economically renegotiable? In reality, are these questions hiding the real question that a new deontology must ask itself: what is medicine in the third millennium, over time sustainable? It is quite obvious that medicine must have deontological and scientific characteristics which cannot be ignored; otherwise, they become distorted. But, it is equally obvious that the apology of Hippocratic medicine is no longer enough. Today, medicine, in order not to be subordinate to the economic vision of the sustainability by governments or insurance companies, must propose an idea of non-economic sustainability, that is, an idea of sustainability through itself through its values and its professionals. What does this mean?

Today, the ideology that oversees the policies of sustainability in medicine and health is that of compatibility, that is, once the limit is established, everything must adapt to it, including medicine. Medicine is sustainable if it is compatible with the economic limit imposed on it. This ideology is not deontologically acceptable. Therefore, sustainability must be defined that is not in conflict with medicine. This way is called compossibility, that is to say that sustainable medicine: it is not a system of knowledge that adapts to a limit, but it is a system of knowledge that transforms the limit into possibilities. The doctor has always had a wide decision-making autonomy. He or she has always been the one who decided what was necessary for a sick person, the outcomes of treatment and the treatment itself. For this reason, he or she has always been, in fact, the one who decided the costs of medicine. When a misunderstood idea of compatibility and therefore of sustainability is affirmed, the doctor begins to lose autonomy. The conditioning of autonomy will open the way to a slow but inexorable professional depletion and that touches the fundamental ganglia of professional deontology. The logical sequence is based on linear assumptions:

- The doctor's practice is a source of expense,
- Conditioning the autonomy of the doctor,
  - Conditions the practice,
    Costs are affected,

This logical sequence must be rethought:

- The doctor's practice is a source of value,
- More autonomy to the doctor to make the practice compossible,
- Compossible practices guarantee sustainable spending.

Autonomy is the watershed not only between an administered profession and a self-managed profession but also between a compatible medicine and compossible medicine. On this value, medicine will have to take a re-elaborated step. Starting from the birth of scientific medicine, different welfare systems are established, and economic conditioning is growing in parallel. This conditioning today is very unprecedented as demonstrated by certain situations and certain facts. Over the years, medicine has sought to respond to economic conditioning by taking the path of the doctor's economic responsibility by resorting to the concepts of appropriateness, efficiency, optimization and evidence. The appropriateness in medicine is an important idea, but judging from the many definitions that circulate it is lacking a univocal meaning.

To understand what this implies, it is worthwhile to use the theory of meaning variance (T.S. Kuhn, The Structure of Scientific Revolution, Einaudi 1962):

- The meaning of the term appropriateness depends on the theoretical context in which it is used,
- Considering that the theoretical contexts of the various definitions of appropriateness are different,
- The appropriateness of a certain theory cannot be considered as having the same meaning, compared to the same terms of another theory.

If you admit with Hanson, that:

- Appropriateness is a theory conditioned by its purposes (theory laden),
- Established that any theory of appropriateness cannot be given as neutral, i.e. independent of such purposes,
- Admitting that the aims of appropriateness are different,
- It can be concluded that the term appropriateness has however different meanings often irreducible or incompatible with each other.

The idea of appropriateness, starting from Donabedian (The quality of health care, NIS, 1990), was born as an extension of the idea of quality, and, in this cultural environment, was conceived both as an epistemological question (use the knowledge and techniques within a true/false or good/bad opposition for the treatment of diseases) and as an ideal of justice (the right thing, to the right person, at the right time, by the right operator and in the right structure). By justice we mean both the conduct adequate to the needs of the patient and the sufficient justifications to demonstrate its validity. Starting from the 1980s, the fusion of these two meanings converges to an idea of appropriateness as a gnoseological conformity of praxis with a demonstrated "degree" of knowledge, and as an epistemological efficiency, that is, the ability of knowledge to simply achieve the goals of care. The appropriateness at the beginning arises as a justification for the doctor to use the knowledge and techniques available to cure diseases. Up to this point, the guidelines, the procedures in general, the protocols are nothing more than gnoseological and epistemological tools. Starting from the 1990s, the term appropriateness and, therefore, the use of guidelines, procedures and other methodological tools change its meaning:

- From the gnoseological epistemological one, concerned with optimizing knowledge,
- We move on to the organizational-management one, preoccupied with reducing the costs of treatment.

Thus, we understand that changing the justification of appropriateness changes the meaning and use of the guideline and of all other methodological tools. The appropriateness that the health ministry proposes today is an administrative justification in the sense that its goal is to find solutions of compatibility between the problems of the economy and the problems of medicine. Today, appropriateness, and therefore the guidelines that are proposed to medicine, tends to be in fact what we have already defined as "administered medicine". A medicine that no longer acts according to the Hippocratic principle of care according to necessity, that is, with respect to an end, but which acts according to the procedural principle of the permissible, that is, with respect to the available means thus granted.

20.3 The Problems of the Scientific Paradigm

Our scientific paradigm was anticipated by Galileo with the introduction of the scientific method based on experimentation and by Descartes with a modern idea of method, but in his doctrinal body it is completed by the positivist revolution initiated by Comte (1789/1857). It follows that in medicine the scientifically unverifiable explanations are considered worthless, and that diseases that are exorbitant from the standard are considered oddities, exceptions and singularities. In essence, scientific knowledge must be based exclusively on a descriptive method, with the clinical facts at the centre, i.e. their objectivity to be studied simply with objective observation. All this today is in the process of rediscussion in the sense that:

- The sick person exists beyond the illness,
- There are things in a disease that are not observable but that do exist,
- Scientific evidence is often falsifiable from experience,
- The patient is no longer reducible to an organ,
- The method is often contradicted by its practical application,
- The clinical trial that defines the scientific evidence is mostly reduced to statistical standards and abstractions,
- Standardization is regularly contradicted by the singularity, the specificity and the individuality of the patient,
- Scientific truth is often no longer polarized between what is true and what is false, and clinical deductions are often independent in the practice of other kinds of inferences.

Medicine must be updated in light of a growing degree of complexity. Depending on how the patient's ontological complexity increases, the clinic will have to multiply its starting premises in order to correspond to the actual patient. The social changes that have taken place in the patient involve unprecedented problems of knowledge, epistemological problems and consequently unprecedented ethical problems. Practices will essentially have to be epistemically adapted to the new ontological reality of the patient. The positivist paradigm of medicine today is therefore challenged by the new complexity of the patient as a disease and a person, language, communication and information enter the premise. The clinical deduction will concern both the illness and the patient, both the language of the body and that of the sick person. The biggest news in the field is the entry of relationship. The error that is generally committed by flattening everything to a generic humanization is to think about the relationship regardless of the way of knowing. One cannot change the form of the relationship that depends on the way of knowing, without changing the form of knowledge. For this reason, the relationship is a question that concerns the paradigm and as such poses unprecedented deontological problems. In the relationship, information and linguistic communication processes are taking place. The relationship is a deontological problem, redefining professional and epistemological practices, and redefining the way of knowing about the disease. In reality, it is impossible for the doctor not to have some relationship with his patient since there is no relationship but so many different forms of relationships. Normally, there is juxtaposition, i.e. a relationship based on the distinction where the distance between doctor and patient is reduced to amiability. The juxtaposition is explained by a definite objective knowledge and for this reason conceived on the clear separation between observer (doctor) and observed (sick). When we say that the doctor must have a relationship with the patient, we should actually say that the physician should change his form of a relationship in another, interactive and therefore relational where the observer is involved in what he observes and vice versa. The interactive relationship between a doctor and a patient is important because it allows us to recover the waste that is created between communication and information. By proceduralism we mean the tendency to subordinate a priori the clinical choice to a procedural rule; that is to say to an algorithm, to a guideline or to a protocol. Complexity of the patient and proceduralism often contradicts each other. From the idea of reducing the complexity of a patient to a procedure (algorithm, guideline, protocol, etc.), some paradoxes arise that concern a fundamental deontological postulate: treat the patient according to his real needs. Today, this postulate must be completed and redefined: treat the patient according to his own complexity. But, if the complexity of the patient is reduced for various reasons to the procedure, it is possible that the patient is not treated according to necessity, or complexity, but only according to procedure. Deontologically, the ideal would be that real necessity and conventional necessity (truth of fact and truth of reason) are coincident. Medicine must ensure that when scientific evidence or guidelines are disavowed in practice, the adoption of another perspective is granted. The big question that arises is the clinical autonomy of the doctor as the first guarantee for an appropriate treatment but also adequate to the complexity of the patient. With the advent of complexity, there is an urgent need to better define the relationships between clinical autonomy and method. The importance of clinical autonomy arises in all cases where there is the possibility of disavowing the method. Without renouncing the scientific method, one must pragmatically give the doctor the opportunity to reinterpret, ad hoc, the methodological rules, i.e. the evidence and the guidelines. If a clinical choice does not work on the empirical level but is correct from the theoretical point of view, then it is the method that must be corrected. If medicine really wants to accept the challenge of complexity, it must rethink its normal ideas of scientific truth as the rigidity of the principle of bivalence (true/false). If there were sufficient justifications to believe something different from the guidelines, then the singularity should not be considered as a denial of the guideline, but simply as the affirmation of another truth not provided for in the guideline. The consequence of the admission of singular truths does not question the value of the method but opens the way to multi-proceduralism.

20.4 For a New Idea of a Scientific Evidence: Chiron Taken to Pieces

The origin of medicine is told through the myth of a "horse … **and** … a man": the centaur Chiron, a conjunction. Prior to scientific medicine, medicine was taught through conjunctions, that is, in complexity. The doctor had to be before anything else philosopher, logical and many other things. Until 700s, medicine was taught in a non-reductive way, with a broad and extensive knowhow. With the advent of scientific medicine, complexity reduces its reduction in the sense that medicine is understood as if it were "nothing more and nothing more" than a science of the body. To the future physicians, one essentially teaches medicine as scientific evidence according to the canon before Galileo and Descartes and after Comte and Bernard. The fundamental function of the university today is to teach scientific knowledge and to teach the rationality necessary for its use, that is, to teach the scientific evidence substantially. Rationality with respect to knowledge is a bit like the "instructions for use" with respect to what you want to use. Rationality is a kind of quality of scientific action. The scientific evidence teaches how to "treat" the diseases, and therefore the "treatments" to be adopted organizing the knowledge according to precise criteria of rationality, that is, according to certain scientific knowledge. It should also be emphasized that the methods of assessment that are used to define scientific evidence are never infallible or exhaustive. Often due to the hyper-complexity of the pathological frameworks and contexts, they can have the most varying degrees of effectiveness and may at most have minimal or no effectiveness. We must accept the idea that there is minimal evidence and maximum evidence, and a variety of evidence exists between these poles. The notion of gradient refers to that of a measure; teaching a concept of a gradient of evidence is not the same as teaching a concept of monolithic evidence. For the first option, we must resort to the polyvalent logic that is an extension of the classical logic and operates with more truth values than the true/false canons, and therefore the principle of the excluded third is not valid in it. For the second, the classical logic of the true and false is valid with the principle of the excluded third. Universities teach classical logic but still do not teach polyvalent logic. Logic is the discipline that studies relationships as a result between utterances, beliefs and knowledge that are strongly intertwined. In general, for anyone to believe, it means that something is probable or possible. In this way, scientific evidence falls within the problems of the guarantees of knowledge, that is, within the need for the doctor to have some basis for believing his knowledge. Medicine is obliged to have certain guarantees of knowledge, that is, of scientific evidence. Scientific evidence in the case of medicine tends to reduce the space between what the doctor believes and his actual knowledge. The notion of scientific evidence for contemporary thought is not as simple and demonstrative as it seems. After all, the real evidence as evidence does not need to be demonstrated. The true evidence is self-demonstrative. Today, universities teach scientific evidences as if they were apodictic truths, and for this dogmatic, that is to say, as truths, being considered conventionally evident in themselves, do not need demonstration. In clinical practice, all the evidence because of the singularity of the patient are exposed to the risk of inaccuracy, so they should not be considered apodictic truth but the opposite only as relatively uncertain and probable truths. Many of the misunderstandings related to the use of guidelines, appropriateness, optimality, best practices and therapeutic protocols derive from a misunderstood notion of scientific evidence that is to consider it as an apodictic truth and not for what is a truth that it should not be simply applied to the case but on the contrary must be interpreted in relation to the case. Nowadays, in no way can anti-technological prejudice be accepted in medicine, and there is a need to better integrate natural observation with instrumental observation. Today, the new question is not *technology* or *no technology*, but the relationship between observation … and … scientific evidence. Sometimes, what one believes to see as evident is not. Sometimes, what is thought to be objective scientific evidence is more influenced by other factors, more than what is believed. The question of observation arises from the physics of quanta. Bohr and Heisenberg have demonstrated four basic things:

- It is not possible to distinguish and separate the system observed by the observing system,
- There is a problem of conditioning the scientific evidence caused by the action of the observing system on the observed one,
- Different descriptions of the same evidence are possible,
- Scientific evidence depends on both what is observed and who observe.

Medicine still strives today to strictly separate the physician, as an observing system, from the disease, as an observed system and to see scientific evidence as an objective property of the disease. Observation is something that mixes the objectivity of what is observed with the subjectivity of the observer, making the idea of scientific evidence more complex. Medical faculties should update their notions of truth. The more complex the complexity grows and the more difficult it becomes to know exactly. Tendentially, the truth becomes verisimilitude. The delicacy of the question is not only philosophical but practical, since today these problems pass directly from epistemology to legality. The scientific evidence is clear and remains a formidable parameter to distinguish the true from the false, the right from the unjust and the scientific from the non-scientific. We cannot ignore that the observation of scientific evidence is particularly exposed to traps and pitfalls. If the premises of the observation are wrong, the reasoning that will follow will also be wrong. The evidence in this case will be wrong. This is the fallacy. What are a virtuous circle and a vicious circle? The term virtuous circle and vicious circle are meant to refer to a stable combination of two or more conditions such that the maintenance of each condition contributes to the maintenance of all others through a positive feedback mechanism. The combination concerns:

- The scientific evidence used to define the methodology,
- The methodology used to define the scientific evidence.

The most classic example is the evidence used to define the guidelines and guidelines used to define any evidence. In this case, one should speak of recursion (recursive definition) between the notion of evidence and the notion of method. The recursion is when to define something (guidelines); the elements of this something (evidence) are used to construct something else (other guidelines). Therefore, the heart of medicine is not scientific evidence as a truth but it is the method that allows one to certify whether or not a truth is scientific evidence. In medicine, it commands the method to the point that it often ends up coinciding with the notion of evidence, that is, to the point that method and evidence are at the end the same thing.

20.5 Hedonism and Economism

Today, all health systems are subjected to accreditation procedures. They concern services, technologies, providers for training, operating procedures and ways of operating them. Anything is considered suitable only if it is in conformity with an authorization procedure. According to the suitability, a training course is scientifically valid only because the provider complies with the procedure that authorizes them to make training courses. But, this does not automatically guarantee that the contents of the course are scientifically valid. Eligibility is another way of making the method coincide with the evidence. Economism occurs when the economic and scientific values of medicine take over the economic reasons, that is, they control economic limits, and the limits are made to coincide with the savings methodologies in the sense that it puts ex ante to the clinical decision the obligation of procedures to be followed from which the expected result is not the cure but a saving. In this case, methodology and financial evidence coincide. When the method and the evidence are the same thing, the patient and his needs are placed between the brackets, the complexity of the medical act is put in brackets and a realistic idea of science is placed between brackets. If the method and the evidence are taught as apodictic truths as impersonal truths, as of the inductive truths, it becomes very difficult to avoid the short circuits and the first to do the expense will always be the sick on the one hand and the good medicine from the other. After all, if the method is a dogmatic truth and the evidence as well, what is the difference between them? It is worth considering them as one and the same truth.

20.6 For a Reasonable Rationality

The great clinicians of the early 1900s, such as A. Murri, recommended their students to stay away, in their reasoning, from conjectures, interpretations and speculations, that is, to think as little as possible. The good doctor was the one who got the scientific evidence from the things he or she saw, in the sense that the scientific evidence was in things, in symptoms and in illness. To discourage interpretations, for Murri, did not mean not to reason but to reason in a certain way, that is, to stick as rigorously as possible to the true source of clinical knowledge that was the observation and description of nature, to be objective. The assumption was that the scientific evidence was exclusively in the nature of the disease, therefore exclusively biological. Today, the problem of scientific evidence is that biological nature, even if prevalent, is no longer enough to explain diseases:

- There is talk of "social determinants of diseases", of historical-evolutionary factors, of environmental conditions, of strong psychosomatic interconnections and of psychic predispositions,
- Biology is like absorbent paper that retains and expresses a great aetiological complexity. The famous "bio-psycho-social" paradigm.

Today, besides describing, we are forced to interpret the nature of the disease within large social realities. The interpretation by profession deals with ambiguous, complex, unclear, multiform things, while the description on the contrary deals with clear and definable things. It is a matter of increasing the degree of realism of scientific evidence by including in it all that is useful for the extended knowledge of a disease. The patient is as if he or she became a "text" to be interpreted as a whole. The doctor, as a simple observer and descriptor, becomes co-author of the text. Teaching both medical and surgical science does not have to see the evidence as notions but it must teach to reason about the evidence and in any case to interpret it. The evidence is notions but also knowledge. The notion is an elementary datum, attributable to a specific knowledge. Cognition is a mental, rational, cultural, logical process that processes notions. Scientific evidence comes from inferences, that is to say, from the logical relations between certain premises and certain conclusions. There are inferences that provide sufficient arguments to confirm the evidence, others that will only give a certain degree of probability, others that will provide us with semi-demonstrative inference and indirect evidence, while others will provide hypotheses useful for explaining certain empirical facts. The thing that must be understood is that the reasoning on scientific evidence is not purely logical or purely mechanical, and less subject to idealization, but something linked to a strong practical necessity. In practice, they must be reasoned as knowledge for the simple reason that they sometimes work and sometimes do not. In general, the doctor explains the evidence of an illness through its causality. Explaining evidence through the cause is like an "absolute demonstration and it is quite easy, the reasoning can be mechanical (if *x* ... then *y*), it is less easy to explain the disease when there is no evidence and the cause is unknown, when there is ambiguity and only relative or plausible evidences are authorized, and the reasoning in this case must be open to several possible inferences. In conclusion: the explanation of an illness generally concerns its scientific evidence. It is made complicated by a lot of things.

If, in the ambiguous situation, besides not knowing the causes, we include the budget limits, the blocking of the turnover, the professional risk, the anxiety of the family members, the broken machines and other variables, we realize that the reasoning that explains the evidence is the result of a lot of clinical and non-clinical variables. In these cases, scientific evidence arises between the truths of science and the situations of reality. Scientific evidence is generally represented by disease models, i.e. by comparing the case with the scientific evidence that can be conventionally correlated with the disease to be diagnosed. Models in general are never perfectly exhaustive of the reality they represent but only approximate and verisimilar. This means that scientific evidence must also be seen with specificity, individuality, singularity, strangeness, atypicality, partial similarities, etc. This is true clinical complexity. Well, in the face of this complexity, we reiterate that it is very important to try to reason practically in the reality of things and cases. We need a practical method that knows how to combine the possible evidence with more clinical truths. In other words, it is a non-meaningful method, but one that is more eventual, more reality possible, that is, a polyschematic method, a practical-deductive method. Rationality in medicine, scientific rationality, is the right to judge well, to know for the better, and to operate correctly, with respect to everything that constitutes the world of the disease. Scientific evidence is the final product of this rationality. It is a great guarantee for the sick person and a rule of intellectual conduct for the doctor, to whom medicine must abide. The problem of scientific evidence obviously does not concern its logical, cognitive principles, or its indisputable truths, but its relations with other rationalities, and with other opinions and visions of the world. The scientific evidence tends precisely because it is considered an indisputable truth, to self-prescribe that is to impose its rules of action on the world. From this awareness in the second half of the 900s, the "bioethics" was born, which in synthesis proposes to scientific rationality, to undergo a principle of responsibility and to measure oneself with ethics, with the opinion of people, with democracy of decisions and with other points of view. Today at the base of the many conflicts between medicine and society, there is a medical rationality felt by different social sectors as "inhuman" because it deals only with bodies and not with people, because scientific evidence is sometimes perceived as unreasonable towards the many problems of a sick person. So, today "the demanding", that is, the one who was once patient, has difficulty in passively conforming to scientific rationality and accepting scientific evidence, even when it is addressed to him as the only solution. Reasonable is the realization by the doctor, that in addition to diseases, there are the sick people who live in complex worlds, but also that the same doctors work in increasingly conditioning organizations. It is reasonable to realize that there is not only rationality. The clinical reasonableness, today, as well as referring, as is obvious, to the scientific evidence must tend to be adequate to the subjects in situations. Scientific evidence is reasonably adequate if it does not overlook the limits that exist in a situation. It is a principle of pragmatic convenience. The patient in the relationship is the measure of rationality not on the contrary.

20.7 Conclusions: For a Pragmatic Medicine

Let's start with a distinction:

- Conventional is the medicine that conforms or follows an agreement on the principles of the rules, and the methods about the cure of diseases,
- Pragmatics is the medicine that modulates its principles, its rules and its methods, i.e. its conventional truths on the basis of an actuality principle of the sick person.

The principle of actuality is very simple, everything is present in a patient either directly or indirectly, therefore illness, persons, society, culture, economy, context, contingency and limits of all kinds. Pragmatic medicine assumes as a reference for its scientific reason, therefore for its rationality and its reasonableness, the principle of actuality as a principle of reality with the aim of becoming more realistic than conventional medicine. The basic thesis: today, conventional medicine must strive to become pragmatic because it gives certain complexity:

- It is cheaper,
- Works more,
- Is more consistent with the changing world.

The moment in which the scientific rationalism of medicine accepts to redefine itself in the actuality of real problems and in the complexity of situations becoming pragmatic, it acquires the characteristics of a new realism, that is a medicine even more rooted in actuality, understood as concreteness. The current rationality for pragmatic medicine means connecting it to the experience, on condition that the experience to which it refers, is to be interpreted in an extended way, not only in the experimental sense of conventional medicine. The actuality as an experience automatically reduces the absolutism of the clinical rationality of conventional medicine. Rationality is as if it becomes more realistic. Pragmatic medicine poses practical questions on scientific rationality, that is, on its consequences. Its basic premise is that logic and actuality cannot be given as automatically coinciding, and less than ever is logic and actuality the same thing. Current events challenge logic and often deny it but not as such, as a standard of rationality. This is why, it is much more congenial that medicine assumes a realistic pragmatic logic. In the ordinary practice of scientific medicine, there are differences between what is rational and what is real. These scraps create important practical problems. So, we must worry about understanding the effects of scientific rationality on the actuality of the patient. This enlarges and complexes the very notion of rationality that is rethought in practical rules for relevant behaviours. The pragmatic address of medicine therefore not only renounces logic but also adds to concepts such as rationality those of common sense, reasonableness, plausibility, practicality, etc. Today, most of the problems defined as "personalization" are nothing but the substitute of pragmatic vision. The issues of aggressive treatment, abuse of technologies, criticism of the use of drugs and methodological obligations are nothing more than the reconsideration of the impact of rationality and clinical logic, on ordinary practices. Today, we are obliged to be realistic and pragmatic rationalists. Pragmatic medicine makes use of an idea of plausibility, which never relies on a single type of reasoning but chooses the most convenient reasoning for the relationship, the patient, the situation, the case and so on. Conventional medicine, on the other hand, adapts its unique rational reasoning to the evidence it observes or constructs. The pragmatic plausibility to decide the efficiency and convenience of a treatment cannot renounce the opinion of the patient, nor the verification of the relationship and less than ever to the results. Today, the fate of medicine is reliant on its degree of realism. Although medicine progresses scientifically, it accumulates degrees of cultural regressivity towards the changing world at every ever-increasing level. Medicine, and even more surgery, cannot afford the luxury of being non-compliant with the reality they face. The path of pragmatism among the many possibilities is that which ensures more coherence with the complexity of reality. In some ways, it is the obligatory way to avoid being administrated by supra-scientific logics. Medicine for social reasons and for economic reasons has lost the characteristic that at least since its conversion into science has always distinguished it, that is to say that it is the scientific self-reference of itself. Today, it has become in spite of itself a regulated political question beyond its scientific goals in order to govern its effects on society and the economy. For this reason, losing the condition of self-reference loses what in mathematics is called a recursive definition, that is, the property of defining its internal changes only by revitalizing its constitutive elements. In this way, the traditional epistemological autonomy is lost, that is the freedom to provide for itself by deciding the rules of the game. Today, the rules of the game are now decided in a heteronomous way by many other protagonists. If the policy or if the insurance decides with cuts or lowering the rates that you must save at all costs, there is no complexity that remains, you just have to save. If the policy or the insurance decides to finance health through the standard costs, of course medicine will in turn be standardized, in the sense that all the variables involved will be subjected to a logic of standardization (exams, therapies and treatments). Theoretically, all the proposed definitions are "open" even those that pursue economic goals tout court.

In this case, the clinical need is always accompanied by theoretical safeguard rules, which have more or less the following logic: respecting the rational use of resources, adopting principles of appropriateness and pursuing goals of optimality. In summary, today medicine has become an affair that goes far beyond itself.

Suggested Reading

1. Cavicchi I. Ripensare la medicina: restauri, reinterpretazioni, aggiornamenti. Turin: Bollati Boringhieri; 2004. p. 273.
2. Cavicchi I. Sanità: un libro bianco per discutere. Bari: Edizioni Dedalo; 2005. p. 351.
3. Cavicchi I. Malati e governatori. Un libro rosso per il diritto alla salute. Bari: Edizioni Dedalo; 2006. p. 226.
4. Cavicchi I. Il pensiero debole della sanità. Bari: Edizioni Dedalo; 2008. p. 290.
5. Cavicchi I. Medicina e sanità: snodi cruciali. Bari: Edizioni Dedalo; 2010. p. 394.
6. Cavicchi I. Una filosofia per la medicina: razionalità clinica tra attualità e ragionevolezza. Bari: Edizioni Dedalo; 2011. p. 242.
7. Cavicchi I. I mondi possibili della programmazione sanitaria. Le logiche del cambiamento, vol. 240. New York: McGraw-Hill; 2012.
8. Cavicchi I. Il riformista che non c'è. Le politiche sanitarie tra invarianza e cambiamento. Bari: Edizioni Dedalo; 2013. p. 218.

Part V

Conclusions

Ferrying to the Future

21

Elio Borgonovi and Dalila Patrizia Greco

The contributions contained in this book have shed light on some trends and challenges for the future of abdominal wall surgery. First and foremost, the professionalism of surgeons is evolving. Indeed, surgeons must acknowledge that surgical outcomes will not depend so much on their knowledge and skills alone but rather on the contributions of many professionals working together in harmony. Thus, while developing new surgical techniques will continue to be important, so will building close-knit teams of people who are motivated to work together to meet the real needs of patients in the best possible way. Members of these teams will have to accept the principle that they can no longer be good at what they do "individually", but rather "together". Thus, the type of leadership required will have to shift from technical/professional leadership to organizational and motivational leadership.

Secondly, the abdominal wall can no longer be seen as a "container" to be repaired and strengthened; rather, it must now be considered an organ in itself, one which must be protected from weakening and rupture, and one whose functional integrity is part of a healthy body and thus must be restored. Scientific knowledge has made advances in the field of biocompatible materials, which are capable of maintaining, strengthening and regenerating tissue; as such, surgeons will have to establish surgical procedures after taking the general characteristics of the patient into account. Indeed, even the field of abdominal wall surgery has made great strides towards "personalized" healthcare. Nonetheless, personalization is not only the result of scientific progress—it also requires a new kind of hospital organization. In that regard, a balance will have to be struck between the rigid standardization of individual healthcare practices and procedures (in this case as related to surgery)

E. Borgonovi (✉)
Department of Social and Political Sciences, Bocconi University, Milano, Italy
e-mail: elio.borgonovi@unibocconi.it

D. P. Greco
Day&Week Surgery Unit, Ospedale Niguarda Ca' Granda, Milano, Italy
e-mail: dalilapatriziagreco@gmail.com

D. P. Greco, E. Borgonovi (eds.), *Abdominal Wall Surgery*,
https://doi.org/10.1007/978-3-030-02426-0_21

and the personalization of the patient's entire experience. Trends in healthcare technology are pointing towards a future in which it will be possible to have a hub-and-spoke design, whereby a central hub will be the anchor point for a number of different surgical procedures that can then be performed at nearby or faraway hospitals. It is possible that the same might occur for abdominal wall surgery. A highly specialized, interdisciplinary team could operate out of a command center, with monitors and equipment capable of providing real-time imaging and vital signs; this command unit could then guide other teams who, in turn, have prepared their patients, and who will be able to request specific support as their own surgical procedure unfolds.

Thirdly, the evolution mentioned above is part of another trend towards patient care networks, which in many countries is regulated by PDTA (Diagnostic and Therapeutic Healthcare Protocols). These protocols organize patient care and healthcare services into networks. Except for emergencies caused by physical trauma or other unpredictable events, the effectiveness and appropriateness of operations—including abdominal wall surgery—depend on the logical organization of the following phases:

- Ability to anticipate needs (very early or early diagnosis phase);
- Scheduling of operations with adequate preparation of patients, in a way that considers the complexity of the health situation and the availability of the best materials to use;
- Performance of the surgical procedure;
- Establishment of a postoperative care program that includes follow-up visits and lifestyle recommendations which facilitate a quick recovery and prevent complications and/or recurrences.

Needless to say, these phases necessarily involve various facilities and professionals, who all must be coordinated. And, that coordination depends on access to complete information all along the chain, which is why it makes sense to work as a network.

Fourthly, this evolution in healthcare models towards PDTA, patient care networks and hub-and-spoke networks means that funding systems for healthcare providers must be revised as well. Indeed, DRG-type systems focus on individual procedures and services (in this case, surgery) with the goal of improving efficiency and productivity, reducing the costs of individual services, and possibly stimulating constructive competition among providers. Nonetheless, when the focus shifts from the service/procedure to a coordinated chain of events, optimizing the efficiency and costs of each individual phase in the process does not mean that the efficiency and costs of the process as a whole will be optimized; the same goes for patient outcomes, which must be the main priority. For example, suppose that the DRG of a complex abdominal wall procedure for incisional hernias calls for a reimbursement of about 5000 euros, which means that the latest generation of meshes cannot be used because they cost too much; and suppose that not using those meshes leads to recurrences or complications in 30% of cases, each of which results in an additional cost of about 2000 euros (hypothesis of 4 days of hospitalization for complications with an average cost of 500 euros a day); the total cost for the healthcare system in this case would be 5600 euros (5000 + 2000 × 0.30). Thus, if there were a funding/reimbursement system in place that was connected to the entire process and lower than 5600 euros, and which reduced recurrences/complications, it would not only be more cost effective, but also more satisfactory for those 30% of patients and caregiver who would no longer have additional health problems. This means moving from current funding models—which operate as if they were in silos or "pipe organs", with no communication between them—to a comprehensive funding system connected to the process, the outcomes (pay for performance) and the value generated (value-based funding).

Fifthly, evolutions in technology, healthcare models and funding models mean that the relationship between sustainability and personalization/Taylorization of healthcare needs to be re-examined. There is no doubt that personalized, precision healthcare in general, and surgery in particular, would become economically unsustainable if the overall approach towards patients was not re-examined. Indeed, the benefits of standardization in terms of productivity and unit costs are lost in personalization/Taylorization. The experience is generally the same in all industries: bringing the service to the customer and personalizing it are ways of charging higher prices. Technically speaking, it is said that personalization/Taylorization increases real or perceived value in the eyes of the customer, who is then willing to pay a higher price. However, a national health service is rooted in principles of universality, solidarity and equity, meaning that any increase in "health value" that may derive from the personalization/Taylorization of care cannot lead to a higher price for the patient. After all, there is no price when the system is funded through taxes. Therefore, an increase in value for patients must be achieved by reorganizing the entire healthcare system in a way that reduces overall costs. And, that cost reduction must be the result of the savings obtained by greater appropriateness in care, eliminating complications and recurrences, and, as mentioned above, organizing healthcare within a network so as to eliminate phases that do not generate value for the patient. Indeed, an organizational change is needed, but it can be achieved by changing the culture of doctors, nurses, other healthcare professionals, managers and those in charge of funding on a regional and national level. The goal of achieving a sustainable healthcare system will have to be pursued within a more general welfare system that—contrary to the past—will no longer be able to rely on an increase in resources, but rather on the best use of stable or diminishing resources.

For what concerns the future sustainability of the healthcare system, it must be underlined that people affected by diseases need to receive effective treatments and therapies that give them the best opportunity for health. However, the resources available may be limited and must be appropriately allocated based on the principles of cost-effectiveness. This requires a revision and an update of the health technology assessment (HTA) process, which was initiated about 40 years ago in response to the uncontrolled diffusion of expensive healthcare technologies. It started out as a multidisciplinary evaluation process, with the aim of establishing itself as a tool to support cost-effective decision-making when allocating economic resources. The process is indeed multifaceted because the impact of technology should be evaluated from clinical, economic, ethical, social and organizational points of view.

In Europe, the first institutions dedicated to the evaluation of healthcare technologies were established in France and Spain in the early 1980s and in Sweden in 1987. During the following decade, HTA programs were established in almost all European countries. Since the second half of the 1980s, European and international networks have been developed to share and compare results and experiences between countries. Starting from the late 1990s, there have been significant changes especially in terms of efforts to coordinate the activities related to HTA among the various European Union member countries. The international drive to harmonize methods for assessing healthcare technologies derived from the goal to guarantee greater transparency and stability in evaluation systems.

At the beginning of 2018, the European Commission presented a proposal to promote cooperation between the EU member states on health technology assessment. The proposal for a regulation—which would cover new drugs and medical devices—lays the foundation for permanent and sustainable cooperation at the EU level on joint clinical evaluations in these sectors. Member states will be able to use common tools, methodologies and procedures for health technology assessment across the EU. In particular, considering the context of abdominal wall surgery, member states will be in a position to perform joint clinical assessments focusing on the most innovative materials and surgical techniques with the most significant impact on patients, in order to choose the most appropriate technology for the individual patient according to a "tailored surgery" approach. The responsibility for the assessment of non-clinical (e.g. economic, social and ethical) aspects of health technologies and of pricing and reimbursement decisions will continue to be referred to individual EU countries. The proposal will now be discussed in the European Parliament and the Council of Ministers. The Commission expects that, once it has been adopted and entered into force, it will be applicable after three years. From the date of application, a further three-year period is foreseen to allow member states to adapt gradually to the new system.

While the European Commission is promoting the cooperation of EU members on HTA activities, on the other hand there is the need to produce clinical and economic data to sustain these activities. Evidence on the effectiveness of drugs or medical devices to inform HTA submissions has conventionally been derived from randomized controlled trials. However, due to patient randomization and inclusion and exclusion criteria, extrapolating efficacy to effectiveness in clinical practice is very challenging. Real-world data (RWD), defined as data gathered outside the context of randomized controlled trials, may be another opportunity to inform cost-effectiveness estimates of new or existing drugs or medical devices in clinical practice. RWD can be derived from numerous sources, including registries, observational studies and case report forms. RWD, which in general consider non-randomized treatment allocation, longer patient follow-ups and broader patient populations, may provide a more generalizable representation of treatment effects in clinical practice. As regards abdominal wall surgery, outcome data on all patients undergoing hernia surgery procedures should be collected in a prospective manner through registries/databases consistent with patient privacy and confidentiality regulations. This process has a twofold aim: to perform cost-effectiveness and budget impact analyses using economic data at a local level, and to evaluate surgeons and centers according to the pre-specified criteria for abdominal wall surgery certification. The certification of surgeons and clinical centers is of great importance to guarantee high quality in surgery. This is particularly important for hernia surgery, which is one of the most commonly performed surgical procedures in the world, because improvements in materials (prostheses, and fixation materials) and surgical techniques mean that the decisions to be made in the management of every single patient are more complex. At present, only Germany has a detailed program in place for the certification of hernia centers, while other countries have no uniform way of classifying hernia surgery units. All centers performing hernia surgery should face up to this challenge and become certified. To this end, hernia societies worldwide should implement certification programs to ensure high-quality standards in surgery.

Essentially, good quality care in abdominal wall surgery requires safe and appropriate: surgical procedures, materials and waiting time. The correct choice of the biocompatible material can prevent recurrences or other complications such as neuralgia or sinus tract. However, appropriateness alone does not mean that the patient will perceive the care as necessary or preferred. High-quality medical care should ensure that every procedure or treatment also meets the patient's objectives for care. It is so very important to involve patients in what becomes a shared decision-making process. In the future, reforms should focus on the improvement of medical care while also taking into account the preferences of patients.

Last but not least, some key questions must be answered: is it possible to design and decide on three- or four-year plans in an environment that is continuously and rapidly changing? Indeed, "Moore's law" implies that every eighteen months the innovation process doubles in potential or halves costs. Once again, the answer is that "disruptive innovation" can be faced with a "disruptive cultural approach". In the past, three-to-five-year plans were defined with the intention of implementing them. Nowadays, and in the future, three-to-five-year plans should be designed with the certainty that they will not be respected or implemented. On the contrary, they should be designed with the goal of imagining possible scenarios in a way that better prepares all involved to adopt solutions day by day, week by week and month by month in response to a given technological, organizational, social, political, institutional and economic context.

Printed by Printforce, the Netherlands